THE LONG WAY TO TIPPERARY

A Revised edition of "I Will Go the Distance: The Story of a "Lost" Sudanese Boy of the Sixties", first published by Pauline's Publications Africa, Nairobi, 2005.

BY JIEL J. AKOL

A note to readers from the author: Strictly speaking, memoirs may point to some historical facts, but they are not history books.

The publisher wishes to acknowledge and thank Dr. Douglas H. Johnson for his invaluable help and support for Africa World Books and its mission of preserving and promoting African cultural and literary traditions and history. Dr. Johnson and fellow historians have been instrumental in ensuring that African people remain connected to their past and their identity. Africa World Books is proud to carry on this mission.

Copyright © 2023 Jiel J. Akol

All rights reserved. It is illegal to reproduce, duplicate or transmit any part of this book in either electronic means or printed format. Recording of this publication is strictly prohibited. No part of this publication may be reproduced, stored in a retrieval system, or transmitted, in any form, or by any means, electronic, mechanical, photocopying, recording or otherwise, without the prior permission of the publishers.

ISBN: 9780645972344 (Paperback)
9780645972337 (Hardcover)

This book is sold subject to the conditions that it shall not, by way of trade or otherwise, be lent, re-sold, hired out or otherwise circulated without the publisher's prior consent in any form of binding or cover other than in which it is published and without a similar condition including the condition being imposed on the subsequent purchaser.

Cover design, typesetting and layout: Africa World Books
Unit 3, 57 Frobisher St, Osborne Park, WA 6017
P.O. Box 1106 Osborne Park, WA 6916

africalogo mono.tif

To my daughter Aker and my son Atem, my grandsons Sean Arungah, Reiss-Longar Arungah, and granddaughter Nyla Arungah: These are your roots.

ABOUT THE AUTHOR

Jiel J. Akol is, in fact, Jacob J. Akol, author of '*I Will Go the Distance*', '*Burden of Nationality*' and two other books. The switch to Jiel J. Akol instead of Jacob J. Akol, is to at last do justice and homage to the eternal name, Jiel, of the Pagong Clan. Jiel, the name that has been long relegated to a mere initial, 'J', by the Biblical name, 'Jacob', was the first-born name given to him when born, followed by Jacob, a name given to him later by Christian missionaries when he went to school and converted to Christianity. According to a Jieng's legend, Jiel Longar, whose son, Longar Jiel, was the first human to live on Dryland[1] and announced *Gong* the Hedgehog as Guardian of his people on Dryland, may now be appeased by relegating the alien usurper, Jacob, to its rightful place: an initial of a name that also remains part of his name.

Jiel J. Akol was born in Southern Sudan, now an independent South Sudan, on a uncertain date in mid-1940s. He was educated in southern Sudan at Kuachjok Catholic Mission up to the intermediate school level. He then skipped in and out of formal education as he led the life of a refugee in Congo (DRC), Tanzania, Zambia, Ireland

---

[1] Jacob J. Akol, (2022) *Myths and Folktales*, Africa World books p.23

and England, where he finished high school, professional studies and, eventually, after a long journalistic career, earned a master's degree in communication arts and media from University of Leeds, England.

As an aid worker cum journalist, he travelled widely in Africa in 1970s-1990s, from Antananarivo in Madagascar through Cape Town to Cairo and from Mogadishu in Somalia to Timbuktu in Mali and beyond - there is apparently more of Africa beyond Timbuktu. He is married to Joy and have two grown up children, Aker and Atem. They all live in UK.

CONTENTS

Dedications — ix
Acknowledgements — xi
Foreword — xiii
Preface — xxi
Introduction — xxiii

Part One: The Herds Boy
    The Importance of Names — 6
    Spearmasters Don't Die — 11
    The Bull Woman — 18
    A Boy's Life — 27
    Stepping Out — 44

Part Two: The Schoolboy
    Village School Ayiel — 47
    Like Mother Like Daughter — 63
    New Dimensions — 72
    The Messenger — 81
    Two Chiefs — 84

In Remembrance of Jesus	96
In Memory of Spearmaster	102
Fear of Soldiers	115
Elementary School Kuachjok	124
Intermediate School Kuachjok	142
The Brewing Conflict	150

Part Three: The Refugee

Way to Congo (DRC)	161
Garaged in Paulis (now Isiro)	170
Way to Bunia	185
Bunia	195
Way to Bukavu	202
Bukavu	209
In and Out of Tanganyika (now Tanzania)	237
In and Out of Northern Rhodesia/Zambia	248

DEDICATION

This book is dedicated to very many people: First, to my mother, Aker Baak, my father's other wives, my very many sisters and brothers, my uncles and aunts, all whose stories told to me at a tender age, have remained vivid in my mind and have enriched my life; to clansmen and many friends at Village School Ayiel and Kuachjok schools, whose lives have touched mine in lasting ways.

It is also dedicated to many people and organisations whose perchance encounter have become very much a part of this story. Of these I mention Valantino Akol Wol, Joseph Bel Kuol, my friend and mentor Emmanuel Abur Matuong, Dominic Muorwel, my nephew Riiny Makoor, Marie Joseph of UNHCR, Mathew Riak, Fr O'Brien, and last but by no means least, my relative, friend and companion, Antiok Athuai Lual, whose story this is, as much as it is mine.

It is equally dedicated to millions of Southern Sudanese children who have lived and still live this story. It is in memory of those who have perished in the bush away from home while in pursuit of freedom. If it represents in anyway similar stories of those who have not like me had the opportunity to tell their own stories, so be it.

ACKNOWLEDGEMENTS

Acknowledgements and thanks are due to relatives and friends who have read the manuscript and given useful suggestions and encouragement. Of these I must mention Raymond and Patti Chalker, Eric and Peggy Messer, my long-time colleagues and friends Jeffrey Phillips and Mike Wooldridge, Rev. Andrew Wheeler, who suggested his own publishers, *Paulines Publications Africa*, who first published this book in 2005, and to Peter Lual Deng of *Africa World Books* who suggested republishing a revised version of the book to reach wider readership. Thanks are due to Nancy Kingsley, who volunteered her time to edit and make useful suggestions.

Special thanks are due to Dr Francis Mading Deng for his encouragement and for writing the *Foreword* to this book. Of special mention is my daughter, Aker, who read the original manuscript and liked it so much that she did not care if it were published or not; now that it has been published, she is also supporting revision and republication of the book, under the original title of the manuscript: *The Long Way to Tipperary*, a county and town in the Irish Republic that was made familiar to me by one whistling Irish Catholic priest in Lusaka, Zambia, just before being admitted to Ireland as refugee in 1964. Tipperary, a county and town I must admit I did not visit until after the first publication of this book, is a great place.

All said, I alone I am fully responsible for any mistakes in this book.

FOREWORD

By Dr Francis Mading Deng

I must confess that I have enjoyed everything I have read of Jacob Akol's writings and not only because of style, but also because of substance. Therefore, I did not expect this book to be an exception. Nevertheless, I found the book to be a remarkable story, told in an engaging and gripping manner. Akol very successfully recreates the drama that he has experienced and makes the people with whom he has interacted come alive with discernible authenticity. The reader relives the experience with Akol and unavoidably marvels at how this young man survived the saga and emerged triumphant to tell his story to the "innocent" world beyond.

Akol carefully puts the word "Lost" in the title between quotation marks to distinguish his story from that of the Lost Boys that caught the attention of the media and therefore the world in the early 1990s (see Introduction), a remarkable journalistic feat in which Akol himself was instrumental. In his dual capacity as a journalist and humanitarian aid worker, Akol was able to return to the very areas under which he had suffered the indignities of a refugee to find them in extreme deprivation and degradation. In 1992, he received word that 12,000 Sudanese boys and girls, who had been forced to flee their country because of the atrocious civil war there, had first gone into refuge in Ethiopia, and had then been forced back into the Sudan by the civil wars in Ethiopia, were now heading towards Kenya.

Akol organized a charter flight and flew to the scene with partners from the international media. As he recalls, "The story of the 'Lost Boys' became instant headline news throughout the world."

The story of the Lost Boys has been told and retold; it has been the subject of numerous articles, several books, documentaries, and a major Hollywood motion picture still in the making. What makes the story so gripping is perhaps the fact that it involves identifiable individual children, in large numbers, who, despite the trauma they have suffered, come across as relatively wholesome, self-possessed, and highly motivated to move on with constructive and productive life, even in the unfamiliar environment of the West.

The publicity around the Lost Boys reminded Akol that "Our stories are being written, interpreted and presented mainly by foreigners who may not have the background or have lived such experience." This is why, again in Akol's own words, "I felt challenged to commit to paper my own experiences of the sixties with the background of culture and political realities that result in so many children being forced out of their homes to live in the bush or in foreign lands."

Indeed, an important aspect of the book that adds significantly to its value is the fact that Akol goes beyond documenting his painful experience as a fleeing young man to provide an expansive and in-depth understanding of the society and the culture which had nurtured his resilience against the trials of life that would later confront him. As he notes, "The story moves through a narrow corridor of Dinka culture, religion, environment and geography, all of which, if considered in detail, would require volumes of their own. But that is neither the intention nor purpose of this book." Although Akol is wise to make that qualification, the book certainly radiates with a deep sense of identity, dignity, self-confidence, and fortitude which undoubtedly contributed to the resilient personalities of the Lost Boys. Reading Akol's book brought back to mind songs composed by Dinka refugees in the Congo, which I recorded in the mid-1960s from former refugees who were then on scholarships in the United States. I later included some of these songs in my book, The Dinka, and Their Songs. Excerpts were also cited in my book, The Dinka of the Sudan. I was deeply moved when I heard some of these early recordings used as accompaniments in the documentary film on the Lost Boys. As I noted in my introduction to the songs, "For a people who had grown up thinking of themselves and their country as second to none, the indignities of refugee life brought lamentation and a feeling of isolation." These are excerpts from one of those songs (some of the characters named in the songs interact with the author during the flight in Part III):

> *Gentlemen grind their grain in the land of Congo.[2]*
> *The Dongolaw, the Arab, has remained at home.*
> *He has remained in our land.*
> *We left our herds tethered in the cattle-camps and followed*
> *Deng Nhial.*
> *Gentlemen beg in the land of the Congo....*
> *Abur Matuong (The Egg Man) left,*
> *He was a determined man;*
> *Wol Majok (The Pied One) left,*
> *He was a determined man.*
> *Then we arrived in Congoland.*
> *When we reached the land of the Congo,*
> *The Congo said, "Dinka are matata."*

---

2   Grinding grain is a task normally left to women among the Dinka.

I turned and asked Ngor Maker,
"What does 'matata' mean?"
Ngor Maker answered,
"He says we are bad."
My heart became spoiled
In the land of the Congo, my heart was spoiled.
And I thought of Anger, the daughter of Wol Ayalbyor.
I wish I could find her to see her again.

In another story, the refugees express their determination to fight for the liberation of their country, however long it might take:

William (Deng Nhial) feud is the task of man;
O Deng Nhial, the feud, the feud
The feud of the Southerners with the Northerners;
Our feud will never end.
The army of Deng Nhial and (Dominic) Muorwel
Are called the Anya-Nya
In Bahr al Ghazal, we shall shoot...
We shall revenge the evils of the past;
And if we succeed in our vengeance
We shall be praised by God
(Oh God), bless us
We are the Dinka
O, feud, O, feud.

Some years ago, at a conference held in the Netherlands on refugees and migrants, I heard a report on a study conducted by German doctors who had studied the Lost Boys in the Kakuma Refugee Camp. The study documented the extent to which the Boys had been traumatized by their experience and what lasting damage they had suffered as a result. To everyone's surprise, the study concluded that the Boys showed remarkable resilience and little evidence of the impact of trauma normally expected under similar circumstances. In seeking to explain this surprising finding, the study argued that the Boys had come from a strong cultural environment that had inculcated in them early in life the values and principles that fortified them against their subsequent travails.

Although I thought the point was overstated, I felt proud of the culture they were exalting, and was greatly flattered, though also humbled, by their frequent references to my writings on the Dinka as source materials on that culture. Jacob Akol's story in a way reinforces the findings of the German doctors, not only because he offers a good example of a Lost Boy who survived that trauma with no apparent damage, but also because of his account of his background and the cultural values it engendered, which must have reinforced him in his heroic struggle against the challenges facing a boy fleeing persecution and imminent death.

Akol explains with appropriate modesty, that while "the book is based on an actual journey and events, it does not pretend to record historical facts." He also notes that "although the incidents cited are kept as close as possible to the original events, actual time periods may be incorrect. Some remembered names of people and places along the route may be either wrongly spelled or fictional. Conversation or dialogue, for instance, is often reconstructed in the likeliness of the original. The focus is on the story." Nevertheless, the book reveals remarkable powers of memory, recollection, and attention to details. The literary form of storytelling, especially through reconstructed conversation or dialogue, is particularly effective. Jacob Akol narrates in a way that evokes confidence in the authenticity of his narrative.

In my interview with Dinka informants for the books,

Africans of Two Worlds: The Dinka in Afro-Arab Sudan,[3] and *Dinka Cosmology*,[4] I begin with introductory remarks in which I liken human beings to trees. A tree with deep roots will withstand even a hurricane, while a tree with shallow roots can be knocked down even by a relatively light wind. The roots of a human being are his/her family legacy, moral values, and cultural heritage. A person reinforced by these attributes is more likely to survive the turbulence of radical transformation, while a person denied these essential ingredients can easily go adrift and be lost. I have also often spoken of the invisible bridge, which ties a person to his/her origins wherever he/she might move. This is a state of mind which allows one to go to and fro between his/her original context and wherever else he/she may happen to move. Being connected with one's origin need not be physical; it is a function of remaining connected, concerned, and conscious of one's contribution, whether through studies in areas relevant to the concerns of the Father/Motherland or through material assistance towards meeting the needs of the people back home.

Most Dinkas, indeed, most Sudanese, remain deeply connected to their families, people, and country, even as they move around the world. The fact that the seeds of this connection are planted very early in life may escape most casual observers. I once received an inquiry from a family that was hosting a Lost Boy. The family was surprised that the boy wanted to send money to his family in the Sudan. How could that be when they thought the boy was lost? They obviously did not know what Jacob Akol reflects so well in his book, that a Dinka child learns very early the genealogy of his/her family, the name of the clan, the village, the section, and the tribe. Even when a child is lost, he/she

---

3   New Haven and London: Yale University Press, 1978.

4   London: Ithaca Press, 1980.

is likely to carry along these symbols of identity through which all the members of the community into which he/she moves can easily trace the details. Many of the Lost Boys later re-established contacts with their families, even though they were often too far apart to be reunited physically.

As much as the book is an account not only of Jacob Akol's experience, but also of the people of the South, it mentions names of many individuals who will be familiar to Southern readers, even though they may have been separated for a long time, and in some cases, forever. I was personally moved by the names of some individuals whom I had known early in school, but had never met afterwards, and some of whom have since perished in the atrocious civil war in the South.

Through his book, Jacob Akol has rendered a multi-faceted service to his people and country. I can only share his aspiration that "the story is told in the hope that other Southern Sudanese may be encouraged to face up to the challenge and tell their own similar yet unique stories. If this book encourages others like me to pen their own experiences, so much the better. The telling of these stories should stand as a testimony to our collective suffering, triumphs over odds, and as definitive of character and destiny of the people of the Southern Sudan."

Francis Mading Deng
Stroudsburg, Pennsylvania
May 29, 2004

PREFACE

The story of "The Lost Boys of Sudan" and the publicity around it reminds me of the fact that our life stories are being written, interpreted and presented mainly by foreigners who may not have had the background or have lived such experiences. As a former "Lost Boy" myself I fell challenged to commit to paper my own experiences of the sixties with the background of cultural and political realities that resulted in so many children being forced out of their homes to live in the bush or foreign lands. This story is therefore written in the hope that it will encourage the so-called "lost boys" and now "lost girls" to tell their own similar yet unique stories in their own language. The telling of these stories should stand as testimony to our collective suffering, triumphs over odds and as definitive of character and destiny of the people of Southern Sudan.

Finally, although this book is based on an actual journey and events, it does not pretend to record historical facts. Although the incidents cited in this book are kept as close as possible to the original events, actual time periods may be incorrect. Some remembered names of people or places along the route may be either wrongly spelled or fictional. Conversation or dialogue, for instance, is often reconstructed in the likeness of the original. The focus is on the story.

INTRODUCTION:

"Unaccompanied Minors" of Sudan: "Lost" or "Chosen"?

In 1992, when I was based in the Kenyan capital, Nairobi, as an aid-worker/journalist, I received information about 12,000 Sudanese children who were heading towards the Sudanese town of Kapoeta near the Kenyan border. The children, who were mostly boys and were once refugees in western Ethiopia but had crossed over to the Sudanese town of Pachalla in the mayhem of Col. Mengistu's overthrow, had been on the road for close to one month, running away from the Government of Sudan's military advance on the town.

Believing that publicity of their plight would highlight their ordeal and support their cause, I organized a charter flight and, along with then Nairobi-based BBC correspondent, Peter Biles and an ABC (Australia) correspondent, James Scofield, flew over to Sudan to meet the boys on the road. The story of the so-called "Lost Boys of Sudan" became instant headline news throughout the world.

As a Southern Sudanese, who at one time in my childhood was in the same shoes as these boys, I was far from being impersonal in my reporting. My objective was not just to report the situation but to paint their plight in such a way that would help their cause. Likewise, I was more sympathetic to the liberation movement, the Sudan People's Liberation Movement/Army, SPLM/A, while naturally unsympathetic to the Khartoum based government."[5]

Following the capture of Pachalla by government troops from the SPLA and the children's flight south, government troops followed some months later and capture Kapoeta. The "lost boys," as aid agencies and the media dubbed them, crossed over to Kenya with the world press hot on their trail. They were soon joined there b more refugees from Sudan. This later group included many women and "unaccompanied girls" or "lost girls" trail. They were soon joined there by more refugees from Sudan. But, as soon as they settled into the routine life of refugees in Kakuma Camp, the media lost interest and rarely talked about them.

However, many years later, some of the refugees had returned to the bush to swell the ranks of the SPLA. Others had dispersed to other parts of East Africa in search of education and work while a few others found themselves asylum in Australia, Europe, USA and elsewhere.

A substantial number of the original "lost boys" remained in the refugee camp until the US airlifted them to America in the year 2000 and resettled them, in a blaze of publicity, under "The Lost Boys of Sudan Programme." I was in Oxford at the time on a sabbatical and the BBC called me in to find out if I had any advice for the boys now venturing into a strange life in the West. In effect, they really wanted to know how I managed when I, like them, started a new life as a refugee in the West. "They will do just fine" was part of my comment.

Four years later they are doing very well indeed as

---

5   Jacob J. Akol, "The Lost Boys of Southern Sudan, March 30, 1992.

individuals and as a group. They have, for example, already begun re-examining their past in relation to their current status and environment. This self-examination has now centered on the very name that was supposed to make them a special group: "Lost Boys of Sudan" and, "Lost Girls of Sudan."

The name has divided the group in the US and elsewhere around the world in a way that was unpredictable. Some of them think the name is part of their history and therefore must continue. Others do not only want to be disassociated from the name, but they also think it is demeaning, offensive and divisive of Sudanese communities and therefore must be discarded or banned by law.

Ironically, and perhaps appropriately, this open and heated discussion and argument raged on for months on the discussion board of a "peace website" called "*Gurtong*" (www.gurtong.net), started by one of the "lost boys" of the 1980s and edited/moderated by one of the "lost boys" of the 1960s; a website dedicated to peaceful and constructive discussions and dissemination of information about Southern Sudan.

In retrospect, this controversy over the taken-for-granted name, "lost boys," would require us to pause and ask: in what sense can they be described as "lost"? It can be argued that the term, "lost boys," was originally used by aid agencies and the media to describe some 30,000 children, also known then as "unaccompanied minors," and to reflect the dramatic stories told by the children themselves. These were stories of sudden and savage attacks on their villages by government of Sudan backed Arab militias in Bahr al Ghazal and Western Upper Nile.

The result of those attacks was widespread massacres and destruction during 1987 and 1988. Crops were destroyed, cattle killed or looted, and young children and women were taken as booty in what the Arab tribes were told and believed was a *"jihad"* (holy war) "against infidels." Famine set in with widespread starvation throughout the two regions. An estimated 250,000 people perished during that period alone as thousands of children trekked to refugee camps in western Ethiopia. "We followed the bones trail", as guide to where they were heading the commonly quoted sentence from many of the boys. This indicates that they at least knew the direction of their destination if not the actual distance.

The condition in which these children were in when they arrived in the refugee camps, after walking hundreds of miles for weeks and in some cases months, left no doubt in anyone's mind that even if they knew where they were going, they had most likely lost other members of their families at the time of departure or on the journey. While some confessed to having witnessed parents and siblings either being killed or captured by the *marahaliin* (Arab militias) or dying on the way, the general picture of separation and departure as they described it was that of confusion and tragedy.

Some of the children's fathers will have already been with the SPLM/A, but the children would have had no idea whether they were still alive or dead or, if alive, had a very vague idea where they could be. In such situations the word "lost" would seem quite appropriate to describe their separation.

There is another sense in which the term "lost boys" or "lost generation" could be applied. Except for the ten-year period between 1972 and 1982, generations of South Sudanese children have lived in a period of wanton persecution by, or through a period of open hostilities with Khartoum-based regimes since August 1955 when Southern troops mutinied in the Southern town of Torit, just four months before independence from the Anglo-Egyptian Condominium.

Lack of both stability at home, and a reliable and steady school education over decades, has resulted in what might be described as "lost generations" of Southern Sudanese children; and in that sense, no generation of youngsters before that was any more lost than the ones to which the label has been applied.

But it is for this generation of "lost boys" or "lost girls" that a counter and legitimate question has arisen: are they A "Lost" or a "Chosen" Generation? The question is in the background of the fact that in their formative years in the refugee camps in Ethiopia, two powerful forces competed for their souls in a supposedly complimentary fashion: the military and the Church.

Although the SPLM/A insisted publicly at the time that the children were not being turned into child-soldiers, it has since become common knowledge that thousands of children in the refugee camps in western Ethiopia received strict military training in the Ethiopian Marxist style of the time in the hope of turning them into future elite troops called "Red Army" or *Jiec Amer* of the SPLA. They would be fearless, ruthless, and totally committed to the leadership of the Movement.

However, the Christian Church also found fertile ground for evangelization in the refugees. In unprecedented solidarity, various Christian denominations came together to administer to the children. Thousands were baptized.

While the SPLA taught them to hate and kill their enemies without mercy, the Bible taught them to love and to have mercy on their enemies.

Out of all that, the boys somehow still saw themselves as a "chosen generation, committed to the liberation struggle but fired by their faith and set apart for the decisive spiritual struggle being fought with the *jak* forces of evil. It is these young people who primarily became the fiery evangelists of Bor and northern Bahr al Ghazal."[6]

In the undeclared war for their souls, the Bible tamed the gun as some of these boys brought strong Christian practice into the SPLA for the first time. Overall, the Bible triumphed over the Kalashnikov, at least for the group that eventually made it over to Kenya.

6　　Werner R., Anderson W. & Wheeler A., *Day of Devastation, Day of Contentment,* Nairobi: Paulines Publications, 2000, pp. 534, 535.

And when in July 1992, they eventually reached Kakuma refugee camp ... the first items to be brought out from their scarce possessions were their red choir vests, their long wooden crosses and Bible rather than Kalashnikov. 12,000 of them settled in Kakuma and became the foundation of a vibrant Christian community there. The march to Kakuma was a crucial bonding experience for the Christian youth of jiec Amer. It was these young people who primarily became the fiery evangelists of Bor and northern Bahr al Ghazal."[7]

But it was not all-smooth sailing. Some were "lost": Those Nuer and Dinka young people who found their way home from Ethiopia without this tight community support more commonly abandoned their active Christian faith and became antagonized, bitter, cynical, and traumatized misfits. Those who had never embraced the Christian faith had nothing but the de-socializing and traumatizing training in violence and brutality they had received with the SPLA in Ethiopia on which to fall.[8]

When the boys arrived in America in 2000, they received unprecedented publicity from the Deep South to the North and from East Coast to West Coast. They were unlike other refugees before them. With innate American generosity they were welcomed with open arms. They were not only "orphans" who needed surrogate parents, they were also innocent "lost boys" of the "Peter Pan" proportions.[9]

They were nobility out of darkest African savagery and tragedy, coming into the bright American paradise. America would teach them how to wash their hands using soap and tap water. They would learn how to use flush toilets cook and use knives and forks.

The American entrepreneurial vein kicked in: "The Lost Boys of

---

7   Ibid

8   Ibid

9   "Peter Pan," a James Barrie fairy tale about a group of boys who never grew up and lived in the "Never Land."

Sudan and then "The Lost Girls of Sudan" would become a trademark for fundraising as well as for publishing books, moviemaking, or any other business. They would learn yet to live the American dream.

Meanwhile, the first signs of culture shock must play themselves out. The following three memos were posted on the Gurtong Discussion Board:

I. Subject: Sudanese in America,
Author: Linda Robison. Posted: 6/27/2002

I work with about 30 Sudanese young men in Tampa, Florida USA. Most came from Kakuma, Kenya and few through Cairo. Like the other boys around this country, they are making a living and have somewhere to live. They are learning to drive and get cars. But their dreams of education as someone told them in Africa are the big problem. They are too old for secondary school, most do not have form 4 secondary school documents, and so they cannot continue education until they pass American high school equivalency test, which is very hard and culturally biased. We are working with the various authorities to get the right program in place for them. They are getting discouraged and frustrated. The dream of America is not what they thought it would be. I wish I knew who was filling their heads with things that are not true before they come here.

II. Subject: Sudanese in America,
Author: Kris Garrison. Posted: 8/26/2002

I also work with a large group of Sudanese from Kakuma. Most are "major," over 18 when they entered America. We've run into the same problem as you have in terms of education. Since our local community college does not require that students have a high school diploma, many of these young men are attending ESL (English as Second language) classes through the community college.

This fulfils their desire to attend college, improves their English comprehension and writing skills, thus putting them in a better position to pass the new GED (General Education Diploma) tests. The federal PELL (Proficiency in English Language Learners) grant covers tuition, books, and a stipend to help with living expenses. Maybe this would be a possibility in your area. Good luck!

III. Subject: Sudanese in America, Author: Sandro C. Juet. Posted: 9/18/2002.

Well... Linda that is a good point. I have been working with [the lost boys of Kakuma] almost for one and a half years, teaching them GED-mathematics and help clear their confused vision about the real things in America. I think they were expecting more than what they found, free education is one of those. As you said they out aged the high schools, and they think that the process of getting a General Education Diploma (GED) is a long and hard way for them. Most of them did get frustrated as you mentioned but for those who do have the will and are ready to adjust to the new environment and culture, success is possible, but that wouldn't happen without consulting and continuous encouragement. Also, there are other options such as community colleges, which they can join if their English and Math's skills improved.

As moderator of the website and a veteran refugee who came to the West in the 1960s under similar circumstances, my response was to thank those Americans who were working so hard to see that the new arrivals were adjusting well to their new environment. I also intimated that knowing the cultural and social background of these boys I had no doubt whatsoever that most of them will eventually get what they want most from America: education.

Understanding and appreciating the social, religious, and cultural background of "The Lost Boys" and "The Lost Girls" of the Sudan is the key to helping them acclimatize to their new environment without the feeling of being uprooted from their deep cultural roots. This is what Fr Dominic Matong (a Catholic priest) praised about the Protestant Church when he talked to Marc Nikkel in 1989.[10]

He compared "the care with which Protestant missionaries and their Sudanese disciples taught the Bible to the care with which a *Dinka benybith* (Spearmaster) transfers his knowledge and authority to a successor. It is the same with Protestants. They have given the real spear of the Bible to their people."

It is my hope that this book will encourage and challenge the so-called "lost boys" and "lost girls" of the Sudan to pick up their pens and tell their similar yet unique life stories.

---

10   Cf. Werner R. Anderson W. & Wheeler A., op cit., p. 532.

PART ONE:
THE HERDS BOY

"A tree with deep roots will withstand even a hurricane, while a tree with shallow roots can be knocked down even by a relatively light wind. The roots of human being are his/her family legacy, moral values and cultural heritage."

— Francis Mading Deng

The Origin of Jieng Clans

In the beginning, people lived in the River under water. There was no disease and no death. But the population grew so big there was hardly room to scratch one's backside.

It was then Longar Jiel, the Spearmaster,[11] went to investigate

---

11   'Bith' is a white barbless fishing spear. 'Alol' is a white barbless spear with two pins on the topside of the blade. Both spears are usually among a small collection of 'Sacred Spears' belonging to a Spearmaster and are used only for invocation by Spearmasters popularly known as 'Masters of the Fishing Spear'. A 'Benybith is also 'Benyalol', "Spearmaster.

the possibility of living on Dryland; but he returned with bad news: Humans could not live on Dryland:

"There are wild animals, diseases and death on Dryland," he told his people and forbade them to leave the River. "Emigrating to Dryland," he said, "was not a good idea after all."

But his people were tired of overcrowding, and they rebelled: "We know why you will not allow us to live on Dryland!" they shouted at him. "You have been sneaking out of the water all the time for Dryland. That's where you disappear to, Dryland. You don't want us to share it with you. Is that not so?" they cried.

Longar stood his ground. "You will have to kill me before you can leave the River. It is wild out there! You will die!" He pleaded with them, but they would not listen. They marched on him.

Longar planted reeds at the exit from the River. He stood on Dryland and waited, his sacred spear was held high and ready to throw. The first person to disturb the reeds he speared in the head, pulled his body out and fed it to the beasts of Dryland.

The killing went on all day until Agoth Cithiik, his nephew, deceived him with a cooking stick with which he disturbed the reeds. Longar split the head of the cooking stick into two with his spear; but before he realised he had been tricked, Agoth emerged from the water and wrestled his uncle to the ground and held him there as Longar tried to free himself.

Meanwhile, people were pouring out of the River on to Dryland.

Longar changed himself into a cobra and bit Agoth on the face. Agoth continued to hold on to him. Longar changed himself into a lion and bit Agoth in the throat. But Agoth continued to hold on to him. Longar changed himself into all sorts of dangerous creatures, which he knew inhabited Dryland. But Agoth Cithiik knew his uncle could do him no harm, for it was written in the beginning: "A Spearmaster's word or deed shall do no harm to his sister's children".

When the River was empty of people, Longar resigned himself to the fact that from then on, humans would never be able to live under water again. They were condemned forever to live on Dryland and suffer the consequences. Agoth then left the Speamaster by the River, seemingly dying of exhaustion and dehydration.

The Gong Divinity: When Longar recovered, *Gong* the Hedgehog was licking his face sympathetically. He picked him up and said: "You will be my guardian and forever my children's and my grandchildren's guardian here on Dryland." He fed the hedgehog with milk and butter and told him to return to his family.

From there on, the offspring of Longar Jiel became known as "the people of *Gong*" the Hedgehog or simply the "Pagong Clan". Even today, members of the Pagong Clan warmly receive Gong the Hedgehog into their homes. They feed him with milk and butter before sending him back to the bush.

Following Longar's example, other heads of families, faced with the realities of a world full of suffering and death, sought protection from other creatures that had lived on Dryland before humans. Thus, we have the Payii Clan or "the people of *Acuiel*" the Kite: they do not kill that bird. The Padiangbar Clan or "the people of *Miir*" the Giraffe: they do not kill or eat that animal. The Padolmuot Clan or the "people of *Koor*" the Lion. They offer him an animal now and again, but they do not kill the lion. And if a lion sheds the blood of a Padolmuot "by mistake", the beast will not touch the bone, for therein lies the bonds of lineage.

Apart from the main relationship with the animal symbols of divinities like *Gong* for the Pagong, other beings or animates have come to be regarded as of sacred importance to different clans through experience. Jiel Longar, the son of Longar Jiel, for instance, added two more "divinities"[12]: *Awar* (a kind of grass: *vetiveria nigritana*) and *Ring* (Flesh). Here are Jiel's separate experiences with *Awar* and *Ring*.

The Awar Divinity: There was great drought in the land when Jiel was a boy. All grass, except *Awar*, dried up. All the cattle fed on *Awar*, but there was no water for the cattle to drink and they began to die like flies, except Jiel's cattle, which he drove to an isolated part of the forest. His animals looked fat and healthy. People wondered why but no one dared ask him.

One day, someone spied on him and discovered that Jiel removed with his hand an *Awar* patch twice a day. Under it was a deep well full of very clear water. Jiel drank first then he let his cattle drink, then replaced the *Awar* patch.

The spy pulled up the same *Awar* patch after Jiel had gone but found no water under it. He threw it aside and pulled up another one and then another but found no water under them. He went home and told the people what he had seen.

The following day, many other villagers spied on Jiel and saw him do what the man told them he had done the previous day. After Jiel had gone, they tried to do the same thing but with no luck. So they killed the man who first spied on the young Spearmaster because they feared what Jiel would do to them for having spied on him. They then returned home and begged Jiel to forgive them and give their cattle some water. Jiel told them: "You should have come to me in the first place instead of wasting time on things you do not understand." He supplied their cattle with water the following day and added *Awar* to the divinities of the Pagong Clan.

---

12   In his book "*Divinity and Experience: The Religion of the Dinka*", Prof. Godfrey Lienhardt would classify 'Gong' as 'yath', "divinity" with a small 'd' as opposed to 'Nhialic (God)', "Divinity" with a capital 'D'.

The Ring Divinity: When Jiel became a man and full Spearmaster, a kite flying over his cattle camp dropped a piece of liver on his lap. He roasted the meat and ate it and found it tasted like no meat he had eaten before. He was intrigued; so, he ordered a hunt and told his people to kill one of each kind of animal and bring their livers to him. But none of the livers they brought back matched the taste of the liver the kite dropped. He made a new list and ordered more hunts; but no liver would match. He began to suspect the liver could have come from a human, but how was he to obtain such a liver?

One day, a young man in the cattle camp died suddenly. The Spearmaster ordered his immediate burial and the departure of everyone from the site of the cattle camp. He told his people he would follow. When he was alone, he dug up the dead man, removed the liver, roasted it and ate it. It matched. Satisfied, he buried the body and prepared to leave.

But someone appeared from behind a bush and informed the Spearmaster that he had seen everything. "You ate the liver of a man, Spearmaster," the man said, "and people should know the truth that they have a cannibal for a leader!"

"Who are you?" asked the Spearmaster. "Are you not the fisherman down the river? What do you want with me?"

"To join the cattle camp and to be as rich as you."

"That's too much to ask, fisherman!" warned the Spearmaster. "Watch your greed."

"Not as much as the shame you will have when I tell the people exactly what you are."

"Alright then, come with me. I will make you very rich, but you must promise never to utter a word to anyone about what you have seen."

The man promised and joined the cattle camp. In a very short time, he became even richer than the Spearmaster. Yet he was not satisfied and wanted Jiel Longar to make him as divine as himself.

The Spearmaster told him that it was something he could not do. "Only *Nhialic* God/Divinity alone can do that." The man appeared to accept that explanation; but he continued to be jealous of the divine powers of the Spearmaster.

One day, the man picked an argument with the Spearmaster, then, in the heat of that argument, blurted out the secret: "You are a cannibal," he pointed at Jiel and added, "you are also a liar if you deny it!"

"I will not deny it," said Jiel Longar calmly, "but I will remind you of your oath."

"What of it!" said the fisherman, believing there was nothing much the Spearmaster could do about his vast cattle wealth and his newly acquired popularity. But a few months later he was back fishing in the river. All his cattle had suddenly died of an unknown disease.

By that time, Jiel had already added *Ring* the Flesh into his list of divinities. Today, all Spearmasters of the Pagong Clan offer a red bull to the *Ring* divinity. The bull is killed at sunrise; the meat is then divided and given to the families of the clan on one condition: the meat can only be cooked and eaten after sunset, never during the day when the sun is in the sky.

Like Jiel, all the leaders of other clans had experiences that made them add more divinities to the original guardian of their clans. Thus, some clans have now relationships with specific trees, others with grasses or insects and so on. As a result, there is hardly a living or inanimate thing in Jiengland that has not a human as a relative and a clan that believes in its sanctity.

The Importance of Names

My name is Jiel *Arunyyiep*[13] (Axe Stroker), son of Akol Atem, of the Pagong Clan. I was about seven or eight years old when this journey began. Not that I could say exactly which day of which month of which year I was born because births and deaths were not recorded in our community because we were all illiterate. But, later, I found the clues from other people's stories that pointed to the fact that I was born on an uncertain date in either May or June of 1946 or 1947.

One story was that told by my sister, Akuch, the oldest child of my mother: She was at a neighbour's house when she got the news of my arrival. She was so exited she forgot to follow the usual path and ran straight through a field of young sorghum crops back to our house. "The crops were up to my knees," she said. As I am the fourth child of my mother, and there is usually an average of two years between children, Akuch must have been around six years old and possibly five feet tall for the sorghum to reach her knees. This could only have been May or June.

It is also said that I was born sometime after the end of *Muunayat*, which was a special tax levied against the Dinka or Jieng to support British Second World War campaigns. This tax was stopped a year or so following the end of the war in 1945; thus, the possibility that I was born in 1946 or 1947.

The naming of children among the Jieng follows an almost predictable pattern. Male children are normally named after their paternal grandfathers, great grandfathers or other long-established male name of the clan. In the case of the Pagong Clan, the traditional names include Longar, Jiel, Gong and Awar.

My firstborn son, for example, could be named Atem after my

---

13   My ox name. All Jieng males are given their own ox names. In his book, *The Dinka of the Sudan*, Francis M. Deng uses the term "personality ox."

grandfather. He could be named Bol, after my great grandfather. The more sons in the family, the more likely an old name, such as Longar or Jiel, or Awar or Gong would be considered for a name, otherwise they would usually be ignored in preference for more recent descendant's names.

Female children are normally named after their paternal grandmothers and great grandmothers. For example, my daughter could be named Ayak after my father's mother. She could also be named Aliet or Athieng or Doot because those are among the long-established names of former mothers of my paternal line of the family. The more daughters in the family, the more likely many old names of mothers of the clan would be remembered.

But a family or a clan name is sometimes dropped simply because such a name is regarded as "unlucky", should the parents recall that such a name was recently given to a child that did not survive childhood.

If the children are twin (*diet*[14]) boys, they are usually named Chan and Ngor respectively. If they are twin girls, they are usually named Achan and Anger respectively. If the twins are a female and a male, they are usually named Achan and Chan respectively. A child born after the twins is normally named Bol if it is a boy or Nyibol if a girl.

A male child born after a stillborn child or after a brother or sister who died before his birth would normally be called Dut or Madut or Manut. If she was a girl, she would either be called Adut or Nyanut. All these names imply 'consolation' for the lost child.

There are, however, other ways new names can enter the family chain of names. My father's name, Akol, for instance, entered the family chain of names when a traveller, believed to have had divine

---

14   Diet means 'birds' for twins. They are regarded as a special gift from God and are believed to have supernatural gifts. As babies they are considered weak and delicate and therefore can 'fly away' (die) like birds any time.

powers, told my grandparents that "the next child will be a boy and must be named Akol (Sun), from where I come and go".

Up to that time, my grandfather, Atem Bol, had many daughters and no sons from his two wives. Since the names of parents are remembered through the male line, they were worried that there would be no son to remember them by giving their names to his children. This would be tragic because the Jieng believe one is truly dead if one is not remembered by naming a descendent after one.

A Male Jieng is also entitled to his own "Mr" as it were. Let me explain: Each male is known by the colour of an ox, given to him when young or chosen later by himself. Thus, someone called Deng may be known as Deng *Mabior* (white ox) or Deng *Mahcar* (black ox) or Deng *Majok*[15] (black and white colours arranged in a certain pattern on an ox).

These "ox names", as they are called, can be highly abstract and metaphorical. For example: An uncle of mine called me "*Arunyyiep*" soon after my birth. This phrase refers to an imaginary stroking of an axe so gently with the palm of the hand and so repeatedly that it begins to shine, reflecting sunrays. This reflection reminds one of a white-colour-patch on the side of a brown ox. Such an ox with such a colouring is known as "*Mabil*". So, while some will address me as "Jiel *Arunyyiep*", others will refer directly to the colour of the ox, addressing me as "Jiel *Mabil*". Although I know of other people who use "*Mabil*" as their ox name, I do not know of anyone else who uses "*Arunyyiep*" for an ox name, thus the uniqueness and attraction of the name for me.

But he could have called me "Jiel *Awet*" (Crown Crane) and the colour of the crane would have become the colour of my ox. I could have changed it myself to such a name, except that I had come to like the ox's colour name given me when I was a baby. It is also a

---

15   A 'Majok' bull or ox is highly valued by the Jieng.

commitment and a sign of respect on my part to the uncle who gave me the ox's name. This same uncle was the one who insisted on my being named "Jiel", despite my mother's objections.

An ox name can be a bit confusing to a non-Jieng because some of them are also people's proper names, and thus the reason for *italics* here to identify them from real names. Machar, Mabior, Majok and Awet are, for example, Jieng proper names. Theoretically, then, a man called Majok could also have an ox of the same name and therefore could be addressed as "Majok *Majok*". Suppose his father and grandfather were also named Majok - which does happen - his full name would consist of four Majoks: his name, his ox's, his father's and grandfather's. To clarify these names, he would introduce himself thus: "My name is Majok *Majok*, son of Majok Majok". I do not, however, know anyone whose given name is also his ox's name.

It should be noted that one does not have to have an ox of that colour physically available in one's family herd in order to be known by it. Thus, Deng *Mabior* does not necessarily have to have a white-coloured bull among his herd. However, if an ox of that colour was born or brought into the family herd, it would nominally[16] be his to look after and brag about.

An ox name to a Jieng man is as "Mr" is to an Englishman. A stranger or a junior addressing a man called Deng *Mabior* as just "Deng" without adding his ox's name, *Mabior*, would sound as disrespectful as if a stranger or junior had addressed a Mr. Johnson as just "Johnson". In this sense, a Jieng male may be considered as having "his own Mr" in the form of an ox name.

Name identification is very important among the Jieng. My elder brother's full introduction of himself to a stranger who is also Jieng would go something like this: "I am called Angui *Majok*, son

---

16 The father or elder of the family has the last word in the way any of the family cattle are disposed.

of Akol Atem, man of the Pagong Clan." He may wish to identify himself even further by announcing his home area, which in this case would be "from Gaikou of Gai Akol Atem." After the other person has introduced himself or herself, the two newly met would conduct business or a relationship in the knowledge of those essential facts.

Spearmasters Don't Die

The qualities of a good man will include bravery, truthfulness, honesty, kindness and generosity. By this yardstick, my grandfather, Atem Bol, clearly failed the last two fundamentals: kindness and generosity. He was often referred to as "mean old Atem".

His malady developed late in life. This was first blamed on the fact that he and his two wives were producing daughters and no sons. On the other hand, his half brother, Rec Bol, and his wives were producing sons and no daughters.

As daughters bring to the family bride wealth in cattle and sons take it out at their marriages, it would seem obvious to a non-Dinka that Atem was more blessed than Rec because he had daughters and no sons. Nothing could be further from the truth. By custom and tradition, Rec would be expected to preside over the marriages of his brother's children, boys or girls, and thereby contribute or receive a sizeable number of cattle. But since Atem had only daughters and no son, Rec could only receive and had no reason to pay out. On the other hand, Atem would be expected to pay out for his brother's sons and receive nothing in return since Rec had no daughters.

Should Atem die without a son, Rec and his sons would be responsible for Atem's wives, unmarried daughters and property; that is to say, in the crude language of modern economics and law, Rec and his sons would inherit Atem's wives and the cattle his daughters brought into the family. "Unfair!" a foreigner would shout, but that's the way it is, a long-cherished Jieng custom which has held families together since they emerged from underwater; few Jieng dare question it.

Grandpa Atem was one of the few who dared break with the tradition in a negative way. Such crude thoughts of unfairness must have crossed his mind, poisoned his judgement and influenced his uncharitable attitude towards his brother, nephews and all around him. The fact that he was blessed later in his old age with two sons seemed to have no positive effect on his paranoia.

By the time my father was born, three of his sisters were already married and Grandpa had already begun to ignore the tradition by conducting the affairs of his daughters' marriages single-handedly. What was more, he kept all the dowry[17] cattle and denied his brother and nephews their rightful share. When confronted for his wayward behaviour, he would tell his brother to do the impossible, that he should turn some of his boys into girls to get himself cattle.

Grandpa was also mean in minor ways too, for example: He ate with his eyes closed to shut out children and dogs that might be watching him eat. This way he avoided sharing his meals with others. He avoided company, became a recluse and spoke only when he wanted to reprimand someone for something.

One day, so goes the story, his favourite dish of dried meat disappeared in front of him. He suspected a neighbour's son and his dog, and he told the boy to own up but the boy flatly denied the theft. Grandpa, the installed Spearmaster of the clan, warned the father of the boy: "who dares steal from me will pay dearly. It is between your son and your dog. Either he confesses or takes the consequences of his lying."

The father of the boy pleaded with his son to confess or "the Spearmaster will call deadly judgement upon you and our family!" But the boy remained adamant that he had done nothing wrong.

---

17   Cattle paid by the groom to the bride's family.

The following morning, a rogue elephant raided the village. When the dust had settled the dog suspected by the Spearmaster lay dead in a pool of blood, crushed by the elephant.

Grandpa ordered the boy be brought to him. When the boy was seated in front of him, he placed his right hand upon his head, spat light sliver on his forehead as a blessing and told the boy to disappear "before I see faults in your soul!"

"Mean old Atem" withdrew into the self-inflicted loneliness of a hermit and eventually faded away from the leadership of the family, the clan and the Gai territory, composed of many other important and minor clans.

One day he announced his own death.[18] He was buried alive with full honours and the pomp befitting a "Great Spearmaster who led his people bravely and wisely." My father, Akol Atem, who was not yet 20, but already had two wives and children, was officially installed as the new Spearmaster, head of the clan and Gai territory, to be known from then on as "Gai Akol Atem."

My father was in many ways the opposite of his father. He was kind, generous and had the excellent leadership qualities required of a Spearmaster. Everybody loved him. Here is his story:

When he was about 15 years of age, he set about repairing the poisoned relationship between the family of his father, Atem Bol, and that of his uncle, Rec Bol. He began by transferring a few cattle at a time to his uncle's herd. When his father noticed he simply told him that the cattle were being given temporarily because, he told his father, "your brother's children need milk-cows, father, and we have so many. I will get them back later."

Grandfather was not a fool. He wanted to know why his son was

---

18   By custom, a prominent Spearmaster is buried alive once it's clear that he would not survive much longer the illness that afflicts him. Spearmasters generally announce their desire "to depart".

also giving them oxen and bulls if he was only providing milk for his nephews. He accused my father of laziness, calling him the son of his mother, an insult for a grownup Muonyjang (Jieng man) to be called a son of woman by his father. He accused him of weakness and warned him that Rec's "horde of boys" would kill him one day and take his cattle and sisters.

Father would apologise to his father, but he never brought back the cattle. That way he was able to give Rec and his sons their rightful share of the bride wealth his sisters brought into the family. Grandpa either forgot about the missing cattle or had come to realise that the torch was passing on to his son. He must have noticed that people who had stopped calling on his family for many years had started coming back, pretending to come to see the Spearmaster, while in reality, they were doing business with the young master who was clearly more level-headed, wise, and approachable.

For looks, father was average: He was below 6ft tall, pretty average for a Dinka man. He had distinct large ears, bowed legs and flat feet. Put those features on a poor man born into a lesser family of lesser wealth and clan and he would be very ordinary indeed. As it turned out, his wealth, clan and family standing, plus an excellent personality and wisdom exhibited at an early age, made him a highly sought-after gentleman, if not by the women he married, certainly by their families. He was in his late 40s or early 50s when I was born. He had 8 wives, including my mother.

I was about five when he married his ninth and last wife. I remember very clearly a ritual visit Malek *Amethpiu* (my half-brother and age-mate) and I made to the young wife in a poorly lit room. She looked very pretty as she rubbed our freshly washed bodies with gee and told us how handsome we were. I remember how proudly we emerged from the room with gleaming bodies and sunny faces. But, what each of us felt but did not articulate at the time was the mild rivalry that had just begun between us.

Our mothers soon exploited this rivalry through a neighbourhood girl called Aluel, whom we both loved and pretended to love us. One day, Aluel would tell other adults in our presence that "*Amethpiu* (Malek's ox name) is going to be my husband. I hear so many good things about him. He is handsome and my mother likes him. He gives her very strong tobacco. I don't know about Jiel though. (Note how she subtly degraded me by omitting my ox's name!). I hear he has been naughty." Malek and I would sneak away, he beaming with embarrassed pleasure, while I suffered the humiliation of rejection. A few days later, her story would change for no apparent reason, and she would announce in the same manner that "*Arunyyep* (that's me) is now my preferred future husband." It took us a long time to realise that the whole thing was a plot concocted by our mothers to keep us straight: "I will tell Aluel if you do that". "I will tell Aluel if you don't do this!" and so on and so forth. We eventually realised that all our older brothers had been victims of such plots "to help them grow up." Some help! Malek and I thought we should complain to our father; but what could he do? He would probably tell us not to be so easily deceived by women. So, we told him nothing.

My father had 9 wives and 25 living children when he died, or rather, when he announced his own death as Spearmasters do. He was buried alive in an elaborate religious ceremony.

I was about seven years old. Although I was aware he had been sick for some time, confined to bed by a cancerous wound on his right hip, it still came as a shock to me. Often, mother prepared food and I accompanied her to see my father at my stepmother's where he was bedridden. Though clearly in pain, he would prop himself up against his cork stool and enquired after us: did we have enough to eat? Did we have enough milk? Were we good children? Were we happy? All to which my mother always replied in the affirmative.

"And what about you, *Arunyyiep*, are you happy?" He either

held my hand or stroked my head with his right hand as he spoke. I would reply to all his questions in the affirmative, though there were times I wanted to say, "I went to bed hungry last night," but could not. It was not the thing to do for boys to show weakness of any kind in front of their elders, fathers. Father would then spat my forehead with light sliver in blessing and told me to go. I was always beside myself with happiness. Nevertheless, I was also delighted to be dismissed and glad to be out and away with my age-mate, Malek, with whom I played, wrestled and sometimes fought over trivialities that seemed important to us then.

Father and mother would talk for a long time before she returned to her homestead. I went back with her only if I was needed or wished to go home, otherwise I played on with Malek until sunset. Often, we disappeared to any one of our father's houses nearby or joined other village children to play.

Although each of us considered his mother's homestead as the primary home, the homesteads of our father's other wives were clearly our second homes. We were fed in any of them when food was available and ready to serve. We were equally taught and disciplined by any adult member of our father's larger family. We were certainly our mothers' children but more importantly we were our father's and therefore members of a larger family and clan.

On the morning of the day my father was buried, Mother told us it was time for father to go. He was very ill, she said, and would not live much longer. We all went to see him for the last time.

When my eyes got used to the dimness of the room he was in, I could see my father clearly as he lay on his back on the ox skin with his head resting on his usual stool. He appeared composed with his eyes half closed. I also noticed that he did not prop himself up as usual. Although he was eventually able to raise his right hand to my forehead, he was clearly unable to speak. A light smile passed over his lips and he slowly withdrew his hand. There were no blessings for the first time. Mother indicated we should go so that other members of the family could come in to pay their last respects.

What do I remember about my father? That he was kind and gentle in the way he talked to me, the way he enquired about my wellbeing, the way he addressed me by my ox's name, *"Arunyyiep."* He conveyed respect and sensitivity for my dignity.

He was a brave man too. Evidence of his bravery and strength was always exhibited by the head of a leopard which attacked him when a young man. He grabbed the beast by the neck, wrestled him to the ground, held him down with his left hand and slit his throat with the blade of his spear. He had the leopard's claw marks on his back, chest, and arms.

The leopard's head, with its mouth opened and teeth bared, was preserved and used to frighten off marauding dogs when necessary. When placed next to meat or fish drying in the sun in a homestead of any of father's wives, dogs knew well to stay clear of that homestead. Dogs to leopards are like mice to cats and dogs know it.

Women fought over the use of the leopard's head until one Cipuouram, a notorious neighbour's dog, responsible for many audacious acts of thievery in the village, snatched the leopard's head one day in broad day light and in front of witnesses. He disappeared into the bush with it. He returned later in the evening, but the leopard's head was never found, and no one knew exactly what he had done with it. Ate it I suppose.

Father was a wise and generous man too. An example often cited far and wide was his decision in a certain year to direct the planting of a quick maturing sorghum crop in all his considerable fields. Quick maturing sorghum does not store well for long and is mostly good for consumption within one or two months after harvest. It is usually allocated a small portion of farmland, as it is only needed to bridge the hunger gap in July and early August. Why then did he do it?

There had been two consecutive years of very poor harvest due to locusts. Limited starvation, he knew, would begin in June and would become mass starvation in July and early August. Although the Aguok people travelled to distant lands like Apuk, Kuach and Malual Giernyang to buy food and seeds, father calculated that such efforts would not be enough to avert severe famine in the land.

He therefore bought plenty of quick maturing sorghum seeds, enough to plant all his fields and some more to distribute to other nearby villages, which he persuaded to do the same.

Then came July. While the rest of Aguok was starving, the vast fields of Gai Akol Atem were ready for harvest. Word spread very quickly, and people came from as far south as Wuuny and from as far north as Agurpiny to beg for sorghum from our fields.

Father directed all our homesteads to give the starving families a basketful of sorghum each, asking them to return the same full basket with the long-maturing sorghum crop once their fields were ready for harvesting. Many families, grateful to my father, returned not only one but two baskets full of sorghum. Such acts of foresight are not easily forgotten.

The Bull Woman

My mother, Aker Baak, daughter of Baak Ngoong, was tall, straight and very pretty, the sort of girl men would compete[19] for or fight over for a first wife. But, according to her family, she fell in love with a man beneath her station. Even when she eloped with him and got pregnant with my sister, Akuch, her lover was totally rejected by her family on many counts, not least his lack of enough cattle to marry into the family of Baak Ngoong.

---

19   Competition usually involves two suitors, none for whom the bride or her people have expressed special preference; in which case who offers most cattle for dowry may get the bride.

Returned from her lover's home, word got to my father that a pretty daughter of Baak Ngoong was available for marriage. He paid an official visit to Kuruech and immediately fell in love with her. "The following morning," mother continued the story, "your father sent emissaries with a token bride wealth of 10 milk cows -not counting calves - 6 heifers, 4 oxen and 1 bull. That was more than expected and he impressed my father very much." She was shortly after ceremoniously escorted to Akol Atem's home. The full dowry was negotiated and delivered much later in instalments.

Mother told us nothing of her own feelings about my father at their first meeting. But the urgency with which she was handed over to my father indicates that her people were not comfortable with keeping her at home for long while they negotiated an appropriate number of cattle for their pretty daughter. If she erred once by falling in love and eloping with a poor man of a minor family and clan, she could do it again. Handing her over as quickly as possible to Akol Atem seemed to be the wisest thing to do. "After all," they must have reasoned, "Akol Atem is an honourable man who has clearly demonstrated his love for our daughter and respect for the family of Baak Ngoong by sending 21 cattle so quickly". He would be alright, they trusted him.

What about Aker, would she still insist on going back to her lover? Most unlikely, at least she did not express, even to her close friends and relatives, any dislike for Akol Atem. That was always a good sign.

As for father, he knew a good thing when he saw one. He knew he had a bargain. Not only was she pretty, but her people were also of a decent and highly respected family. On his part, it seemed he respected mother's opinions and overlooked her flaming temper. He even admired her outspokenness and bravery because he was the one who first dubbed her "Bull Woman".

Her honesty and no-nonsense approach to business was respected and accepted by members of the Akol family. When there was something to share, such as dried fish which father sometimes bought in bulk from distant lands like Twic, mother would be the one to share it out. On official occasions such as marriage celebrations, mother would be the one to share out food and drinks.

Her dominance was based on a few principles: no favouritism, no underhand dealings and no fear of anyone who wanted to corrupt. I know that her own family came last in her considerations when sharing out communal goodies. As a result, we (her family) often got the smallest share or nothing at all because she would rather her own children had nothing than see someone else go without. Those traits made her the natural spokeswoman for the Akol family in business issues involving women of other families or clans.

Father's respect for mother must have increased as she presented him with one son after another. Of all his nine wives, only mother had four living and healthy sons. Over time, the bride wealth given to her family jumped to over 100 cattle, something unheard of for a seventh wife who came with someone else baby!

Her submission to the wishes of her family in marrying father and making an excellent job of it made her "an honoured daughter" in her father's household. Because she was well married, she could walk into any of her father's homes or her brother's homesteads and helped herself to anything she liked. Their wives dared not challenge her. After all, was it not the cattle she brought into the family that enabled their husbands to pay a dowry for them? If her marriage to my father broke down and father reclaimed all his dowry cattle and their offspring, their own marriages could break up because my father would trace all his cattle to those marriages. A daughter well married was not to be trifled with!

Mother was well off in her own right. She was entitled to up to five cattle from bride wealth brought into the family by any of her younger sisters or nieces - and she had plenty of them. And mother was not the sort of woman to let her brothers get away with her rightful share of bride wealth, even if they tried.

Although these cattle from mother's side of the family were part of Akol Atem's cattle wealth and father could do anything he liked with them, they remained mothers. We (Aker's family) had priority over the milk cows from our maternal source.

Aker Baak's homestead consisted of herself and her five children. One other very important member of our family was a man called Lual *Mangar*, Lual Kon. He came from the Panhial Clan and was therefore a maternal relative of my father. We called him 'Uncle' though at first, I thought he was our elder brother.

He lived with us and did most of the man's work about the house. His duties included gathering firewood for making fire in the centre of the compound in the evening[20]. He worked very hard in cultivating and harvesting our fields. He dug and mixed the clay from a nearby pond for the building and repairing of any of the walls of our homestead. He designed and supervised the actual construction of the walls. He selected, cut and transported wood from the forest for roofing to our homestead. He made and repaired ropes for our cattle, sheep and goats. He taught and showed us our duties as boys and supervised our activities. He was the handyman of our homestead. Father had distant relatives like Lual *Mangar* working for him in his other homesteads.

One day he received his payment: Father married him off by paying a lot of cattle for the hand of a girl from a family somewhere near the Jur River. He moved out there, but he and his wife came back just before my father died. They stayed with us, and it was great to see him and his wife again. She was pregnant, expecting their first child.

Lual *Mangar* and his wife moved out as soon as my elder brother, Angui *Majok*, was initiated to manhood and was then to do most of

---

20   This wood is not to be confused with the firewood gathered for cooking by women.

the tasks Lual *Mangar* used to do. But Angui spent much of his time at the cattle camp. I don't know how we coped without Lual *Mangar*.

Sorghum is our staple food. It is prepared and eaten in various forms. The simplest way is to boil the grain mixed with tamarind seeds or groundnuts until they are thoroughly cooked and soft to chew. Salt is sometimes added. But a woman who feeds her family this way too often is not only considered lazy but uncaring.

The most common way of eating sorghum is in the form of thick porridge. The grain is first pounded into flour, which is then cooked and presented as porridge or bread. This took a lot of mother's time and energy to prepare. First, she soaked the grain in water to clean out any dust, sand or pebbles and to soften the grain because dry sorghum could be very hard. She would then put it in a hollowed block of mahogany wood, which was partially buried, hollowed face up, in the ground and pounded it with a heavy wooden stick.

The first pounding loosened the skin from the grain. It was then removed and cleaned of the featherweight fluffy skin. Any course flour out of the first pounding was of "inferior quality", but she kept that for other uses - such as beer brewing. The grain was then pounded for the second time and the fine flour was separated and kept aside. The remaining grain was pounded once more to abstract more fine flour. Any sorghum not turned into flour at that stage was kept separately as fine grain.

Mother added the fine grain into a boiling pot of water first. That was stirred into thin, soft porridge with a wooden stick, fitted at one end with a piece of bladed backbone of a sheep or goat. But mother always warned us to keep away from the pot when the small grain was breaking up into porridge because blobs of hot porridge were thrown out at random. If one of these caught your eye you would get a nasty burn, or you could be blinded for life!

Fine flour was finally added then stirred into thick porridge while the pot remained on the fire for a few more minutes. The hot pot was then removed from the fire, usually with bare hands. I often wondered how mother did it without getting her hands burnt!

Anyway, to give the porridge flavour, sour milk was sometimes added into it while still cooking. Other times we added fresh milk to the porridge when it was being served. On rare occasions, fresh butter or gee was added to the porridge while still hot. For those dishes, oyster shells were used as spoons. Children and women might elect to use their fingers. This was not normally an option for men.

The most preferred way of flavouring the porridge was to prepare an accompanying dish of meat or fish broth, cooked in peanut butter sauce and vegetables, such as ladyfingers. Sometimes, sesame butter was used instead of peanut butter. The broth usually required an extra dish per person or per sharing group.

Father had his own dish. Often, he came home much later in the evening when we had all eaten. Sometimes he did not turn up at all and we assumed he was staying in any one of his other homesteads for the night and unlikely to turn up hungry anyway. So, we ate his food if we were still hungry or ate it in the morning.

There are no strict rules about having to share with others or who to share with at an early age but if Malek was around, for instance, he and I would always share from the same dish. When we got older, we shared more often from one dish with those of our own age. At the age of seven or thereabout, Malek and I shared food together more often than before and generally waited for each other at mealtimes.

The sharing of food with people who did not live in the same household involved moving from homestead to homestead. It was both exciting and exhausting yet a rewarding one. For instance, if one's mother decided not to cook, which they often did, or it was during times of food shortages which were frequent, there was always a homestead with food available and ready to eat; thus, one did not have to go to bed with an empty stomach very often. It was clearly beneficial for one to share with others.

After the evening meal, conversation would usually begin with children trying to find out about things that puzzled them. We would want to know, for example, why the sun rises from the east in the morning, sets in the west and comes up again from the east in the morning. We were told convincing myths, like the one which says that when the sun wanted to marry the elders refused, saying that if the sun had a wife and two children in the sky people would burn.

It was not until the sun promised that he would keep his wife and the children away from the sky, that the elders agreed. So, the sun married two wives and kept his wife and children out of the sky. One wife and her children live in the east while the other wife and her children live in the west. So, he travels across the sky to give people light and sneaks back along the horizon to the east during the night. Mother explained all very convincingly.

Stories of slave raiders were also told repeatedly after evening meals. My great grandmother, Angeth, was kidnapped by Arab horsemen when she was a young woman. The men of the tribe were away in a battle with a notorious Arab slave trader the Jieng called Adhal *Manyi*el, most likely a distortion of Arab name 'Abdalah' with a bull's name added. When they returned home after defeating and killing him, they found that Angeth and other women and children of the village had been taken by the slave raiders. The men followed, caught up with them and rescued the women and children, including my grandmother.

Although the slave raiders had split her head with a whip when she tried to run away, they still forced her to carry a basketful of sorghum on her head and she had a very swollen wound when she was rescued.

It was at such times and at that early age that we were told about great Jieng heroes, like Chief Ayok Lual, who resisted slave traders. We also heard of rare Jieng traitors, like Lual Ngor, who had his own army armed with guns and cooperated with Arab slavers.

We were also told about other Jieng tribes and their peculiarities.

For example, we were told that Agaar Dinka, were not circumcised and that they could change themselves into lions. The Malual Giernyang and the Twic had peculiarities that were abhorred by our own Rek Jieng.

The closer people to the Jieng, we were told, were the Nuer, but even they were often described in unflattering terms, such as not being circumcised and untrustworthy. You could feed a Nuer one moment and the next moment he gets up and spear you. They were also said to be afraid of hand-to-hand fighting, preferring to hit and run.

As for other tribes, they were lumped together as just '*Duor*' (plural) or 'Dor' (singular) and cannibals because they were all thought to be submissive and, unlike the Jieng, did not remove their six lower teeth. They were also described as very small people with red skins and walked one after another like army warms.

Jur Mathiang, were Arab horsemen who in the past raided our people and took children and women into slavery. They were described to us as brown in colour like their horses. A horse, we were told, was much bigger than a bull, but in fact it was just a big dog-lion because it had neither a hump nor horns. Unlike a bull, it had upper front teeth like a dog.

Turuk, a corruption of the word Turk, referred to the white man or white men who governed the country. They were said to be "Dinglith", a corruption of "English" and that they came from a land very far away. Turuk was different from the Arab or the Kawaja, a term which referred to local Greek traders.

The first time I saw a white man was when my brothers Atem, Malek and I were playing a game of *aweet* in the shade of a tree. He came suddenly upon us on a horseback. It was also the first time we saw a horse. The animal was breathing smoke, so we thought! It looked like a strange bull, and I wondered why it was called dog-lion, though I understood why it was also called "*mathieng-jong-koor*", a combination of the three: "brown-dog-lion".

But the white man! He looked exactly like Mother said. His whole face was covered with thick red hair with his big nose protruding out of it. His mouth and the red lips looked like a red smear on a bird's grass-nest. He smelled awful, a combination of soap and cigarette, odours with which I was not yet familiar! When he parted his lips to smile and speak, we saw a row of teeth both up and down. A cannibal we thought! So, we ran off before he said whatever he was about to say.

We sneaked back later when he had gone to mother's compound where he was drinking local beer with my father. Malek and I kept a good distance from the visitor. While keeping an eye on him, his horse was also an object of both fear and fascination. Awien Baak, father's youngest wife, joined us.

When we asked if that was *Turuk? (*White man*)* she said it was not, that the man we were looking at was called "*Abundit*" (senior priest) who collected children from villages and took them to his house to learn books. His house, she said, was located in a place called Ayiel, near Gakrial town. His other house was said to be in Kuachjok, further south from Gakrial.

One of my half brothers, Malueth, was taken to school once by the priest; but he was always getting sick, and his mother convinced my father that he would die if he returned to Ayiel. So, he gave up school after three years. My father did not replace him as was expected by the priest. That was the main purpose of his visit. If Malueth was too sick to return to school, then my father must give him another boy. He was speaking in Jieng with a very funny accent.

He was telling my father that as Spearmaster and leader of his community he should show a good example. He told my father that our people were backward and that our people must take their children to school. But father told him the children were needed to look after cattle. Besides, he argued, there was no good food for them in school and that without milk in their diet they were always getting sick. Also, father said, the children they had taken to school were only servants in towns and that they had no respect for their elders back home.

The priest argued that things were changing very fast, that the English were returning to their country soon and without education, our people would be enslaved by the Arabs. My father dismissed this as nonsense, but, when the priest insisted, he looked around for my brother Atem, who had made himself scarce because he knew what was coming. My father had often mentioned him as replacement for Malueth.

The priest fixed his eye on me and called me to come to him. I refused and moved further away from him. So, he said he could take me to school. My father said no that I was too young. He looked around for Atem once more and when he could not see him, he told the priest that the children were not interested in going to school and that was that.

A Boy's Life

Father departed in January, the last month of Autumn and first month of Winter. It was very windy during the day and cold at night. Tall elephant grass was plentiful in the usually summer-flooded lowlands around our village and in the open areas of the nearby forests. But it was drying up fast.

We boys started burning grass nearer home in mid-January and continued burning it progressively further away from homesteads through February and March. The generally accepted rationale for burning grass was to clear out snakes, make footpaths easily accessible and prepare the soil for fresh grass in spring.

However, from our point of view, we set the grass on fire not only for the sheer joy of it but also to kill fat grass-cutter rats, which we beat up with sticks as they escaped from the fire and smoke.

Sometimes they ran into a network of holes underground but once the grass was burned to ashes, we dug them up with sharp sticks and fishing spears and chased them. Some we killed but many somehow managed to escape.

Anyway, we barbecued the lot over an open fire in the bush. Unlike those small and dirty house rats, which no one would touch, those grass-cutters were fat and juicy and a great source of meat for boys.

But, despite our activities, there was always a big population of these brown grass-cutter rats. Sometimes they invaded farms and homes in millions. No matter how many we killed there were always many more to eat the crops. It was no longer sport for us when there were so many to kill, and we would lose interest in killing and eating them.

We had to watch out for snakes when waiting for rats to emerge from the burning grass. Sometimes a snake came out instead of a rat and bit anyone that was not quick enough to get out of the way. Also, snakes were sometimes found in the underground network of holes made by rats. Most of our snakes are very poisonous and many people were bitten and killed each year.

January was also the season when the main herd was driven to the permanent swamps, a two to three days walk in a north-eastern direction. The nearest *Toc* to us was *Tony* Apuk, normally occupied during January through February. When it got dryer at the beginning of March, the cattle and their herders moved on to Low, where we met up with the Nuer.

The Nuer were a funny people, so we were told. Their men were not circumcised! We also "knew" they were sly fighters. They attacked then ran away. And when you thought they had gone, they turned around and threw more of their thin-shafted flyweight spears at you, always at a distance mind you, then disappeared! They did not like hand-to-hand fighting, so we were told. They were also not to be trusted! "Feed a Nuer when he's hungry; when he is satisfied, he gets up, spears you and runs away!" That was a popular belief in our area, and I had good reason to believe all the negatives I had heard about them. I myself had had a bad experience with a Nuer once at Grandma's - but more about that later. Let's get on with the story.

The last grain was harvested in December, the month summer floods began to disappear very rapidly in a matter of days. The receding water left many varieties of tropical fish stranded in drying up pools. We boys had great time fishing in the shallow pools for mostly catfish and the tilapia. We speared them with fishing spears or caught them with our bare hands. We then roasted them over open fire under the trees in the bush and gorged ourselves with them. Often, we threw away the leftovers; but sometimes we took home some raw fish.

There was always plenty of fish in the pools in December. Birds like the pelicans, the marabou storks and even the vultures indulged in an orgy of fish killing and eating. Even large and poisonous snakes got on the act, and we had to watch out for them when fishing in the pools.

My half brother, Bol Akol, was bitten and killed by a snake when crossing a local pool near our village. Also, an adder by a pool near our homestead bit my elder brother, Angui. He almost died! Lual *Mangar* had to leave immediately that evening to see a man in the Gok area. He returned the following afternoon with dry roots of a strange plant. This was ground into course powder, dissolved in water and then forced down Angui's throat. Shortly after, he vomited a gooey brown stuff, so sticky that even the great green fly could not free itself from its grab. I knew a lot of people who were bitten by snakes. We thought of snakes as horrible and fearful creatures, almost as frightful as the lions!

April, May and June were the months when young boys like Malek and I spent a lot of their early evenings gathering palm fruits. Palms trees were important in our lives. We even gave them names, like Luenh Kuol, which towered over our homestead.

Palm fruits come in three sizes: The biggest one has three stone-seeds in it; the medium one has two while the smallest has only one stone. When they are fully mature, they are so heavy that small boys find it difficult to carry more than two in their arms.

The fruits stay up on the tree for months, glued to their individual sockets until they are ripe, red and juicy. Sometimes we suspected they would never come down. But then, one day, in April or May, one would come crashing down through drooping dry leaves with a force, which would hit the ground with a WHUM! Really deadly! One day one of Luenhkuol's fruits hit one of our cows, right on the head. The cow went mad and had to be slaughtered for meat.

But no one in our homestead was ever injured by a falling fruit though we played a lot under Luenhkuol. Often, we were warned by the "whoosh" sound of the leaves as the fruit fell and we scurried away before it hit the ground. We then prided ourselves in being quick enough to get out of the way, but I guess we were just being very lucky.

Luenhkuol had delicious fruits, unlike the palm tree at the east-end of our sandy field. The flesh of her fruit was tasteless. Unless one was particularly hungry, her fruits were better left alone. We boys knew that. That's the nature of palm trees. A few have sweet fruits while a few others have awful ones. Most of them are in between. We children knew which was which among the more than 300 palm trees we had in our village.

On an evening in April or May, boys of different ages would gather near the largest group of palm trees and played games or told stories, while their ears were keenly tuned to the 'whoosh' sound of the dry palm leaves made by a falling fruit. We could, for instance, be playing "the game of "*The Orphaned Ant*". Participant children would sit close together on the floor and stretched their legs out. The conductor/referee of the game would touch the stretched legs one by one while reciting:

Ant why are you crying?
It is my mother.
Who has beaten her?
She's beaten by my father.
Just be quiet. I will take care of you.
What sort of care? That of an orphan!
You are pinched and pulled in!"

The leg on which the finger rested on the phrase "pulled in" would be withdrawn and the reciting began all over again until there was only one leg left in the field. The owner of that leg was declared the loser and was tickled by everyone.

But boys considered the game of Ant as a girls' game and prepared to tell stories that normally began with someone calling: "Our old home" and the rest answered, "All of us." This was supposed to stop nightmares about stories just heard.

But even a short folktale rarely finished before a palm tree dropped one of its fruits. At the 'whoosh' sound, any game or story in progress was immediately abandoned and a rush towards the direction of the sound would follow. In the dark, the fastest boy did not always get the fruit, as it might have hit the side of the trunk and rolled a long way away from the tree. A frantic search would follow and, sometimes, the slowest or the youngest boy in the group would come upon the fruit and claim it.

Sometimes two or three boys would find the same fruit at the same time and a struggle to get possession of the prize would ensue. This could develop into a fight involving wrestling, hand blows and bites. Other times, a big bully would rob a smaller boy of his possession but repeated too often, this behaviour could prompt older relatives or friends of the younger boy to intervene, and nasty fights could follow for days. In the end, the boys either made peace among themselves or adults would be forced to intervene. In the absence of clear guilt being apportioned, all the boys in that group could get a whipping.

A Boy's life was far from being just fun in Jiengland. When my elder brother, Angui, was initiated into manhood, he ceased to do boys' work, such as milking cows and making dung fire in the cattle camp or at home. My brother, Atem, two to three years older than myself, assumed the duties that were assigned to Angui, which meant he spent much of his time with young men in the cattle camps away from home.

I would have naturally assumed the duties previously assigned to Atem but I was away at Grandma's, doing exactly what Atem was doing back home. So, my younger brother, Bol, took over from Atem.

A boy's life in our village was dictated by activities that were in turn dictated by the seasonal rains and the flooding when River Jur (Bahr el Ghazal) overflowed its banks. The rains began reluctantly in April and May, then became urgent in June; very heavy through July, August, September and much of October; they lessened from the end of October and tapered off through November. December was a drying up period that faded into mid-January when the full-blown dry season set in, becoming very hot and bone-dry through February, March and April.

All that gave us five distinct seasons in a year: The Winter, from mid-January to the end of March; Spring, from April to the end of May; Early Summer, from June to July; Summer, from August to October; and Autumn, from November to mid-January.

Summer was a very busy period for boys at home. Up to 30 cattle, consisting mainly of milk cows and their calves, a few heifers and a bull, would be brought home from the main cattle camp. At Grandma's, it was my duty to know which rope and which peg belonged to which animal because each cow must be tied up with its assigned rope and tethered to its assigned peg in front of the byre at sunset and in the morning. It was also my job to milk the cows and then lead them one by one to their assigned pegs inside the byre. With the help of my nephew, Majok, it was also my responsibility to take the cattle, goats and sheep out of the byre early in the morning and tether them one by one to their individual pegs in front of the byre.

My next jobs would include cleaning up the byre by collecting the cow dung and depositing it in an assigned area outside the main compound; then I would get down on my knees and, with both hands, spread the dung to dry in the sun. Back in the byre, I would use the shoulder bone of an ox to scrape up any messy mixture of dung and urine from the floor. I would then spread fine ash from burned cow-dung over the floor to soak up the damp and then clean it off the floor. With the help of Aunt Atong, I would then milk the cows before releasing them into the pastures. I would eat a meal or drink some milk before following the cattle to the grazing areas.

Out there in the forest or meadows with the cattle, there was really nothing much to do except play with other boys, while watching the cattle grazing peacefully. But there were scary moments when bulls started lowing and wanting to fight each other. It was the duty of the boys to keep warring bulls apart. But there was really nothing boys could do to stop two determined bulls from battling it out. Bulls in a fight could inflict terrible wounds on each other and it was not uncommon to see a bull gored to death by a rival. Men boasted so loudly about the sharpness of the horns of their bulls, which they constantly sharpened and polished; but it was the boys who got punished when the bulls used those horns on themselves and wounded or killed each other. The unfairness of it all!

Anyway, before returning the cattle to their evening post, I would leave them near the homestead and go home to perform one important task: making fire in the centre of the byre, a job that required certain skills a Jieng boy must master very early in life. First, he used the shoulder bone of an ox as a spade to open the remains of the previous fire. He then spread it into a circular shape, making sure the red-hot embers were placed at the edges of the circle. He then poured the semidry dung into the centre of the circle by basketful until it just about covered the hot dung at the edges of the circle. He had to be careful not to smother the fire by dumping too much dung on the embers. Such a structure would naturally conform to a conical shape.

Properly made, the burning dung would quickly generate thick smoke, which escaped through the door, the windows and through the grass roof. Anyone who had not seen this before would assume that the byre was on fire. To moderate the burning, a boy would hold his breath and dash into the smoke-filled byre, smother the burning parts of the dung with old ashes and firm the rest of the structure with his hands before rushing out of the smoke to breathe. The fire would then burn slowly until much of the smoke was dispersed before the cattle were led into the byre for the night.

It might be thought that with so much to do at Grandma's I was overworked and therefore unhappy. Far from it. They were, overall, two very happy years. Like mother, I was treated with great respect and dignity everywhere I went in Kuruech village. I was, simply, "Jiel Aker", forget about Akol Atem, *Arunyyiep* and all that. Ever heard of the saying that "a child is well spoiled by his maternal relatives?" I was not exactly spoiled but I got away with things that I would not be allowed to get away with back home.

Aunt Atong, the first wife of Uncle Madut, was a very beautiful woman. She was also the kindest and gentlest woman I knew. She never raised her voice even when she was upset. She thought the world of me, and I thought the world of her too. I know that Grandma loved her very much and she would never dream of letting her move out of her homestead, even when her youngest son, Aleu, was married.[21]

My uncle, Madut, thought the world of me too until the encounter I referred to earlier with the Nuer fellow: He accused my cousin, Majok, and I of insulting him. Uncle Madut lost his head because he found it particularly humiliating that we insulted his friend and guest in his house. We were thoroughly thrashed, and I resented it very much because I was totally innocent. Atong Marach's son, Majok, was the culprit. He was often my problem!

Majok, a boy much younger than me, had a loose tongue. He always caused me trouble with older boys because he would shoot his mouth off unexpectedly, then I was obliged to stand by him in the many fights he caused. This time, however, it was a grownup Nuer he insulted, believing he was asleep.

It was when we returned home for our mid-day meal that we found the Nuer fellow sleeping in the byre. Without thinking, Majok set his tongue wagging: "He is uncircumcised, he sleeps so deep that his spurt would wake you up next door. The spurt of the uncircumcised is so rotten it will knock you off your feet." I tried to shut him up, but it was too late.

The Nuer fellow stirred and propped himself up on a stool and told us in no uncertain terms that we were bad boys, "to insult a guest like that!" He would have punished us himself but "because I am not a bad man," he said, he would tell everything to Uncle Madut, his friend. Majok knew what the result would be if his father heard of it, so he begged and begged the Nuer fellow not to tell his father. "I am very sorry. I will never do it again!" Majok pleaded in vain.

The Nuer fellow told Uncle Madut that we had insulted him, and we got a real thrashing that evening, as Uncle Madut was not

---

21 Traditionally, the youngest son's first wife inherits the mother's homestead. The rationale is that it is the duty of youngest son to take care of his mother in her old age.

listening to any denials from any of us. So, you see why I was inclined to believe anything bad about the Nuer?

Majok was also the one who started me on the wrong footing with Athuai, whom he accused of stealing his toy bull. You see, we played a game of cattle herding under the shade of a tree in the dry season. The game consisted of shells, which came in different shapes and sizes.

We collected the shells from the dry pools in February and March, then polished them up and shaped them into different colour-pattern by scraping off their skin with broken shells in appropriate places. The very small shells were "calves"; the soft, smooth and broad ones were "heifers" or "cows", depending on the size; the big, sturdy-built ones were "oxen"; and the very tough shells, usually found in very small numbers, were "bulls". The long, more upright shells, also found in very small numbers, were "dogs". In a season, the richest boy would own up to five hundred shells in total. Such a boy would therefore be able to conduct business, including friendship and marriages, very easily.

A game would start with the unearthing of shells buried for storage at the end of the last game. They would then be arranged in an inverted triangular shape, with the oxen at the furthest edges around the cows, a bull in the centre and the calves at the thin end, closer to the fireplace where the herder and his dog or dogs would sleep.

On the day I met Athuai, Majok and I started together from home at about mid-day and headed for the playground. For reasons known to Majok alone, he started running off and left me behind. By the time I got to the playground, a full battle was already going on between him and Athuai, a boy of my age. Athuai had wrestled Majok to the ground and was dealing him blow after blow with one hand while at the same time trying to wrestle a shell from Majok's hand with his other hand. Majok was fighting back like a cat while at the same time screaming. I jumped in, separated them and threatened to take on Athuai, blaming him for everything.

"You should take on people of your age!" I said menacingly to Athuai.

"He called me a thief!" he said, threatening to slap Majok again.

"He is a thief!" Majok bellowed. "He stole my bull! This is my bull!" He held up a shell in his hand.

"Give it back to me!" said Athuai, breaking out of my grasp. I forced him back. So, he turned on me. "Who do you think you are? He stole my bull, and he kicked my cattle and scattered them all over the place! You tell him to give me back my bull and arrange my cattle!"

"Leave him alone!" I spoke. "He says it is his bull."

"But it is mine!" He jumped at Majok again. This time he succeeded in snatching back the shell while still going at Majok. When I tried to hold him back, he gave me a mighty blow on my left ear. We exchanged a few heavy blows, then paused to reassess the situation. We were about to resume talking when older boys suddenly arrived on the scene and encouraged us to battle it out.

"Time to see which of you is a woman!" said one of them.

"Yes," said another, "come on, Athuai! Show this *Buothanyith* what *Agurpiny* boys are made of!"

"Come on, Jiel Aker," said a third boy, "are you not the son of Akol Atem?"

"Give Majok back his bull!" I spoke.

"It is my bull. He is lying!" said Athuai.

We exchanged a few more blows. Then I wrestled him to the ground and prepared to settle on him. But he was as quick as a monkey. He flipped himself up. I tried to wrestle him off and down again, but, before I knew what was happening, he sunk his teeth into my left cheek. It was painful but I struggled bravely, concentrating on getting his teeth out of my cheek. When I eventually managed, his teeth were red with my blood.

I was furious! I threw blow after blow at him. He tripped and

I got him while still on the ground and sunk my teeth into his left cheek. He struggled hard to shake me off; but I held on fast. All the boys were shouting: "Finish him! Finish him!" Athuai struggled very hard, but he could not throw me off. In the end he yelled. "Get him off me! He is killing me! Get him off me!"

"Finish him! Finish him!" shouted the other boys. Athuai began to scream at the top of his voice. That was what the older boys were waiting for. By crying, Athuai had given up the battle; but I was not going to let him get off so easily. So, I held on to his cheek. Two of the older boys pulled me off. Athuai got up and ran off with a bleeding cheek.

But the fight that sealed my superiority over my age-mates at Grandma's was not between Athuai and I, but between an older boy called Anai and I. Anai was the son of mother's half-brother. He had a finger missing on his right hand and was nicknamed "*Mator*", which implied that he had only one testicle. How a missing finger transferred to a missing testicle was never explained but "*Mator*" stuck.

Of course, only boys of his age or older boys dared called him "*Mator*" to his face; but I did it one day. I don't know why, and he told me to take it back or else. I refused and a fight between us was fixed for the following morning at an isolated place, where there would not be any adults to stop us.

A large crowd of boys was present when we started fighting. It involved slapping, wrestling and biting - in which I had the advantage because I still had my six lower teeth while his were removed. Use of sticks was not allowed. We fought until our faces and hands were swollen by mid-day when adults eventually arrived and chased us off. Neither Anai nor I had the stomach to continue the fight after that. Anai eventually dropped the idea of getting an apology from me and I voluntarily restrained from calling him "*Mator*". It was a win-win situation. But boys of my own age like Athuai learnt from that fight that I was stubborn and would not give up a fight if talked into it and they left me relatively in peace for the two years at Grandma's.

Following that fight, Athuai and I played a lot and rarely fought. The last time we fought resulted in what was thought a serious injury to my chest. It was at Athuai's home. No adult was there, and we started playing; then argued and, eventually, the whole thing deteriorated into a fight. He was fighting and screaming very loudly when his older brother, Akot, suddenly appeared on the scene and joined the battle on his brother's side. I fought hard but the two of them were too much. I beat a retreat, hoping to turn it into full flight. But Akot picked up a heavy stone of a palm fruit and threw it at me. It caught me under the right shoulder blade, and I fell flat on my face; but I got up quickly and ran off.

I thought little of it until later in the evening when I could not breathe properly and felt pain in my chest. My ribcage felt as if a stone had been inserted. Until then, I had not told anyone about the fight with Athuai and Akot earlier that day. When I mentioned Akot's involvement in the fight, Grandma was outraged. Off she went to see Aluel Pot, Athuai's mother. She returned shortly with Aluel Pot in tow. In fact, you could hear the two women a long distance away before they arrived.

"Come and see what your sons have done to the child of my daughter, Aluel Pot! Come and see with your two eyes! They have killed the child of my daughter, your boys, they have! What shall I do! What shall I do! "

"What is becoming of children these days, Nyiron Chok, tell me: Why do they want to kill each other? Why do they do these things?"

"Because we let them get away with it, Aluel Pot, that's the reason!

"I will kill that boy, Akot, I will kill him if he comes near me! I will kill him! Why he has gone and injured Jiel Aker like that, I don't know! I don't know! I will kill him if he comes near me, I will!"

"He won't come near you," said Grandma. "You will be lucky if you see him in the next two days."

"So that's why they have disappeared, he and Athuai!"

When they arrived, Aluel Pot was all over me: "Son of my brother! (She is of my clan). Son of my sister! What have those brutes (her children) done to you? What have they done? Oh! Oh! They have broken your ribs! That's what they have done! I will kill them! I will kill Akot! I will! Why does he not take on people of his own age! I will kill him!"

I tried to explain that it was nothing, but I don't think she was listening to me. Aluel Pot was bent on killing her children, especially Akot. I was convinced of that; only to find out later that he was still alive and kicking.

Aunt Atong took me home to Gaikou the following day. Mother was concerned but she was more rational, level-headed and more practical about the whole thing. "It is terrible," she said, "but boys will always do these things. They never learn."

A local "bone fixer" was called in. He asked for hot water and oil and then told me to lie down on my stomach. He used the oil and water to massage around the bruised spot on my back. Very painful! His verdict: He declared that there was no bone broken and that I would mend. So, I did.

The next thing I heard about Athuai was that he had gone to Gakrial and had not returned home. Some said he was in school at Alek or Ayiel or Kuachjok. Others said he had gone to Wau. I didn't really know, and I didn't care. The injury he and his brother had inflicted on me sent me home from Grandma's and in a way gave me a longish sort of holiday. As I was expected to return to Grandma's any time, I was not required to do much at home because my younger brother, Bol, was coping very well. I helped him now and again, but he did not want me to take over from him. What really kept me back home was the fact that my mother had not given all clear for me to return to Grandma. "Before the rains, maybe," she said when I pressed her about my return to Grandma's. She had been like that, indecisive, since my father passed away.

Sometime after I returned home from Grandma's, following the fight with Athuai and his brother, I accompanied my sister, Akuch, to Gakrial. It was the first time I had been to a town, and I saw many great things: First, there was this lorry, which met us on the road to the town. I saw it coming a long way away, with dust billowing behind it. Then, suddenly, it was upon us. The front appeared to swell in my eyes as it got closer and closer. Then, "BROOOM", it went by, as I attempted to get further away from the road. We were covered with dust. I could not see the back of the lorry in the white dust, and it was gone in no time at all, while the dust and a horrible smell lingered on for a long time. I pinched my nose to block out the smell.

"That's the spurt of the lorry," said Akuch, as she held her own nose. "You will get used to it. There are many of them in the town."

I wanted to know where the lorry was going and Akuch could only tell me that it was going to Alek. I also wanted to know if the road ended at Alek or not? If not, where was it going? Akuch concluded that the road had no end, in fact that it was going to the end of the world.

I could not comprehend the distances involved to the end of the world, so I kept quiet, for a while, trying to imagine how long it would take me to Alek, then beyond! Alek, in fact about six to seven miles from my village seemed so far away.

Then a very bright object on the southern horizon caught my eye. It looked like the sun burning brightly through the branches of distant trees. But I could see the sun halfway up in the morning sky, so it could not be the sun returning from the west to his first wife in the east. My sister told me that the shining thing was the roof of the shop of Gorgor (Gregory), our local Greek trader. I tried very hard to keep my eyes on the shining object, but it hurt, and I had to look away.

We walked on. To our right was a big rectangular building on a high ground with a wall built with baked bricks. Its roof was made of grass, and it was as high and as big as our Great Byre back home.

Akuch told me that it was the house of God and that school children prayed there. This was Ayiel, the school run by the priest who came to see my father, the first white man I saw.

Akuch said the school was not a nice place because father said they did not treat children well there and that was why our brother, Malueth, was always sick.

I looked at the buildings critically from afar: They consisted of nine round mud-walls and thatched-roof huts, each as big as our Big House, widely spaced out in a semicircle facing the Church and the main road to the town. Akuch told me that the school children slept in those houses.

At the north-end of the semicircle, nearer to the Church, stood a long rectangular building with walls of red bricks and a grass roof, with its back to the Church and facing a big semicircular compound. Akuch did not know what that building was for.

Nearer the road was a well, a garden, a large fig tree and a large brick and thatch-roofed building with its back to the main road. Together with the other buildings, they circled the big compound, in which a lot of people, mostly boys, were walking or kicking about a round thing, which sounded loud in my ear when kicked. We could hear it clearly from the main road to the town.

Under the fig tree were also a lot of people who appeared to be pounding something. Akuch told me they were school children pounding sorghum for their food. They prepared and cooked their own meals. "There are no women to cook for them", Akuch explained sympathetically, "that's why they fall sick." I fully appreciated then why my father did not want me to be taken to school.

We continued our way to Gakrial. What caught my eye immediately was the number of people in the town. So many people in one place, walking up and down, never seeming to settle down!

Never seeming to mind what anybody was doing! Also, there was food everywhere in the market and in the shops. There were loads of clothes, hides, salt and beads, loads of them in various sizes and colours. There were many men and boys riding bicycles and there were many lorries loaded or empty, standing idly or making a lot of noise and moving about slowly with loads of sacks or hides on them.

There was also drumming, singing and ululation coming from distant houses. But the smell! There were a lot of odours in the air that weren't just the spurt of lorries. There was everywhere the nauseating smell of the priest who came to see my father. There was so much else in the air; none of it, I feared, was any good for health.

When Akuch was buying beads in the big shop of Gorgor, a man said to be the richest man in Gakrial town, I was watching a fight between two boys. One was big and fat. The other was his opposite: small, short and lean. The big fellow swung and kicked very wildly. Both used fisted hands to box each other. This to me was a new technique, though it seemed inefficient. Back home, we used fully opened palms to box. It was more effective that way because you could block air in and out of your opponent's ear. Very painful! Those town fellows appeared not to know how to fight.

But what the small fellow did next seemed stupid at first, but I will not forget the result: He clinched his teeth, stretched himself upward, grabbed the big fellow by both ears and pulled his forehead against the top of his own and "Bang!" The big fellow was suddenly flat on his back! It all happened in one swift move. Blood was whooshing from the big fellow's forehead. I thought he had killed him but no! The fat fellow stirred. The small fellow was walking arrogantly around his victim. Other boys were cheering, just like we did back in the village. I wondered what new tricks Athuai was learning wherever he was.

Stepping Out

Aguatguat, our herd dog, barked; I woke up with a start and looked around me. There was nothing to worry about. This was, after all, Roor Mabior, no lions. If there were a lion about, we would have found out much earlier in the day. In fact, whatever the dog was barking at could not be a lion because everyone knew that dogs did not bark at lions. They were so frightened they could only squirm with fear. And it could not be a hyena because hyenas slept in their holes during the day and did not come out until dark. That fact I knew. Aguatguat was simply bored and wanted activity or to go home.

It was already late in the afternoon, and I must have slept and daydreamed for hours under a tree. It was the heat of spring that did it and I supposed it was time we headed home. I got up and immediately Aguatguat dashed off to round up the goats and the sheep. She was so excited about going home that she failed to notice I had not actually moved from under the tree. I watched the animals disappear behind the distant trees towards our village, then sighed, turned my back on them and took a step in the opposite direction. Although I did not realise it as yet, it was certainly the biggest step of my life.

But I was thinking of Akec *Ngardit*, as I walked out of the forest into Pap village and then on to the main road from Gakrial to Alek. He was the son of Doot, one of my father's many sisters and the man who assisted with prayers at father's burial. His mother died at his birth and his father, Ngor Chok, Grandma's younger brother, the one who escaped from slavers when a child with his elder brother Thony, rejected him and claimed his dowry cattle from our family. Grandfather swore to have nothing more to do with Ngor Chok and his family and he treated Akech like his own son; and that was the only good deed Grandpa was believed to have ever done. But if Grandpa was alive when my father married mother, he would have rejected the marriage because my great grandmother, Angeth, was the mother of Ngor Chok.

When he died, he instructed my father to continue looking after Doot's son and never allow Ngor Chok to claim him, though this was his blood-right to do for a boy. Normally a son would return to his father on becoming of age. But Akech never wanted to do that despite Ngor Chok's belated change of heart.

Father kept his promise, at least in part. Akech's marriage was a grand affair, heard of throughout Buothanyith and still talked about long after it had happened. Our family paid over 200 cattle in dowry for Akech's first marriage. When their first child, a boy, was born, he was named Atem, after Grandpa. What was more, Atem Akech, age-mate of my brother Angui, was to be of the Pagong Clan, not of the Papech Clan of his father, Akech, son of Ngor Chok. That was my grandfather laying full claim on the son of his sister.

Atem Akech was just like a brother to us and was treated as such by the whole extended family of Akol Atem. The making of Atem Akech into a member of the Pagong Clan was legitimised by the fact that a sacred bull and a few sacred cows dedicated to the clan's divinities of the Pagong were included among the dowry cattle given for the marriage of his mother. Ngor Chok's blood ties were thus overridden.

All that was not, however, the main reason Akech *Ngardit* was very much in my thoughts that afternoon. It was just that I found him a little eccentric and this caused me a lot of worry each time he challenged me to a game of *Aweet*. When I won, he beat me because he claimed I was cheating. When he cheated openly and won a game, he punished me because I insisted on pointing out where he had cheated. The only time I won and got away with it was when we had witnesses; but then he always lost.

But of late he had developed the habit of surprising me at home when there was no one around. He then harassed me to accompany him to one of the large fig trees under which *Aweet* game was played. He seemed obsessed with the idea that he was a better player than myself and I was determined not to oblige him with an easy win, either by losing a game intentionally or admitting to having lost a game I hadn't lost by overlooking his cheating habits. It was for me a game of wits that I was not prepared to lose, even at the cost of being punished; but I wearied of the whole thing sometimes.

When I told my brother, Bol, that morning that I would look after the goats and sheep one more time before returning to Grandma's, it was really to get away from Akech *Ngardit* bullying me about the game of *Aweet*. I had no idea the escape would lead me to the big step I had then taken towards the main road to Gakrial and Village School Ayiel.

PART TWO: THE SCHOOLBOY

"The ruin of nation begins in the homes of its people."

- Ashanti Proverb

Village School Ayiel

My intention was to walk up to the main road just to see a lorry go by. I could not understand the swelling on the front part of the lorry when I saw it approaching for the first time on the road to Gakrial. But when I got to the road, I saw a lot of people and no lorry, not even a bicycle. If I turn right and walked north, that would have taken me to Alek, and I did not want to go to Alek. If I turned left, I would end up in Gakrial, some five miles south. There were many lorries in the town when I was there; so, I turned left and walked along the road towards Gakrial, expecting to see a lorry any time. If I saw one, I would have returned home. No lorry came my way; and yet the town was pulling me like magic. I walked on.

Meanwhile, it was getting very late in the afternoon. By the time I realised I would not be able to get to the town in time to see a lorry and return home before sunset, I was very close to Village School Ayiel. "Coming this way is not such a good idea after all," I told myself and I was about to turn and head back when I saw two men walking towards me.

One of the men smiled at me, bent down to see my face and announced that he recognised my features as that of Akol Atem. He immediately assumed that I was on my way to school. But they laughed at me when I told them that I was on my way to Gakrial to see lorries, then, I would be on my way back home.

They introduced themselves and said they were teachers at Ayiel. Then they set about convincing me that it would be too dark to go back home that evening and that it would be wise to spend the night at the school. I did not think it was a good idea to spend the night at that school. The things I had heard about Ayiel were not encouraging. But the thought of meeting a lion on my way back home was more persuasive.

It was close to sunset when we reached the compound of Village School Ayiel. There were small boys of about my age as well as big boys of different ages. There were also many grown up men mixed in with the boys. They were kicking about a brown ball as big as a fully ripened three-seeded fruit of a palm tree. That was what they were kicking about last time Akuch and I looked this way from the main road to Gakrial. We were a little far away and the ball didn't seem so big.

Now that I could see it close, I could not understand how anything as big as that could be so light to kick about and fly in the air and bounce about without breaking up! They all seemed to be shouting at each other as they chased the ball. My sort of crowd in fact, but, that thing! It rolled over towards us. With swift movements, one of the teachers, who introduced himself as Arel Akol, let lose his right foot and kicked the brown thing with a loud "bang!" The ball flew up in the air and over a house at the far end of the compound. There were loud cheers.

But this was soon interrupted by the loud shrills of something I later came to know as a "whistle". The whistling was urgently repeated, and the ball was immediately abandoned, followed by a sudden rush towards the whistle blower. "That's your uncle, Abiem," said Arel Akol, pointing at the whistle blower.

The man had the whistle in his mouth while he dragged one of his feet through the sand while moving very fast towards one of the houses. Behind him was a line across which no one was allowed to cross. Two other men made sure that no one jumped over the line to the other side; so late arrivals were forced to try to get behind the line by going through the narrowing gap between Uncle Abiem and the house in front of him. But soon that alternative was closed. But most boys had crossed the line anyway into the circle. Only three boys could not get behind the line in time.

Uncle Abiem approached the three boys and pointed to the sandy floor in front of him. One of the boys lay down on his stomach and Uncle Abiem gave him three lashes on the buttocks. The boy got up and ran into a line, still scratching his backside with both hands. He gave three lashes each to the remaining two and walked to the front of what was now a very neat assembly of over 100 boys and men standing at attention in four lines. I noticed that the smaller and shorter boys were in the front lines while the tallest among them were at the back. It made the lines slope forward.

I glanced at the two teachers. They seemed to be watching the whole thing with detached bemusement. "The Overseer is counting them to see who is missing," Arel volunteered the information. "He also wants to know who has or has not done what today. Then he will tell them anything new and what to do tomorrow." The assembly broke up shortly after with loud cheers.

Uncle Abiem walked over and Arel Akol began to introduce me: "This is the son of your…"

"Don't tell me", the overseer interrupted. "Is this not a son of my Uncle Akol Atem?" He immediately assumed that I had come to school to fill in the space left behind by my brother, Malueth. When he heard that I was on my way to Gakrial to see lorries and that I intended to return home in the morning, he laughed loudly. He insisted that God and my departed father had all got together and sent me to school.

"Spearmasters don't die!" said Uncle Abiem firmly. "If you don't see them, they are still there. That's why you are here this evening. It's your father who wants you to come to school. That's why you are here."

I told myself that it all made sense. How else could I have decided to walk away that afternoon from my goats and sheep without much thought? Where did the idea of my wanting to see the smelly lorry come from? Uncle Abiem was right. It must have been my father who made me come to school. His spirit I supposed. But, that place!

Uncle Abiem introduced me that evening to two men students of my clan: Gong Awar and Akel Awar and said they would take care of me.

"Take him to the store tomorrow morning and fit him with uniforms," he said to Gong and Akel. "I will be going to see his mother and his uncle, Bol Atem. I will see you tomorrow evening." He left me with Gong and Akel.

I could not envy his going to break the news to my mother in the morning. He would find out why she was called "The Bull Woman," I said to myself.

I faced my newly met clansmen. Apart from their fathers having the same name, Awar, Gong told me that their mothers were also called Nyibol. But, as far as I could see, that was as far as similarities went between the two men.

Physically they were worlds apart: Gong was a giant of a man. He towered over Akel and my head barely reached his waist. He had huge thighs and arms and very strong legs. He looked extremely powerful to me.

Akel, on the other hand, though average in height, was small in body and had the peculiar look of a weakling. Everything about his physique made him look as if he had been buttered down by the creator. It is hard to explain but his body had no clear curves: On Akel, an arm looked like one continuous piece from wrist to shoulder with hardly any noticeable break at the elbow. The same thing could be said of his legs and thighs. His buttocks, hardly noticeable under his khaki shorts, appeared to be a continuation of his barrel-like trunk.

"He is a mongoose, isn't he?" said Gongdit with his deep resonant voice responding to my curious stare at Akel. "His name is Machuot", a nickname befitting his peculiar shape.

"Don't listen to him, son of my uncle," said Akel in a rather boyish voice for a man of his age, "He's not a good man!"

"Who? Me! Not a good man!" said Gongdit. "Who rescued you from the well last year, was it not me? Who is always protecting you from bullies? Is it not I, Gongdit, 'Gong Awar, Gong Nyibol' saving you 'Akel Awar, Akel Nyibol'? Are we not of the Pagong?" he laughed loudly. "Anyway, son of my uncle," Gongdit turned to me, "you shouldn't call him 'Machuot'. He will kill you if you do. He is not as smooth as he looks!"

There were a lot of coded messages in all that Gongdit had said and much of it became much clearer to me much later. To begin with, Akel did indeed fall into the deep well at the edge of the school compound. As he could not swim, he struggled to hang on to the concrete wall of the well. Those who were there when he fell in panicked and flapped about like frightened chickens.

Not Gongdit. When he got to the well and saw Akel struggling at the bottom, he climbed down quickly, balancing himself with his hands and feet against the concrete wall of the well. He grabbed Akel by the hand, but, having done that, he was unable to move upwards with Akel in tow. Besides, he was so big that he blocked any view of Akel from the top of the well; thereby causing a hue and cry as the word went around that "Gongdit is stuck in the well on top of Akel" and that Akel was probably drowning or dying of suffocation. All they appeared to be doing on the top of the well was fight for a peep at the unfortunate men; but in doing so they blocked out the light and air for those at the bottom of the well. Gongdit once again had presence of mind and shouted to those on the top of the well to lower a rope. He gave Akel the end of the rope and told him to hold on to it. He then asked for a second rope, which was lowered. He grabbed it with both hands and told them to haul him up.

"It took ten people to pull Gongdit out of the well," Akel mused later in the presence of Gongdit, "and it took only Gongdit to pull me out. They were all afraid that Gongdit would block the well and they would have no water to drink." That was the maximum amount of fun Akel dared poke at Gongdit.

However, Akel was rumoured to have said out of Gondit's hearing: "They were afraid that Gongdit would 'spoil' the water." 'Spoil' implied many things and, therefore, had unacceptable connotations for Gongdit. Gongdit threatened to beat Akel up, but, according to Gongdit, Akel pleaded thus: "Gong Awar, Akel Awar, Gong Nyibol, Akel Nyibol: Ha! Ha! We are the Pagong!" Akel told me that was exactly what happened between Gongdit and himself that he begged for mercy in those words. I accepted that as the truth, but later events gave me reason to believe that was not exactly what happened between Gongdit and Akel.

You see, many months later, Gongdit and I were waiting for Akel to come for dinner as we three shared from one plate. Gongdit told me to call Akel with my sharp voice, as there was a lot of dins going on around us. Without thinking, I called out loud and clear: "Maachuoot!" The din ceased. They all knew the caller and the called. How was Akel going to react to this? They all wanted to know without saying so. Akel, having heard my call, soon turned up, grabbed my right hand and led me to a nearby hedge, presumably to get a slim branch from the thicket to whip me with as punishment for my insolence.

"Son of my uncle," said Akel as we approached the hedge, "I don't want to beat you, but you must pretend that I am doing so. I don't want others to think that I can be insulted at will by anyone then get away with it. My dignity is at stake, do you hear?"

I nodded my head gratefully.

We looked back at the houses in front of which interested parties were seated and to ascertain that they could not see us clearly in the dark. He then got himself a slim stick from a bush and began to beat the ground next to me with it while I shouted at the top of my voice, begging him to stop beating me, that I would never insult him again. "Run back to Gongdit," he whispered, "and I will chase you. Keep crying." I did as told and ran straight into Gongdit's protective arms. A total farce that they - except Gongdit, perhaps - swallowed hook and bait. If such was my arrangement with Akel, then I see no reason why the same understanding could not have been reached between himself and Gongdit in the so-called "Akel's begging Gongdit for mercy."

I was taken to Class One on my first day in school by Gongdit, after having been fitted with a khaki uniform, and handed over to the teacher: "This is Andrea Ayok", the Headmaster of Village School Ayiel," said Gongdit, "and this is..."

"Yes, we met yesterday. Sit down," Andrea Ayok pointed me to the front bench and continued with the teaching. Gongdit disappeared to his class. He was in Class Three, the final year at Village School Ayiel. So was Akel. All the classrooms were in the same long building, which Akuch could not tell me what it was used for.

Beside me sat a round-cheeked little boy of about my age. The bench on which we sat was built with bricks with the surface smoothed over with concrete. A wooden plank, balanced on two brick stands, served as the writing and reading surface for exercise books and reading books. The boy next to me had both his arms folded on it while responding enthusiastically with singsong answers to singsong questions from the teacher. I looked around me. There were at least 40 boys of different ages plus a few grownup men in the class. They were all behaving just like my desk-mate. Translated from Dinka, the singsong exercise went something like this:

Teacher: Who made people?

Class: God made people.

Teacher: Who made people?

Class: God made people.

This was repeated many times before the teacher moved on to another question, which was also repeated many times and then on again to another question. Here are a few more questions and answers:

Teacher: Why did God make Human?

Class: God made Human to know God, to love him, to do his command on earth, and to go to his house in happiness.

Teacher: Where is God?

Class: God is in heaven, on earth, here and everywhere.

Teacher: Do we see God?

Class: No, we do not see God because he is white divinity without a body.

Teacher: Does God see us?

Class: It is true God sees us and things we think and things we say God knows.

The teacher then turned his attention to me. "Come up here." I stood up and went to him. He told me to face the class, then he introduced me as "the son of Akol Atem of the Pagong Clan from Gaikou." He then told me to face him. "I am going to teach you how to pray," (in Dinka) he said. "Put your left hand over your chest like this, hold it there. Touch your forehead with your right hand like this. Then say, 'In the name of the father'. Then bring your right hand down to your chest like this. Then say, 'and his son'; then with the right hand touch the top of your left and then the right shoulder while saying, 'and of the holy spirit'; then bring both your hands together like this on your chest under your chin, then say, 'amen'. He repeated the whole thing himself, first slowly then quickly and said: "Now your turn."

I was sweating. To begin with, it was the first time I was wearing clothes and I was uncomfortable in them; then this complex nonsense! I attempted the 'Sign of the Cross' for the first time and failed miserably. The words were either mixed up or my right hand was moving faster or slower than the right words. I stumbled over words, and this elicited hearty laughter from my classmates.

That was it, my mind was made up. As soon as my mother turned up sometime in the day, I told myself, I would be on my way back home. I never liked being made fun of back home and I was not going to put up with it here either. I decided not to co-operate with the teacher.

But the teacher insisted on my getting it right and the situation got worse and worse. I knew he wanted to break me, like Akech Ngardit tried to do back home, and I refused to yield. So, first, he used a wooden ruler to inflict sharp strokes on the inside of my right palm, then on the back of my hand. It was very painful, but I refused to cry. Eventually, he told me to "get out and learn it well before tomorrow, else you get the same beating!"

I got out of the class, feeling both triumphant for having resisted tears and sorely sorry for my misadventures of the previous day. Only if mother would come!

The rest of the class soon followed me out and my desk-mate came to me. He offered me a hand to shake and introduced himself as "Manyoth Machot, from Agaar country". This was a big shock to me. The Agaar were said to live so far away from us that not a single person in our village had ever been to the Agaar country or seen one of them. But legends about the Agaar were plenty: "The Agar (plural) are able to change themselves at will into lions and vice versa. They can change themselves into vultures as well and fly away."

And now, right in front of me, was one in flesh and bone, albeit a small one, who looked just like me! I extended my hand uncertainly and introduced myself. Then I broke off the handshake rather abruptly. Manyoth mused: "You think we are lions, right?"

I told him he did not look like one; yet I asked him if he could change himself into a lion? He said he would if he were angry enough. That made sense. Anything can happen when one is angry. I looked down at my feet, scratched the dust with my big toe, and said nothing.

Manyoth wanted to know if I knew how to write my name. I said nothing because I did not know what on earth he was talking about. He told me to sit down and then he began to scratched the sand with his index finger and left some puzzling marks on it. "The marks are:" Manyoth spelled them up, 'J', 'e', 'l': 'Jel'. That's your name. You write it."

Akel appeared from nowhere and told Manyoth that was not how to write my name. He said the right spelling was "J, i, e, l: Jiel."

Gongdit appeared and said, "I suppose Manyoth has been telling you he will change himself to a lion if you annoy him?" When I said nothing, he added, "It is all rubbish! Agar cannot change themselves into lions or anything. Only ignorant people can believe that."

Manyoth laughed but insisted later that he would change himself to a lion anyway if I annoyed him; but he was not convincing any more.

Uncle Abiem *Amethweng*, the Overseer, returned to school in the afternoon and informed me that my mother had agreed to my staying at school, that she and Uncle Bol Atem[22] (my father's half-brother) would come to see me the following afternoon. I could not understand why my mother had so readily agreed to my becoming "a son of *Abun*". I remembered how she resisted father's plans to have my brother, Atem, taken to school. What had happened?

I found out part of the truth the following afternoon when she and Uncle Bol turned up at school. *Amethweng* would not leave us alone as we talked. Uncle Bol began an uncharacteristic speech: "Things are changing, son of my brother, things are changing. There is no future in the way we live today. Men are going to come from the children of *Abun*, not from cattle camps, you hear! School is the future for our children. Now that you have decided to become a child of *Abun*, work very hard and be an example to other children." He handed a bag of money (all in coins) over to Abiem *Amethweng* and said to him: "Look after him, son of my father, look after him," he concluded and said to my mother: "let's go home, Aker, let's go home. He will be fine."

---

22   Although Atem Akol inherited the leadership of the Akol's family when Father died, the overall 'Guardian' was Uncle Bol Atem, who had the seniority, experience and wisdom to garnish the respect of all the members of the family. He was the spokesman for our family in external issues.

Mother just looked at me and said nothing; but I could see sadness in her eyes. I walked over to her, and she opened her arms and embraced me. Then she looked up at Uncle Abiem and said, "Look after him, son of my father." "He will be ok wife of my father. I will take care of him," said the overseer, took my hand and led me away while Uncle Bol and mother returned home.

What I could not understand was where from Uncle Bol had got his sudden conversion to school education. All the nonsense about future men coming from "the children of *Abun*, not from cattle camps" was so unconvincing and sounded like something planted into his head! I suspected Uncle Abiem.

Uncle Abiem, the school overseer, lived in the school compound, house No 3, with his wife and two children, Abiem Junior and Beek. Although both boys were very bright, the most interesting of the two was the younger one, Beek. At the early age of four or five, he was already a budding poet of sorts, with an ability to string together nonsensical verses that demanded attention. For example, when I asked him what his name was, he replied in a singsong tone:

> *I am Beek*
> *The Axe Head*
> *The Spitting Ass Mongoose*
> *Like stampeded weasel*
> *Takes the vulture's shit*
> *To her baby mouth-feed.*

"What sort of a name is that?" I asked him, but he continued:

> *Mangar and the Chief of Children*
> *Mangar and the Cook*
> *Mangar and Backbiters*
> *Mangar and Kitchen Thieves*
> *Mangar and…*

All that Beek wanted to say in so many words were that he had more than just the one ox name, *Mangar*, which he would match against anyone, from his father, the overseer, to whoever else he fancied.

Beek had already got the news that I had problems with the "Sign of the Cross" earlier in the day. So he asked me if I had learned how to do it yet. I told him "No," that I was not interested. Beek piped up:

Mangar in the Name of the Father,
Mangar and Can't Pray!

Then he ran off before I got my hand on him.

When I told Gongdit and Akel about the funny little boy, Gongdit told me that "Beek got all that nonsense from Akel. You should hear Akel. He's a very bad comedian (*alueeth*).[23]" Akel then cited one of his "nonsensical verses" as requested by Gongdit for my benefit. Here are a few lines from a long verse:

I swear by God.
The lizard escorted the snake.
The mouse boasted his mouth.
I hate the words of the big impotent man who can't speak
up. He with a head like the axe-handle of Bol Monycek.
A gentleman's head cannot be like a giraffe's head.
That has fallen into Maroor Wol's trap-hole.
I called upon a great girl at our Tony Abuok.
A great girl with vaginal cord
as thick as the hind-leg of a baboon…

---

23   While the word, "*alueth*," normally means "liar", it can mean different things in different contexts. Here it means "comedian," a phrase said with tongue in the cheek.

I laughed my head off. After that I asked Akel to give me some catechism lessons. I liked him.

On the second day in Class One, not only was I able to make the "Sign of the Cross" without mistakes, I was also able to cite a few answers to catechism questions and the teacher was greatly impressed. And so was I. After all, I was not a village '*ping*' for nothing.

My first Sunday morning at Village School Ayiel was marked by a high state of preparation that began on Saturday. Manyoth informed me that "*Abundit* is coming tomorrow! You have to wash your clothes and iron them this afternoon for Church tomorrow." I had forgotten about '*Abundit*', the one who visited father some time back. Village School Ayiel, I thought, was his home; but where was he? I had not seen him since I arrived. "Where is *Abundit*?" I asked Manyoth.

"In Kuachjok schools, of course, that's where he lives."

"Where is Kuachjok?"

"Alelthok (where iron-stones soil begins), at Kuach."

I turned my full attention to the business of washing clothes. We had been issued with a bar of soap each and told to use it for washing our bodies and clothes for a week. Manyoth and I went over to the well and drew some water with a bucket tied to a rope and lowered into the deep well. We then shared a large tin tray for washing the only garments we had: the khaki shorts and a khaki shirt each. It was then I noticed that Manyoth was uncircumcised. I laughed and pointed out to him that he was not yet circumcised.

"So what?" said Manyoth. "No Agaar girl will marry you if you are circumcised."

"So, all the Agar are uncircumcised?"

"That's right. In Agaar country, we compose terrible songs against the Rek for being circumcised."

"This boy knows a lot", I said to myself. The "Rek" word was something new to me as well. "Who is Rek?"

"The people who are circumcised like you, from Kuelchok (Tonj) to Gakrial. They are all Rek and they are circumcised. It is a shame no Agaar will put up with!"

We finished the washing, put our clothes on the nearby grass to dry and skipped off happily naked to kick the brown rubber ball about with other boys, most of them without any clothes on, having washed the only ones they had in preparation for Sunday.

On Sunday morning, all the 120 children[24] of Village School Ayiel were assembled in four neat lines in front of the Church, awaiting the arrival of *Abundit* from Kuachjok, 19 miles south of Gakrial.

I was expecting to see the priest on a horse, just as I first saw him back in the village that day when he turned up unexpectedly. But he turned up on a big, thunderous, motorbike. It was the first time I had seen such a vehicle and my attention was concentrated on its movement and the noise it made. The motorbike and the rider disappeared behind the back of the Church, where there was an adjacent building, and we did not see the priest again until we were seated in the Church. Now that he was off the motorbike, I could see him clearly for who he was not.

"That is not *Abundit*!" I said rather loudly to Mnyoth, "that is some Big Red *Abun*."

"That is *Abundit*," said Manyoth firmly. I protested even louder than before; but everyone around us shushed. So, we shut up and I paid more attention to what was going on inside the Church.

Everything inside the Church was new to me. The candles, for instance, were a fascination: "how can something burn unceasingly without firewood under it and no smoke?" I murmured at Manyoth, who shushed me: "Don't speak in the Church!"

There was movement behind the candle as Arel Akol got up from his front seat and gave a signal for everyone to stand up. He then

---

24   Some were grownup men with wives and children at home. There was hardly an age limit for Village School Ayiel.

started a hymn in Jieng. Everyone, except me seemed to know the song; but that did not bother me.

My attention was fixed on the procession approaching from behind the platform on which the candles burned. Four boys, each dressed from neck to ankle in what looked like a smart *jalabia* (Arab dress) were followed by the Big Red *Abun* in similar attire. Big Red held in both hands something covered with a green piece of cloth. They walked to the front seats, then turned their backs on us and walked up to a platform I later came to know as the Alter.

The boys then divided into two as they stood aside and let Big Red walk up to the Alter on his own. Big Red placed whatever he had in his hand on the Alter. He then opened a small chamber on the side of the Alter with a key, placed the thing in it, closed it again, made the Sign of the Cross, knelt, got up again and joined the boys at the foot of the Alter. They knelt in unison. While the boys remained on their knees, Big Red turned to us, raised his arms above his head and broke into singing a strange hymn in a strange voice in a strange language. Again, everybody except me seemed to know what he was on about.

We mingled aimlessly outside the Church when the Mass was over. No one seemed to want to go away. Then Big Red joined the crowd, shaking hands left and right and beaming with infectious laughter. He spoke good Jieng with an accent that made it difficult for me to understand what he was saying. No matter: I was fascinated by the way he glided through the crowd with an amazing ease in his long *jalabia*. He was loud! One could hear his voice and laughter a mile away.

"He is not *Abundit*!" I said with finality to Manyoth.

"But he is!" insisted Manyoth.

"I know *Abundit*. He came to see my father!"

"May be not. This one is call *Boldit* (Botilotti). There are many of them in Kuachjok.

"So, there are many *Abundit*?"

"So many. They have different names."

This Agaar, I said again to myself, how does he know so much? I thought he had only been in school for just a month before I turned up. But he now told me that he was in many schools in Agaar country before he came to to Ayiel. But his mother wanted him out and his father, a chief, agreed with the Mission to bring him as far as Gakrial for a year "to stop my mother from bothering the school." I did not know whether to believe all that or not, but that was his story - and he certainly knew a lot. We became fast friends, and I brought him home with me during a two-weeks break in August because he could not make it home to Agaar and back in two weeks. Besides, I was enjoying his company.

Like Mother Like Daughter

Our homestead was crowded with strangers when Manyoth and I arrived; but mother was very excited to see me and my new friend. I introduced Manyoth and adding, rather cautiously: "He is from Agaar." Mother showed no surprise at all: "You are welcome in our home son of Machot", she said and gave us some food to eat.

All these strangers, about ten of them, were seated on papyrus mats near the byre. With them were Uncle Atemdit, Uncle Bol Akol, and other senior male members of the Akol family. They appeared to be in a serious conversation.

Then uncles Atem and Bol saw me and called: "The son of *Abun* is home! Come here." I went over and shook hands with all of them, including the guests. "This is Akuc's other brother who has gone to the home of *Abun* (school)," said Uncle Atemdit. He did not say who the strangers were and what they were doing in our house. "Whose son is your friend over there?" he indicated Manyoth, who was still sitting with Mother in front of *Big House*. "He is Manyoth Machot, from Agaar. His father is a chief," I told them. Again, no surprise that I had an Agaar (a lion) for a friend. They called him over and Manyoth shook hands with everyone as was expected of juniors. "I know your father," Uncle Bol told Manyoth. "He is a great chief!"

Back with mother, I enquired after everybody. My younger brother, Bol, was out in the common grazing areas minding the home cattle, sheep and goats. "I would have been doing that if I didn't become a "child of *Abun*," I said to myself and went on asking after the other members of my immediate family. Angui and Atem were, of course, at the cattle camp nearby and were expected home later that evening. Akuch was at the homestead of Amiir Agany with her half-sisters and age-mates.

I turned my attention to the visitors: "Who are they?" Mother informed me that they were Akuch's future in-laws and that they were there to discuss the dowry and marriage arrangements with our men folks, led by Uncle Bol Atem and Uncle Atem Akol. Mother told me the guests came from Nyarkach, halfway between our home and Gakrial. I needed not ask if Akuch's future husband was among them because, at my age, I should know that discussions for preliminary marriage arrangements were generally between elders and did not require the presence of the groom.

As for the bride, she should have been around, serving the seniors of her future family. It would be their first chance to observe her beauty and manners. Though respectful, they would nevertheless poke fun at her, such as knocking a water or milk container out of her hand "accidentally", just to see how she would react.

I was sure that Akuch, though around the age of 14/15, was mature enough to handle such a situation admirably. She was, after all, a sister to four brothers, many half-brothers and had recently spent considerable time at the cattle camp where teasing girls (unmarried women) is the preoccupation of young men. Having many brothers alone was widely considered as enough character credentials for a girl by her future family-in-law. Not that girls were always appreciative of this fact, as one little girl is said to have remarked in frustration: "Mother! I will never marry a man who was ever a boy!" But why was Akuch not there? Mother explained simply that Akuch had already met the visitors and that she did not want to be around when the men were discussing the dowry cattle. "Go and see her," she said.

I suddenly had the desire to see my 'big sister' (always so to me) who never seemed to get any fat on her bones, no matter how much she ate. People always said that what she ate added to her great height everyday. She was already as tall as mother, but they said she would stop growing any taller soon. "Girls always do," they said. But I was not so sure.

When Akuch saw me, she grabbed me and held me tightly in her arms, then embraced me and burst into tears of happiness. "What a fuss?" I said to myself. It was as if I had been away for years, not months. After all, I was away before at Grandma's for over a year and she did not behave like that when I came home. What was the matter with her? Maybe she believed I was lost and would never come home?

"That man!" she cried, "That man ---"

"What man?" I interrupted.

"The man who came to tell us you had gone to the home of *Abun!* O, he threatened to take Mother to prison and to take all our cattle if Mother insisted that you came back home. He threatened to take all the boys and... you know mother! She went mad! It was Uncle Bol *Yoom* who saved the situation. You are not going back to him, are you?"

"You mean Uncle Abiem? He is OK. He's the overseer, I told her; but I was beginning to fully understand what happened that day when Uncle Abiem left me in school and came to announce my whereabouts. It was her that must have made the lecture repeated by Uncle Bol *Yoom* back at school. My mother was not giving in until the overseer threatened her with "imprisonment and fine by the government." My village folks didn't know if such orders existed or not; I did not know either; but Uncle Abiem accomplished his mission all the same.

He then persuaded Uncle Bol to bring cash for my uniform and for food, since it was too late in the year for my family to give the annual contribution in grain given by parents to the school. One of our he-goats was therefore sold for the cash and that was the money handed over to him at school that day by Uncle Bol.

To be fair to Uncle Abiem, he had been giving me some money each weekend to buy whatever I liked and could afford with such little amounts in town. Often, Manyoth and I spent it on fried pancakes or roasted peanuts which we liked very much. Also, his wife often fed me, along with her children, when I was around. So, the money didn't just disappear into his pocket.

I assured Akuch that uncle Abiem was alright and that he was good to me.

I introduced her to Manyoth, pointing out that he was from Agaar. I told her his father was the chief of all the Agar. I don't know from where I got those facts. Manyoth must have told me, for he did not correct me. She shook his hand and told him he was welcome; then she asked him if it was true that the Agar were also lions.

Manyoth told her it was not true. That was the first time I heard him deny it. Akuch accepted this statement without any more questions and turned her attention back to me:

She wanted to know what I had learn in school. I told her I had learnt to read and even knew how to write people's names. It was then a small game started. I introduce people Manyoth did not know by writing their names of the sand and Manyoth read them out. This produced a great excitement as the group of children and adults swelled around us.

The general conclusion was that school children were top wizards. But, although the term, "wizard", is normally derogatory and intended as such, it was not taken seriously in the normal sense of the word. No one expected Manyoth and I to invisibly pick up sand or stones with our eyes and insert them into people we didn't like. 'Magicians' may be the closer thing to what they intended to call us, for they thought that we were merely playing tricks they could not understand or cared to know.

Nevertheless, I felt for the first time a lot closer to Manyoth than to my own brother, Malek. Only Manyoth and I in that crowd understood there was nothing magical about writing and reading; that it was only signs representing sounds that we all make. We tried to explain that they also could learn to read and write but they would not listen. None of them saw any point in learning such outlandish things that had nothing to do with the art of minding cattle.

My half-brother, Malueth, who went to school for three years, faced such a fate when he returned home and tried to teach reading and writing to his brothers and sisters. He might be the only one who understood what we meant by reading and writing having nothing to do with magic; but he himself had practically forgotten his alphabets. Besides, he was no longer interested. Society had got him squarely back to where it believed he belonged: minding cattle. To them, nothing else mattered much.

So, it seemed like I was going to be the only schoolboy in my big family - indeed in the whole village of Gaikou and the villages around. But that reminded me of Athuai, the only boy of my age from my area that I knew had gone to school, but which school? He was not at Village School Ayiel and no one there had ever heard of him.

I turned my attention to Akuch. She had grown. I think she looked more like what I imagined my mother would have been at her age: tall, straight, very pretty and slim. Childishness appeared to have suddenly deserted her. She listened more attentively and was more contemplative. She was, in a word, mature.

She would not talk to me about the man who wanted to marry her. But I gathered later from others that the man was already married to one wife. Pretty and strong-minded girls like Akuch were generally opposed to the idea of being married off second or third or whatever number, other than first. Was that the problem? Maybe but she was not telling.

A couple of months later, the family of her intended husband-to-be had already given Akol Atem's family 25 cows, 10 heifers and 5 oxen as down payment, because Akuch was young and needed a year or so to fully mature. More cattle would have to follow, of course, indeed a lot more if a family as large as that of Akol Atem as to be satisfied and won over.

It soon became known, however, that Akuch did not like the man, leave alone love. What was more, it was also discovered that she was in love with another man. The man she loved was called Arol Madut, who lived far away in Nyinakoi village of the Agurpiny, near half a day's walk from our village, Gaikou. But distance or being of a different sub-tribe from Buothanyith was not the problem. After all, Mother was from Agurpiny. The problem was that his family was considered by our family to be of meagre means (not rich in cattle) and of a minor clan. It looked like Mother all over again!

Uncle Atemdit was outraged: "Does this man not know someone has already declared his intention honourably. Does he not know there are already 40 cattle on Akuch! He is a son of nobody! Fishermen of the river! That's what his people are!" He told the young men of our family to "deal with the intruder" if he showed his face again near our village.

The man, however, kept turning up and meeting Akuch in unexpected places at unexpected times, as some of her half-sisters and age-mates were in cahoots. By the time my brothers got to know, he had already come and gone. Akush was threatened with beating and even death if she continued to meet the man.

Meanwhile, the family that put down 40 cattle doubled the number instead of pulling out. Many men would be too proud to continue with the marriage after the girl had said publicly that she did not love the intended husband. But, as far as this family was concerned, there was nothing wrong with their son. Akush, they contended, would eventually learn to love him. Young girls, they believed, always behave like that. Before long, they increased the number of cattle 100. They then put pressure on our family to hand Akuch over to them, arguing that she would run away with her young lover.

My family, led by Uncle Bol, refused point blank, making it clear that 100 cattle were not enough for a large family like ours. They also resented the suggestion that Akuch would run away with her lover. Such a thing was unheard of in Akol Atem's family. But they also argued: "Who are you going to deny the right to have something small (like a heifer) from a marriage of his sister?" Uncle Bol asked them rhetorically, so they went back to reconsider the matter.

Meanwhile, Akuch's lover was in earnest and was reportedly turning up secretly almost every other day, while Akuch's movements and activities were becoming hard to pin down. One would suppose that his aim in turning up so often was to persuade Akuch to elope with him. Only with Akuch's connivance could he hoped to marry into the family of Akol Atem. As it turned out, this was indeed his plan, while Akuch resisted, fearing the consequences.

The man turned up one night at Amir Agany's homestead and aske for Athieng (my half sister and Akush's age-mate and confidante). Athieng saw him and went to fetch Akuch. While on her way, Malou (Athieng's boy brother), became suspicious and ran next door to inform two of our brothers, who quickly rushed to where Akuch's man was waiting. Recognising that his cover was blown, he tried to ease his way out with nice words, such as "I don't want any bloodshed", but my brothers would hear none of it.

"You were warned never to show your face here!" one of them said and let fly his stick. The man, a more mature and experience stick fighter than the young men attacking him, deflected the stick and mounted his own counterattack. The two of them went at him with their sticks while he defended himself gallantly defended himself. The sound of stick-on stick could be heard in the nearby homesteads. Hue and cry followed. More running feet approached, and Arol Madut decided it was time to beat retreat. He vaulted and outran the whole village, something not so hard to do in the dark.

Not much injury was done, no blood was spilled, just a few bruises. The fight did not involve spears because the intention was merely to frighten, not kill him; and this appeared to have been accomplished. They did not expect to see his face for a while.

However, Akush disappeared that night and no doubt where she had gone when, two days later, she was not in the homes of the relatives she would have been expected to when upset. Soon, a messenger from Nyinakoi informed uncle Bol Akol that Akush was in the house of her lover's uncle at Nyinakoi. There was no way she could have crossed Roor Ayi on her own that night to reach Nyinakoi. Her lover must have told Athieng where he would be waiting if he were discovered. Athieng of course insisted she had no idea where Akuch had gone that night. If anything, she speculated, Akuch might have committed suicide the way she had been treated. It had been known to happen, especially with girls forced to marry men they did not like.

More messages came the following day, with the ma's uncle calling for peace and offering to meet with Uncle Bol Atem and Uncle Atemdit. His message was that the intention of the man's family was honourable and that they wanted to marry Akush into their family.

But Uncle Atemdit was so angry he swore an oath not to have anything more to do with Akush, because "she has disgraced the family. Uncle Bol Atem was, however, able to swallow his pride and was willing to negotiate. "There is nothing to be gained by refusing to talk. The girl has already eloped because we wanted her to marry a man she does not love. Do you want her to kill herself?"

So, although Uncle Atemdit continued his oath against Akuch, Uncle Bol went ahead with marriage negotiations. It turned out that the family of Arol Madut was not after all just "a bunch of fishermen." In the end they scraped up more than 80 cattle in dowry, not enough but acceptable under the circumstances.

Uncle Atemdit was allocated his share of bride wealth and he mellowed a bit. Eventually he agreed to reconcile with Akuch and her husband, but because he, a Spearmaster, had sworn an oath, he could not drink milk from Akuch's dowry cattle or eat any food from Akuch's marital home until a ritual to revoke the original oath was performed. The ceremony, carried out a year later and a half later, at an appropriate when Akush returned home for a visit with her first baby girl.

Mother decided to mov house from Gaikou to Wunchuei a year after Akuch eloped. So, our new homestead was now located near the homestead of Awien Maroldit near the river. Mother did not say, but I think the attitude of Uncle Atemdit towards Akush was hard for her to bear; moving a distance away from Gaikou gave her space to breathe. Also, apart from being near Awien Maroldit's homestead, Akuch's marital home, Nyinakoi, was closer to Wunchuei than Gaikou.

My elder brother, Angui, probably agreed with mother on issues concerning Akush, without appearing to be in open opposition to Uncle Atemdit and in agreement with Uncle Bol Atem. Though respected as head of Akol Atem's family, Uncle Atemdit was, after all, our brother, not our father. If anything, Uncle Bol Atem, who was senior to Atemdit and clearly demonstrated wisdom and farsightedness in difficult situations, carried more weight with his brother's family. In agreeing to mother's decision to move house, Angui was in a way asserting a degree of independence from Uncle Atemdit, who was likely to face more challenges from rebellious sisters. For my unmarried half-sisters, Akuch became their heroine for defying the family and married the man she loved.

New Dimensions

BY The end of the first school year (April - December) at Village School Ayiel, I was able to read and understand the contents of the *Dinka Primer and Reader 1*[25]. While the alphabets were stuck somewhere in the middle, the book began with simple sentences such as: *Get up. Sit down. Come here. Go out. Turn your backs.*

Sentences increased progressively in length and complexity from page to page as new elements were introduced. Page 5, for example, had a picture of a woman pounding something in wooden mortar with a wooden pestle. The words next to the picture read simply: *It is my mother. My mother is called Achol. She is at home.* Another little shadow sitting on a stool on the same page was that of a man smoking a pipe. The words next to it read: *This is my father. My father is called Dut. He is smoking tobacco.*

The fact that these pictures were merely abstract representations of real people did not present me with any difficulty because, back home, on the outside and inside walls of *Little House*, many human forms were expertly drawn with charcoal and decorated with colourful ashes mixed in oil. The only difference was that the pictures in the book were on a piece of paper instead of a wall. They also had written words to explain what the pictures stood for; and that was the point of departure, a new dimension.

Animals illustrated included creatures as fierce and dangerous as the lion, the crocodile the buffalo, the hippo, and the snake and

---

25   *Dinka Primer and Reader 1,* The Rev. Father Nebel. (First published 1954).

graceful ones like the gazelle and the giraffe and giants like the elephant. Again, although we could draw these animals on walls back home, the words under each picture left no doubt as to what animal the picture represented and what the animal was supposed to be doing. Words added dimensions and soon took the central stage; thus, relegating pictures to mere illustrations of stories told in words.

I found the stories short, familiar and interesting. Here is one:

A man finds a monkey drinking in a well. He aims his spear at the monkey. Frightened, the monkey jumps out of the well and runs for cover. The man laughs at the monkey for being such a coward as he was only joking. He puts down his spear and goes to the well to drink. The monkey returns, picks up the spear, and aims it at the man. The man shakes with fear. The monkey says, "It's joke for joke". He then puts down the spear and runs off.

The book also introduced the Cathedral at Kuachjok Catholic Mission, 19 miles south of Gakrial. It looked imposingly big and beautiful. The words read:

The House of God at Kuachjok. It is big and very beautiful. Palms trees are painted on the wall. It is covered with metal leaf. God the Divinity who created people. Good people pray to God.

Numbers and signs, simple additions, subtractions, multiplication and division in the book were also learned and understood. They made counting, adding, subtracting, multiplying and dividing things look like child's play. Although the full impact of such knowledge was not yet fully understood, the possibilities for its application seemed unlimited. Cattle, for example, could be counted and their numbers represented by a single number or few figures instead of, say, 50 pieces of sticks for 50 cattle as we do back home. It was definitely a new and exciting dimension.

The final installation in the *Dinka Primer and Reader 1* set out to explain why school education for children is important. Here is my translation of the full Dinka text:

The Things Children Gain Through Education (Ka ye mith yok piocic):

> *Children must be told of the very important things we learn and the things we do, so to be good. And Son of God himself, called Jesu Kristo, taught us things that make us good before God. And people who listen to his word and do his bidding are his people and good Christians. What God wants very much from a person is for the person to listen to the word of God's representatives. God's representatives are the father of the homestead and the chief of the country. A country (or people) without a ruler (or leader) falls apart. And the important thing children must learn is that everyone is a child of the Creator, so they must love each other like children of one man. If people in a country love each other, that country will prosper. A person who loves other people will not kill another person, will not be difficult to others and will not steal other person's property. If he sees a poor person, he will comfort him. Children are taught to protect themselves from disease, so not to be tired at work. And a person must guard well the body given him by God. But he should not love his body more than his soul. The good things from a person's heart are greater than the body's, and they are a lot better. A person is not highly praised because he has a strong and big body. Illness can destroy a person's body very fast, and many animals are stronger than any human. A person is well praised if he has a clean heart. You school children, let your hearts be advised to know the right things for your country.*

Catechism lessons, which began with the Sign of the Cross on my first day at school, were continued at a steady pace throughout the year. By December, I was able to recite the first catechism book by heart.

The reading of the Bible (in Jieng) was also a daily lesson. I had no problem with the fact that the God of the Bible created everything in six days and took a rest on the seventh day. Adam and Eve could have been our own Deng and Abuk or Garang and Abuk. That they lived in "Paradise" where there was no suffering and death; that they offended God who cast them out of Paradise to suffer and know death: all that sounded very much like our own stories concerning the origin of Man from under water to dry land.

The Angels, Jesus, Virgin Mary, the Saints and all that sounded familiar and brought up no serious contradiction with our own idea of the hierarchical set up between Man and God. Still, the story of God and Man in a single book, the Bible, was a radical dimension because our own stories about God and his relationship with humans is scattered in the minds of so many people; so, adopt a different form when told by different people.

Big Red priest who came on my first Sunday at school turned up punctually for mass for three consecutive Sundays. Always on his big and noisy motorbike which, for all I knew was the only one in "our country"(Aguok), his approach could be heard as soon as he emerged out of central Gakrial, a mile or so south of the village school. He always came to the Church via the main road. When he left for Kuachjok he went by a footpath leading into *Malakia*, an area of Gakrial which housed the main local beer brewing, sales and bars. The place was also notorious for prostitutes. Akel told me the priest went there to preach to the sinners and prostitutes. But Gongdit said the priest loved the local beer and went there for a drink before returning to Kuachjok. Whatever, he seemed to enjoy his weekly visits away from the Mission.

On the fifth week, however, the Big Red priest who visited my father sometime back turned up in a green truck. He joined the boys outside the church compound after the service.

But the boys who knew Fr. Passino well were watching him like hawks and jumped out of his grab with excitement as he tried to catch them. I got the idea but when he reached out for me, I was too crowded in to get out of his way in time. So, he grabbed me by the shoulder, hoisted me off the ground, tucked me under his left arm and started to tickle me with his right hand, laughing as he did so. I tried very hard to resist laughing because I knew that was what he wanted me to do, and I did not like people who laughed at my expense. I struggled even harder to free myself, but he was too strong, and he continued to tickle me. Eventually I gave into uncontrollable laughter and all the boys went wild with laughter at my expense. I clawed at his hairy face and got nowhere until he suddenly stopped. He put me down and peered at me: "Say, is this not my little friend from the village? So, your father has agreed at last to bring a son to school? This is very good. How is your father?"

"Uncle Akoldit passed away in January this year, Father," said Uncle Abiem. The priest made a quick Sign of the Cross and mumbled an inaudible prayer.

"Jiel decided to come to school on his own," Uncle Abiem explained "and I have already sorted things out with his Uncle Bol Atem. All is well."

"That is good," said the priest, "God bless you, my son." He made the Sign of the Cross once again, this time for me in a new dimension of blessing. He then returned to his quarters and then off to Kuachjok.

Fr. Passino continued to come to Village School Ayiel most Sundays. Boldit zoomed through on his motorbike most weekends on his way north to Panliet and Mayen Twic and usually arrived back at Ayiel at about 4:30pm and 5pm on Sundays on his way to Kuachjok.

When we heard the sound of a motorbike, we knew it was Boldit coming, and we rushed to the main road to wave greetings to him.

First, we saw a streak of dust bellowing through the trees before we could see the motorbike and the rider; but Boldit and his bike were soon upon us, and we waved and cheered furiously. Boldit waved and shouted back greetings. Suddenly it was all over, the whole exercise having taken not more than two minutes; but we enjoyed it all the same and looked forward to next Sunday. I am not sure which of the two we most wanted to see: Boldit or his motorbike? I have a sneaky suspicion that it was the big greyish and noisy vehicle we wanted to see more than the priest.

Sunday was the only day of rest. The rest of the week was very busy. Apart from lessons, there was always in the wet season the creeping grass weed to clear around the school compound to keep at bay snakes, mosquitoes and other nasty insects like scorpions. We used sickles to cut the grass short, though it always seemed to regain its full height within a week. Some of the weeds had to be uprooted altogether by digging them up with hoes.

But, although we managed to keep snakes away from the main compound, getting rid of mosquitoes and other insects was never that easy. Bedbugs were even worse than mosquitoes. Sometimes the health department in Gakrial turned up and dosed the whole place up with DDT chemicals: sleeping mats, floor, ceiling, the wall and anything in the rooms turned white with the chemical for weeks. Mosquitoes and all sorts of insects like bedbugs died like flies on the floor of our sleeping huts, in the kitchen, the classrooms, the Church, everywhere! The dead were swept away, and we had a few weeks of relatively bugs-and-mosquitoes free houses; then they were back again in force before the smell of the DDT had even disappeared completely. I think we hated the smell of the DDT more than the bite of mosquitoes and bed bugs. In the wet season, malaria was as common as the common cold, but I think our bodies had long learned to cope with it.

Attempts were always made to keep the pit latrines clean, but this was very difficult for children not used to burying their body waste in holes. They either missed the hole or avoided pit latrines altogether for fear of being bitten by black cobras which lurked around the huts over such holes. Apart from snakes, the possibility of meeting a man-eater lion, a leopard or rogue hyena discouraged the use of latrines at night because they were in the bush, a good distant away from the compound. The clearing of grass and excrement along the paths to the latrines was one of the dreaded jobs one had to do if assigned. But no matter how hard we worked at keeping the place clean, there were always giant green flies buzzing between the latrines and the compound. Chronic diarrhoea and even dysentery were our regular companions.

There were also school fields to be planted with groundnuts, weeded and harvested. There was the school garden with bananas, lemons, papaws and oranges to be taken care of. None of the fruit ever seemed to reach our table, but we did not care much about such fruits because they were strange to us and did not miss them anyway.

We were also busy making bricks for a new Church. Clay soil had to be dug up, mixed with water, put into shape with brick trays, covered up with grass and left in the sun to dry. Dried bricks were then piled up in the shape of a pyramid with tunnels under it. These tunnels were then filled with semidry firewood, then fired and fed with firewood for at least three weeks.

Another important daily activity involved food preparation. Firewood for cooking had to be gathered from the nearby forests. But the hardest job was the daily preparation of sorghum for breakfast, lunch and evening meals. Several children were selected and issued with half a kilo of sorghum each morning. Often there were not enough wooden mortars and pestles at the school. Those who failed to secure these tools had to go looking for them in the neighbouring homesteads.

Some boys got away with light jobs. These included those assigned to teachers' houses. Boys assigned to teachers (all men) houses were not required to cook for them because, even when a teacher was not unmarried, there was always a woman or a girl relative who would do the food preparation and cooking. The assigned boy did odd jobs and errands for the woman and teacher. In return, he often ate good food at the teacher's house. Overall, such a boy did fewer dirty jobs and used a clean latrine at the teachers, usually equipped with *The Messenger*, a feather-weight Mission newspaper, which somehow found its way into the teachers' pit latrines and was used as a fine toilette tissue. I know because I was assigned once to a teacher's house.

Among the cushy jobs was that of the cook's assistants. They invariably looked "very healthy" (fat) the longer they stayed in that job. They were always envied and suspected of eating the best pieces of meat.

Dreaded were the prefects, who often seemed like a collection of sadists who enjoyed making others miserable. Not only did some of them appear to hate dirtying their hands, but they were also always finding faults with everyone else who had to: "What are these? You call this firewood! (Spits). These are twigs! Two bundles on Saturday afternoon!" He would put it on a piece of paper to aid his memory. "That will be after normal work." If one tried to explain or argued with such prefects, one was either shushed up or shut up with a kick or a slap. That was how cruel and arrogant some prefects were. If you did not do the job well on Saturday, you got a more serious punishment, such as lashes on the buttocks. We learned not to argue with prefects!

Sometimes, however, they overstepped their authority and all of them, including their head, would be thrown out of power and a new regime of prefects appointed. We went wild with happiness over the change. Some boys composed nasty songs against any prefect thought to have been particularly nasty. Some of these songs could be so outrageous they could not be repeated here. But here is a translation of a comparatively mild one against someone I call So & So:

Leader: So, & So is dismissed, ehee!

Chorus: He is returned to work
To stay at home
To clean latrines
when you tell So & So not to shush[26] people
He hears it with his ass!

Boys smaller or weaker than So & So would of course participate in singing such a song at their own risk. The solution for them was to join a big group so that So & So had no chance of singling them out, otherwise they sang the song when the target was out of hearing.

However, such songs were usually dropped as soon as the new team of prefects became more unpopular than the previous lot. Previous prefects like So & So would join in maligning the new team. None of this, of course, lightened our load, but it gave us the satisfaction of laughing at authority, albeit a token one.

But the significant thing about all these work activities was that we, boys and men, had to perform jobs normally done by women back home. Our idea of the little things that we thought were important to manhood was thus undermined and given a different dimension.

The Messenger

One day I was busy pounding sorghum at the house of Guot Malual, a neighbour a few hundred yards away from the school compound,

---

26 One may "shush" a dog or a donkey, not people.

when the old lady of the house called me. "Come here, my son, come. Sit here." I sat in front of her while she silently examined me critically. "Tell me", she said at last, "are you a son of Akol *Arialbek* (*Marial*)? Are you a son of Akol Atem?" I told her I was. "I thought so! I thought so!" she said with satisfaction and relief in her voice. "Ayak! Come here! This is a son of a gentleman! Children of these days don't know what a gentleman is. So, you listen to me, Ayak, my daughter! What is going on? How come a son of Akol Atem is allowed to do this woman's work in my house? Don't you know..."

Ayak, was the young wife of Guot Malual, son of the old lady. Her mother-in-law told her how my father saved starving communities with his quick-maturing sorghum. After grilling her daughter in law, she instructed me to bring to Ayak any sorghum given me any time. "Ayak will prepare it for you. You also eat here. Ayak you hear that? The son of Akol Atem will eat here in my house. I don't like what they eat in that school! They give them sand! That's what they eat! You will eat here any time."

Neither Ayak nor I had any say in the matter. We both knew we would have to accommodate her wishes as far as practically possible. I knew that if I turned up too often, that would not be appropriate. If I came infrequently, she would blame Ayak for my absence. As it turned out, Ayak and I understood each other perfectly well and things worked out just fine. I called there at least once a week. I would have "home-cooked" meal and returned to school with the best-prepared, sand-free, sorghum flour.

These arrangements between Ayak and I were unexpectedly interrupted by a teacher called Deng Luil who selected me to work in his house during working hours. It saved Ayak and I from pounding school sorghum. I was no longer required to do jobs such as collecting firewood, weeding and the building of the church. It also saved me from attending roll calls, which always took place early in the morning and at sunset. While others ran like mad at the sound of the whistle, boys working in teachers' houses walked the other way, pretending to be doing errands for their masters.

Deng Luil was a bachelor. He ate little and drank a lot of local gin, an illegal brew. Sometimes, he would send me to buy the gin from nearby homes. One day, I bought two bottles that turned out to be "flat".

"Come here!" he was angry. "Let me show you how to choose a good bottle. Pick up the bottle by the neck like this between two fingers and the thumb of the left hand. Hold it up and flick the bottle with the big finger of the right hand like this. "Do you hear that? Very low notes. It sounds like water! And that," pointing at the bottles I just brought, "is water! Good gin has high notes!" Ting! Ting! Ting! He tapped the bottle. "Do you hear that?"

I heard him very clearly. I didn't want to lose my privileges. Mistakes like that could return one to the mess.

I was never sure how often Deng Luil ate and where. He was out most evenings and I assumed that he knew a family or woman somewhere in town and went there to eat. The evenings he was at home, Ayak, the young wife of Guot Malual, brought him prepared food, which he generously shared with me. Ayak, a very pretty woman would wait around for her plates while saying very little.

Guot Malual had a pretty daughter called Arek by his first marriage. Arek's mother died when she was very young and Ayak, her stepmother, stepped into her shoes. Guot Malual had some school education and was therefore prepared to send Arek to school. As there was no girls' school nearby, she went to a boarding school far from home; but she often returned home on leave when our school was still functioning, and I got to know her very well.

On one of her home leaves, Arek and I were conversing when she said something out of the blue: "You know what is going on, don't you?"

I looked puzzled.

"You know what is going on between Deng Luil and my father's wife."

I just looked at her and said nothing. Now that she mentioned it, it suddenly became clear to me that Deng Luil and Ayak have been having an affair, that they both used me to carry coded messages between them.

"Well," she resumed, "people think that you are the go-between. I think you should leave the house of Deng Luil."

I did not have to make the decision because the following morning the school was closed because there was fighting going on in Equatoria between Southerners and Northerners. The situation was not yet clear, but the school was closed anyway.

Their affair soon became public knowledge. Deng Luil was heavily fined. Ayak either left Guot Malual voluntarily or was divorced by him. I never found out which.

Guot Malual later came up with these songs:

> *A woman says:*
> *"It is Guot Ngokdit who has failed"*
> *And Ayak has slipped*
> *You can't hold people to a joyless bed."*
> *The child says:*
> *"It is Guot Ngokdit who has failed"*
> *And Ayak has slipped*
> *You can't hold people to a joyless bed."*

> *When I sleep with the woman*
> *She tells me this:*
> *"You are killing me!*
> *You Guot Ngok the sexy*
> *You are killing me!*
> *Give me small space*

So to find my soul
You are killing me!"
I swaggered proudly swaggered
I am a man who satisfied a woman!
Yet I am being exchanged for a man
With whom to build a home.[27]

Two Chiefs

For meat, an ox was slaughtered each month for the 120 boys then at Village School Ayiel. The meat was sun-dried and rationed out each day for broth. But we were often short of meat, so the rations were very small. To augment the number of oxen available for this purpose, "greeting visits" to leading personalities of the Aguok sub-tribe were regularly organised. Our home was visited once by school children before I was born.

At Ayiel, I remember at least two "courtesy calls": One was to Malek, home of the family of Agoth Agany, whose sons, Kuanyin Agoth and Wek Agoth were both "court chiefs" - as distinct from tradition chiefs/spearmasters. Though the visit was ostensibly to bring greetings and prayers to "our great chiefs," the real purpose was to solicit for an ox or two - if we were lucky.

Both chiefs lived at Ayiel village, very close to the school. When I asked Gongdit why we had to go to Malek instead of just calling on the chiefs next door, he explained, "To visit them here would be less dignifying for them and would yield poor results for us. At Malek (about five to six miles from the school), whole villages will turn out in force to see the children of *Abun* marching and drumming and to listen to their songs of praise for the two chiefs and their family. In the presence of so many people, the chiefs will be flattered, and we will get a big fat ox - maybe two if we are lucky!"

---

[27] Ayak and Deng Luil did not become man and wife, thus the sarcastic line.

The two chiefs were informed about the planned visit to Malek and on the date it would take place. New songs in praise of the two chiefs were composed and learned before the visit. The day before the visit, drums were rolled out and left in the sun to dry, thus tuning them up.

Near the village, Uncle Abiem blew his whistle and we all fell into four neat lines, with the shortest boys in front and the tallest at the back.

"Ateeenchon!" shouted the overseer at the top of his voice. We all stiffened up like soldiers; followed by a mighty and uniform stamping of the left foot on the dusty ground. "By the left quick march!" and off we went, perfectly timed with the drums. Two pre-selected song leaders would start with any song but eventually would have to come up with the one praising the two chiefs, preferably in their presence.

Even though this was before the national independence from Britain in January 1956, a legislative assembly was already set up in Khartoum and most administrative posts were already taken over by Sudanese, the vast majority were occupied by Northern Sudanese or, in the language of the time, Arabs. Those who composed the songs must have been very aware of the political changes then taking place in the country and the unfair way these posts were being distributed.[28] There was no doubt that the chiefs understood what was going on near and far, unlike most of us.

The visit was a roaring success: the brothers gave us two big bulls and promised more soon.

Another "courtesy call" was made to the grandsons of Ayook Lual at Ajoong, near Alek and Marial. At Alek village, we were shown the spot where Ayook *Kerjok* decided not to go any further with his captors. We were shown massive scars on the bodies of giant

---

28 "Only 8 out of 800 posts were given to Southerners. Fransis F. Deng, War of Visions.

palm trees, many of them thriving despite gapping scars from deep wounds accidentally inflicted on their trunks by cannonballs fired at the "Battle of Ayook Lual". The trip to the home of the descendants of a historically revered Spearmaster and war leader, earned us a fat ox and an important history lesson.

These "courtesy calls" were not made to just anybody. They were made to those individuals and families considered important the history and continued well-being of the Aguok people. They were the leaders and protectors of the land of the Agok.

The neighbouring sub-tribes, like Apuk, Kuac and Awan, called our sub-tribe Agong (Aguok) Wek or Agong Mou, after our two chiefs Wek Agoth and Mon(u) Akeen. But what exactly made up a sub-tribe like Aguok? Who did the chiefs represent and how did they come to be chiefs in the first place? Who appointed them? What was their background and how were they regarded by the Aguok people? In their eyes, were the two chiefs of equal status? If not, why not?

After my "expansive education," attained from Village School Ayiel, I was now able to sum up the whole geographical environment of the Jieng thus:

My village, Gaikou, is only a small place, one of many that makes up Gai Akol Atem's territory. Gai and Dhok Aken Mou together make up the Buothanyith Section with their *Wut*[29] centre at Dhok. The youth of the clans making up Buothanyith meet at Dhok annually at the end of July or beginning of August to dance and introduce competing new songs of the year called "*week loor*", (lit. songs of drum). Other symbols of a clan's importance, an individual's aesthetic beauty and standing are also displayed at such dances. The unity

---

29   "*Wut*" in this context is a Centre where young men of clans of a section, in this case Buothanyith, bring their cattle annually at about the end of July or beginning of August for a 8 to 10 days celebration at *Loor Ker*, literally "Drum of *Ker*", a short seasonal period which falls between Spring and Summer.

within this group is very cohesive, with a lot of intermarriages. Any fight between Buothanyith and Dhok are usually limited to skirmishes between the youth. Weapons used in such fights would rarely, if ever, involve anything as lethal as spears.

The Buothanyirth Section (*Wut*: Dhok), together with Agurpiny Anau Thiik (*Wut*: Kurue*c*), Wuny Agoth Agany (*Wut*: Malek), Atukuel Muou Ajok (*Wut*: Atukuel), Marial Ayook (*Wut*: Marial). There is a lot of intermingling within Aguok, involving intermarriages between the sections. A battle between any two sections, say between Buothanyith and Agurpiny, may involve the use of spears though it rarely does.

Other sub-tribes of the Rek Dinka include the Apuk people of Jok Tong and Giir Thiik, the Kuac of Nyok, the Lou of Ariik, the Gok of Kuelcok (Tonj), the Awon people of Mou Ring and the Awon people of Can Nyal. Interaction between sub-tribes is generally common at the borders and at certain times of the year, such as winter (dry season), when the young men of the sub-tribes drive their cattle to *Toc*, the swamps, where grass and water for cattle are plentiful. Any serious fight between any two sub-tribes of the Rek tribe would most likely involve spears.

The Aguok and the Apuk often fight serious battles involving spears. Such battles are sometimes provoked by something as little as a quarrel between two youths or a fight between two bulls. Sometimes, an exchange of insults between individuals may develop into a war of insults between sub-tribes. Terrible songs are then composed against each other, as it happened recently between Aguok and Apuk, (referred to below).

Other tribes of the Dinka I have heard about are the Agaar, the Malual & Abiem, the Twic, the Ngok of Deng Kuol, the Boor, and the Atuot. Apart from the Agaar, the Twic and the Malual, I have not at this stage met any member of the other tribes. All I know about the Boor and the Atuot is in association with certain breeds of cattle. A *boor* bull or cow has extensive long horns. An *atuot* cow or bull has thick, long, straight and tan-coloured horns. Beautiful! Both breeds are rare in our area and are, therefore, highly valued. One is sure to get oneself a wife very easily if one has an *atuot* or *boor* bull amongst one's herd.

What about Aguok, is it Agong Mou or is it Agong Wek? I asked, Wol Lang, a boy of about my age from Wuny area, which of the two chiefs he thought was the greatest?

"Wek Agoth, of course," Wol replied. "Everybody knows that he is the cleverest of the two." He proceeded to justify his assertion with a popular song:

> *Even if judged by all.*
> *And Wek has not expressed opinion.*
> *It stays lob sided.*
> *It stays as lob sided as*
> *The two-stoned palm fruit stays lob-sided.*

There was no question about the legendary wisdom of Chief Wek Agoth. I myself saw him in action at court in Gakrial a few years later. The first case involved my brothers, Atem *Mawut* and Malou *Bungajok*. They had recently been initiated into manhood, when Malou's unmarried sister, Doot, became pregnant (another blight on Uncle Atem's dignity). She went to the home of the man responsible. For one reason or another, the man could not marry her and the case was settled with the usual number of cattle given to the family of the girl in such cases. Doot was given to another man and that was that. So, it seemed.

A year later, the first lover, the father of her now young baby, was seen lurking in the vicinity of Doot's new home; then she disappeared.

Believing that Doot had gone to the home of this man (which indeed she did), Atem and Malou could not bear "the insult" any longer. Without telling anyone, the two of them invaded the home of Akoon, their sister's lover. Finding him at home, they attacked him with sticks. The man, older and more experienced than the two of them, defended himself gallantly; but they were two. Atem's stick found its mark on the topside of Akoon's head. Blood spurted out but Akoon fought on. A hue and cry were soon raised and a few young men from the village came out in force and gave chase to Atem and Malou. They managed to get away from Akoon and his relatives, but not from the law - and Wek Agoth.

Everyone who spoke in court before Wek condemned the violence, but they were all "very understanding of the humiliation the family of Akol Atem had been subjected to by this man" (the victim) and sympathised with the way the young men reacted. The insult inflicted on Akol Atem's family by this man called Akoon, was "difficult to suffer in silence" and on and on. We all thought Atem and Malou were going to get away with only a fine and a warning. But that was before Wek Agoth opened his mouth.

Chief Wek surveyed the courtroom with his eyes, like a hawk. Then he looked at Atem and Malou and ordered them to "stand up while I speak:"

"Where is Atem Akol? Where is Bol Atem?" he asked, knowing very well neither Uncle Atemdit nor Uncle Bol *Yoom* were present. "The family of Akol Atem is falling apart! The girls are running here and there like prostitutes! The boys know no law! What will Akol Atem think? That we have closed our eyes to what is happening to his family? No! Not me, not me! You boys are being misled by recently acquired testicles. But let me tell you: those testicles are only squirrel's, and you are dealing with an elephant. This is me, Wek Agoth! You are never going to boast again even in my absence!"

There was silence as he surveyed the courtroom once more. "Do you know what Squirrel said to his wife and children when he returned to find them in the rain because Elephant had accidentally destroyed their home and the tree they lived in?"

He looked around. Everyone knew the story, but no one dared say any thing. The point was not the story per se; rather, it was what the citing of it forebodes for the two young men.

"Well," the chief resumed, "Let me tell you: Squirrel boasted, 'OO, absence is like death! That's why Elephant dared pass through my village!' Imagine that! When Elephant heard what Squirrel had said, do you know what he said?"

Once again, the chief surveyed the courtroom to let it all sink in. At last, he said: "Elephant said: 'Blokes like Squirrel will get themselves misled by big testicles.' You boys have got yourselves misled by big testicles which you think are bigger than the law. Tell Bol Atem to hand over a pregnant heifer to the family of this man here, injured by his boys. Tell him this is the word of Chief Wek Agoth. And you, Atem, you inflicted a serious injury, and you are going to prison for two years. When you come out, you will be telling other young men they should not be flaunting their testicles carelessly in my path. As for you, Malou, go and sort out your sister. She needs you. Atem Akol and Bol Atem seem to be incapable of controlling the girls - and now the boys! I warn you, never to cross my path again. Do you hear! Court closed."

Sometime later, when I was about to go into exile, a young man called Joseph Bel Kuol, earmarked as our leader and guide on the dangerous journey we were about to take out of the country, was in serious trouble over a girl he slept with in Gakrial town. A dashing young man, born a few miles north of Gakrial who had recently returned from England after doing an Airport Management Course there, Joseph was then the rising star of the Gakrial community. If he were not the only Dinka who had been to England for such training, he was certainly the first for Aguok. Great things were expected of him.

The girl he went to bed with probably thought so too, because she turned up the following morning at the home of Joseph's senior relative and declared that she had come to be his wife. Joseph said he was neither ready for marriage nor interested in marrying her. In the village, such a case would have been resolved between the families by returning the girl to her people with an appropriate compensation for the lost of her girlhood. But the uncle of the girl in whose house she was staying in Gakrial town, wanted to take the case to court, believing that the young man would either be forced to marry the girl or that the family get better compensation.

Normally, such a case would take two to three weeks before it came up in court, but Wek Agoth suddenly decided to bring up the case before that. While all spoke of "arrogance and irresponsibility of our educated children," Wek Agoth took the opposite view, berating the uncle for bringing the girl to town. "I tell you!" He shook his index finger at the girl's uncle, "Gakrial is not a place to bring up a young girl. Even so, what sort of a girl is she who would jump into bed with a man within a few minutes of meeting him, eeh? How is she different from the prostitutes in this town? Tell me that! Tell me that! If you want to get anything out of this girl (pointing at the girl who was sitting shyly in front of him), then take my advice: Get her out of Gakrial as quickly as possible and find her a nice man back home to marry her. That is my advice. The people of Bel Kuol will give her father a bull as compensation. That is my word. As for this young man here (pointing at Joseph), I would advise him to watch the front of his trousers. There are greedy and uncouth women around here who would like to see what's in there."

There was general laughter as the court closed; a mere paragraph thus added to the legendary wisdom of Wek Agoth.

Wek Agoth was long known as "chief without teeth" because a good number of his upper teeth were missing. Adding this to the six missing lower teeth usually removed at childhood by the Dinka, the chief's lips appeared collapsed, making him look like an old man. Gaunt in appearance, the missing teeth were thought to have contributed to his unflagging seriousness, his seeming mean demeanour and his no nonsense approach to court cases. Even when he later went to Khartoum and had all his teeth replaced by a dentist, thus making him look incredibly young and meant he could smile freely when he wanted to, he was always identified with tight lips and seriousness. If one did not respect Wek Agoth, one had to fear him.

Nevertheless, Wek's rise to power was often ridiculed. His commitment to law and order made him appear very much like he was more interested in serving the interests of what was seen as an alien government than serving his own people. He was seen to be "sucking up to Government" and, as such, his chieftaincy and meteoric rise was seen as reward for his submissiveness to alien authority, something the Dinka abhor. The bottom line, it seemed, was that there would be no Chief Wek if there were no Government. He was often the target of many derogatory songs. This short song, for example, referred to the time when he had no teeth:

> *People laughed with gums at court.*
> *Chiefs with broken teeth are playing wizards.*
> *They have bewitched my case,*
> *A court person turned his backside to the wall.*
> *To eschew my case eeehe!*

Chief Mon(u) Aken was the opposite of Wek Agoth. He had a respectable amount of beef on his frame, and he was easy-going and surprisingly fit. Unlike Chief Wek, who cycled a mere mile to court and back, Chief Mou walked some six miles from his home to Gakrial and back. He always had a crowd bustling around him and was said to know everyone by name. Unlike Wek, he joked and laughed a lot with the youth and his age-mates alike. Even when he threatened to tell the family of any youth who blatantly showed disrespect, everyone knew he would never stoop to such lowly demands for respectability.

Mon Aken, I heard it said repeatedly, was very much "a child of the cattle camp" (*e manh wutic*), where Dinka children put the final touches to their manners. Among many codes of conduct, a *manh wutic* was always polite to elders, tactful and not easily derailed by cheap favours. Not to be *manh wutic* was to have greatly missed out in Dinka etiquette. Being a *manh wutic* himself, the chief knew very well that if a youth, indeed anybody, crossed a certain undefined line to show disrespect to him, such a person would soon be warned off by others.

Mon(u) Aken was also the son of Aken Mou, the name that had been closely associated with Aguok before Wek and Mou. Even in the 50s and early 60s, Aguok was still referred to as "Agong Aken Mou".

Most importantly, the family of Mon(u) Aken belonged to the Payi, a traditional clan of spearmasters, a clan as spiritually potent as the Pagong. But, though the Pagong and the Payi had become the two leading spiritual leaders of Aguok, the Pagong were recent immigrants to Aguok from Apuk. My own family could trace its presence in the Aguok territory to only four generations. This historical fact left the Payi very much the long-time spiritual leaders of Aguok. Mou Aken was, therefore, seen as the legitimate leader of the Aguok people.

Nevertheless, change was thought to be very much in the air. Wek Aagoth's chieftaincy and his rise to prominence in Aguok's politics signalled this change. The fact that Chief Wek had risen to rival Mon Aken and overshadowed his elder brother, Kuanyin Agoth - also a chief in his own right - empathised the change even more. In addition, there was no denying Wek's keen mind, his dedication to work and his incisive judgement of cases. In the minds of many, he deserved all the praise he got.

His popularity, however, put him in the firing line on controversial issues between Aguok and other sub-tribes. While Mou was seen as a symbol of praise for Aguok, Wek was often seen as the symbolic object of insult when one wanted to criticise or insult the Agok as a people.

At one time, Aguok and Apuk, entered a serious war of words. What began as a quarrel between two Agok (people of Aguok), developed into insults and then into insulting songs which, as usual, became popular with the youth. These two Agok hired professional composers, one who happened to come from the Apuk sub-tribe. Somewhere along the line, the two composers turned on each other. Before long, the whole thing turned into a full "war of insulting songs" (*bi koc ket*) between Aguok and Apuk. The original quarrel between the two Agok was forgotten.

Terrible songs were composed against innocent individuals and families on both sides. In such wars, few were spared. Women and children alike were insulted at will. The contents of such songs were mainly fabrications. For example: my aunt Ajok (mother's half sister), married to Chief Giir Thiik of Apuk, came home to Aguok for a normal visit. Out came a song, which implied that Giirdit had done shameful things, which caused my aunt to run back home; thus, making it appear as if my aunt had divulged something previously known only to herself and her husband. Giir and my aunt ignored the nonsense and got on with their lives.

Wek Agoth, being a chief of Aguok, was the target of many diabolical songs, along with his family and clan. Songs likening his artificial teeth, which were small and bent inward, like a dog's "scratching its backside" were comparatively mild insults indeed. Mon(u) Aken and the Payi Clan, and sometimes the whole of Aguok, were presented as victims of Wek's evil schemes; for tolerating Wek, Aguok had to suffer.

The Pagong and the Payi and their leaders were not touched by both sides, a testimony to the high regard the Jieng attach to the power of Spearmaster's divinities.

The whole thing got so bad it eventually ended in an actual battle between Apuk and Aguok at Panacier, an Apuk village at the border between the two sub-tribes. The government sent in armed police from Gakrial, but they arrived after many lives were lost.

The composition of derogatory songs did not end until a court ritual was performed in Gakrial town. This involved both sides singing all the songs thus far composed in front of chiefs and elders. At the end of the singing, the two composers sat on a low branch of a tree. The branch was then cut with an axe until it fell with the two men on it. The symbolic cutting and the fall of the branch ended the whole episode.

As for the two chiefs, Mon(u) Aken was seen as the custodian of traditional leadership. But change was nevertheless thought to be very much in the air. Wek Aagoth's chieftaincy and his rise to prominence in Aguok's politics signalled this change. The fact that Chief Wek had risen to overshadow both Mon Aken and his elder brother, Kuanyin Agoth - also a chief - empathised the change even more.

There was no denying Wek's keen mind, his dedication to law, order and justice and his incisive judgement of cases. He, more than Mon Aken, was aware of the national political intrigues then taking place. Even though he was known to be strict in his application of the law, he knew when it was politically appropriate to support the cause of Southern Sudan. He knew it was "illegal" for a southerner to leave the country with the possible intention of joining the rebels abroad. But he also knew that if he delayed Joseph's case and he was arrested by then military dictators of the time, it would not be in the interest of the South. Wek could have said to Joseph to "disappear," but this to his way of thinking would be unacceptable, as he would see it as failure to dispense justice. So, he speeded up the case and passed judgement.

Aguok was doing just fine with its two chiefs. It did not matter much under whose name it was known.

In Remembrance of Jesus

Preparations for Christmas celebrations began in October. New songs were composed, learned and rehearsed repeatedly as we marched up and down the school compound for many of the remaining Sundays of the year.

One of the teachers visited Bush School Alek to teach the children there the new songs. They would join us on December 21 for the walk to Kuachjok Catholic Mission. Alek and Ayiel formed a competing unit and represent the Aguok. At Christmas, we competed against schools from Apuk, Kuach, Awon Mou, Awon Chan and Tuic.

Besides these schools were the Teachers Training College and Trade School. They were also primed up for the Christmas celebration.

We were issued with new khaki uniforms, the second in a year, and were told to keep it new for the celebration. They were washed, ironed and tucked away for the big day.

We arrived at Kuajok two days before Christmas and camped in the compound of the Teachers Training College. Awon Mou, Awan Chan and Mayen Twic joined us later in the day. The Apuk and Kuach were accommodated in the compound of Kuachjok Elementary School.

It was my first time in Kuachjok. The differences in soil and vegetation were already apparent. While all that I had ever seen was black cotton soil and clay, here was red soil with large red stone boulders strewn all over the place. The largest stones I had ever seen back home were pink or white round stones, usually found in the forest near anthills; but they were small and could be picked up with one hand and thrown at game birds with apparent ease. We called them "hyena stones" because it was thought that beast swallowed them when he was hungry. At Kuajok, there were big stones that could not be lifted even by two men. The trees and the grass out of this soil looked different too and the land seemed dryer even in December.

Akel Awar, who had been to Kuachjok on two previous Christmas occasions, decided to show Manyoth and I the lay out of the Catholic Mission we had heard so much about. He took us to the top of the T-junction, where the road leading into the mission meets the main road from Gakrial to Wau.

"You see that building at the end of the road?" asked Akel, "That is the Church of Kuachjok Catholic Mission."

There was no mistaking it. Even at this end of the road, half a mile away, we could see clearly the famous giant palm trees drawn on the face of it. The road itself, leading east to the front of the Church, was very wide and dead straight. It was framed between two well-trimmed edges of a foreign plant I saw for the first time at Ayiel. We called it *sim* (Arabic) because it was said to be very poisonous. Any way, it was green throughout the year, even in a very dry season.

We walked up the road towards the Church. Immediately right near the junction of the two roads were big houses with walls of stone and corrugated iron roofs. To the left were a couple of similar houses. Akel told us that the houses belonged to "the teachers of teachers" but that one of them belonged to the headmaster of Kuachjok Elementary School.

We walked on, past the Teachers Training College to the right. Further down was the Kuachjok Girls Elementary School, their dormitories and the Sisters Quarters, just to our left and right of the Church. To our right and left of the Church were the Fathers Quarters, beyond that the Trade School. All these quarters and the people who moved about in them could be glimpsed through the thick foliage of mango and strange trees.

The Church itself was truly big and magnificent. Built with stones and red bricks with a corrugated iron roof, I had never seen a building as big as that before. Above the wide entrance was an arch, on which pictures of angels blowing trumpets and floating on clouds around the unmistakable radiant figure of Jesus Christ on the cross with his crown of thorns. A dove-like figure from the clouds poured on Jesus brilliant sunshine from its beak. On the wall on both sides of the door and the arch were painted the famous giant palm trees, stretching from just above ground level to the corrugated metal roof. They looked so real with their red fruits seemingly ready to fall.

We walked around the Church before we entered. I could hear loud musical tones coming from the far end of the Church. I asked Akel what it was, and he explained it came from and instrument called an "organ."

"Is it like an accordion?" I asked. I had seen an accordion only once when Father Passino brought it to our Church at Ayiel. I was fascinated by the way it made the sound when opened and closed, but I forgot all about it when the Church service was over. Now I remembered it because of the strange musical sound.

"No!" said Akel. "It is something … it is something you kick with your foot, and you play it with your fingers… It is … Why don't we go in and see!"

We walked in behind Akel. Following his example, we dipped our fingers in a stone dish containing water. We made the Sign of the Cross, knelt on the right knee, made another Sign of the Cross and walked stealthily towards the organ and its player. But every move we made seemed to echo very loudly between the beats. The organ player glanced over his shoulder and glared at us. It was Father Passino. We almost bolted but he beckoned us and turned his attention to the organ. When we got close, he motioned us to sit down near him, then began a hymn he recently composed in Jieng. We knew the hymn, but I had never heard it sung with an organ as accompaniment:

> *Our grandfather Joseph*
> *A great man indeed*
> *Our grandfather Joseph*
> *Guardian of Christians*

You guard, and you guide
When we live here on earth
We are children of Jesus
We are Christians
Guard us and guide us
To save our souls
Yeehee!
Bless the Pope
And our Bishop
People of God
All Christians
Jieng (Dinka) and Jur and homes eehe!
And fields and cattle
We beg you eehe
Great saint indeed.

He got up and led us out of the church. He then shook hands with us and welcome us to Kuachjok. He told us to follow him. When we reached the gate of his compound, he told us to wait there. He went inside, plucked three ripe mangoes from a tree in the compound and returned with them. He gave us one each and bade us farewell. We ate the mangoes as we walked towards the boys' elementary school. They were delicious.

Kuachjok Elementary School was of grander scale than Village School Ayiel. There were two large T-shaped oblong buildings with walls of stones and bricks and thatched roofs at the back of the Church. These housed the four classrooms of the school, the headmaster's office and the teachers' common room.

Beyond the classroom buildings was the playground/football field, bordered on the far side by five large dormitories. Only a few large trees screened the dormitories from a large expanse of open grassland between the school and the River, punctuated by scattered trees here and there. Undoubtedly, this large expanse of empty lowland must be flooded in the wet season, thus the absence of trees and villages on it. A dirt road, built with stones, broken bricks and clay, led eastward towards the river, a couple of miles away.

"This road goes to the river (Bahr el Ghazal)", said Akel. "When the mission's steamer comes in October from Khartoum on its way to Wau, it stops there for Kuachjok to unload their goods."

We return to our sleeping place by sunset. Overall, I was very impressed with what I had seen of Kuachjok thus far. The Mission was much grander and more beautiful than I could have imagined. The Cathedral was breath-taking.

On Christmas Day, all the visiting schools went to Church at midnight. The rest went to Mass in the morning with services at 6, 7, and 8. Nine to ten was left for preparations. All the schools were gathered at the Teachers Training College, TTC, near the T- junction. Kuachjok Elementary School for Girls led the parade, followed by Kuachjok Elementary School. Wunkuel, representing Kuach, (where Kuachjok is located) followed; They were followed by Aguok, Apuk, the two Awen (plural for Awon), Twic, the Trade School and, finally, the TTC. Everybody, excluding the girls and the TTC students, were dressed in smart khaki uniforms. The girls wore blue skirts and light blue shirts. The TTC students wore khaki shorts, white shirts, white canvas shoes and long white socks. By the time the last group started for the Church, most schools who had already arrived, stood aside for the others to arrive and take their allocated places in the widening semicircle.

The show began in reverse, starting with the last school to arrive: the TTC. They sang a few songs and made smart drill moves, then quickly got out of the way amidst thunderous cheers. They were not in the serious competition between the six sub-tribes. Neither were the Trade School, and the two Kuachjok elementary schools for boys and girls. They, nevertheless, sang their very impressive songs and did fantastic drills; then got out of the way.

The competing schools were led by Kuach, followed by Twic, Awan Chan, Awan Mou, Apuk and Aguok, in that order. In the audience and among the judges was His Lordship the Bishop, who decided that year to honour Kuachjok Catholic Mission with his presence at the celebrations. He was flanked by numerous priests, nuns and "brothers" (non-ordained technical experts of the Mission), many who came with him from Wau. They were joined by the teachers and local dignitaries.

Aguok, whose songs I knew best, included an array of soul-searching songs that year. Here are a few:

Loud sheers and clapping of hands followed the end of this lead song. It was followed by some of the songs that got His Lordship up on his feet and earned us standing ovations:

There was a prolonged standing ovation after this last song. Even the Bishop was on his feet much longer than before. Aguok walked off with the prize, the Mission's flag, for the second year running.

There was drumming all day all over Kuachjok Catholic Mission. People from the surrounding villages, though not necessarily Christians themselves, joined in the celebration. Milk and local beer for sale was plentiful in the local market. Several oxen were slaughtered for the feast. Loads of sweet bananas, oranges and sweets were brought in from Wau. There was food everywhere you turned.

In the evening, Kuachjok boys and girls' elementary schools, the Trade School and the TCC entertained the visitors with drama and comedy. There was even a biblical play, displaying the wisdom of King Solomon. We did not go to bed until well after midnight.

At sunrise, I said goodbye to my friend, Manyoth. He would be heading south to Wau, then east to Agaar later that morning, after breakfast. I, like a few other boys, decided to skip breakfast and headed north back to Gakrial, then to our various homes. We did not have much to carry and 19 miles to Gakrial did not seem like a long journey. I expected to be back in town by noon or early afternoon, then arrive at Gaikou by 4pm at the latest. Plenty of time to reflect on what had been learned thus far.

In Memory of Spearmaster

We arrived in Gakrial town at about two in the afternoon. Wol and I had our first meal of the day and said goodbye to each other. He headed west to his village while I continued north.

Just beyond Village School Ayiel, I noticed a small band of mostly young men, girls and boys going my way. Their faces and bodies were decorated with white, red and bluish colours of ash from burnt cow-dung, mixed with gee. Their necks and waists were adorned with colourful beads arranged to suit the latest fashion and individual taste.

Girls (unmarried young women) wore around their necks a large collection of colourful beads. Some girls added two plated loops of beads, one passing over the right shoulder and under the left armpit; the other passed over the left shoulder and under the right armpit. The two loops overlapped at the back between the shoulders and in front over the chest. The rings of beads framed their breasts, thus making them prominently pointed, a sign of beauty, youth and maturity. In addition, most of the girls wore a *geer*, an intricate mat of colourful beads that covered the trunk from hips to navel. On each leg was a long coil of aluminium rings covering half the leg. Below the coil around the ankle on each leg, was added one or two steel bangles with chambers containing two to three small metal balls that knocked against the metal chambers and made a loud tinkling sound. Apart from a narrow patch of hair, stretching from forehead to the back of the head, their heads were shaved clean.

Most of the men had around their necks what the Jieng call *biing*, a thick mat of beads, usually of one type and of fewer colours like *majok*, a large bead of black and white. This gear was donned mostly by young men who thought it matched their top-of-the-head hairdo, a conical piece of artwork which, when bleached red or blond, stood out distinctly on their black heads. It was known as "the Nuer hairdo" and the youth loved it.

At the other end, the older generation hated the Nuer hairdo and loved the "old-style" that looked like a giant red or blond mushroom. With the old style, the trick was to let the hair grow under a tied piece of black cloth, bought specifically for the purpose. Under the cloth, the air was irrigated daily with cow's urine until it bleached red or blond. When the cloth was removed, a dome of tightly knotted red or blond hairdo was the result. It also gave this type of hairdo a peculiar smell which the youth derided as "the rotten leg of a goat".

Songs were composed against each hairstyle by those that did not have it. One brief dance song composed by a youth, told the domed hairstyle man to:

Implying that the Nuer hairdo youth was too poor to purchase cloth for the old hairstyle, a mushroom hairstyle man replied:

More and more people joined the path as I approached Rumbel, the village just south of Gaikou. Two young men caught up with me. They were singing a duet, usually composed of very short songs call "roots" (*mei*). One of them sang this well-known song[30] as they passed me:

His duet-mate started another song, as they jogged away from me. The sound of the drum I heard way back at Nyarkac was now clearly coming from our village, undoubtedly, the peculiar sound of *Mangongdit*, father's drum. It was then I realised what was happening.

---

30   Francis Mading Deng has a slightly longer and different version of this song in his book: *"The Dinka of the Sudan,"* pp. 161-162. He adds these relevant footnotes: "There are 100 piasters in a Sudanese pound (approximately $3). There are 10 miliems (malim above) in a piaster. Both the buying and cooking of food are traditionally done only by women." Tharip is half a piaster. Sudan now uses Dinar instead of the pound.

It was now nearly a year since my father died. The Buothanyith Section of Aguok sub-tribe was out in force to remember the departed Spearmaster in an elaborate celebration in dance, song, prayer and offerings to divinities and Divinity/God. The feast began over a week back when I was on my way to Christmas celebrations. It had two more weeks to go.

The fields around our homesteads and those of the neighbouring villages were dotted all over with wooden pegs driven into the ground. The cattle were still out grazing in the forests and meadows.

When the cattle returned just before sunset, the calves, which were separated from their mothers during the day, were already tethered to their individual pegs in the field. The mooing of cows wanting to see their calves as well as the response from their calves; the lowing of bulls protecting their territory and the lowing of oxen and others - just for the hell of it - permeated the air. The dust raked up by their feet and the smoke from numerous dung-fires were mixed and hanged in the air like warm, heavy, fog.

There were cattle everywhere, among them boys and young men sorting them out. To a non-Jieng, it would seem such a mess that it could never be sorted out. But all the thousands of cattle were tethered to their individual pegs before daylight was completely gone. All that din decreased and almost disappeared as the cattle settled down to ruminate and rest.

Throughout the night though, a bull or oxen would pipe up here and there with a melodious low. Its proud owner might loudly respond with praises for his bull or ox or family or clan. No one would complain at being bothered or kept awake by a noisy bull or oxen or by its bragging owner. To a Jieng, all that would be a sign of wellbeing.

Each day began with various activities, some running concurrently. For example: Two or three clans might independently decide to offer a bull[31] to a divinity of their choice or to God (*Nhialic*) on the same day. Each one would independently go through procedures like these:

At sunrise the bull would be led by people of all ages through the village, singing war songs and hymns. Men with shields and spears would play war games as they run forward and backward and around the crowd and men tugging at securing ropes tied around the neck and the base of the horns of the bull, now perfectly wild with rage for being pulled along unwillingly. The procession would usually begin with a walk and short repetitive war songs and hymns:

These hymns would be repeated while walking until the leader called out *Macardit*, the black divinity, in metaphorical terms such as 'ant' (*angic*) and the chorus would reply with affirmative "Yes!" The crowd would start running with the bull until the leader returned to the original hymn. The same activity would be repeated at sunset. The bull would then be sacrificed in the evening or early the following morning, depending on the divinity to which the bull was being offered and for what purpose.

Early mornings and evening activities would also include young men singing their songs of praise or lament about their individual families or clans. Each man would lead by a rope his personality ox as he sang. A trained and experienced ox would follow its master voluntarily as he went around various cattle camps and homesteads, with the owner showing it off and praising it. An ox would fall into a rhythmic and dignified walk in front or behind its swaggering master. Francis M. Deng[32] described this activity very clearly in these terms, followed by a short exemplary song:

---

31   Apart from reproduction purposes, bulls are usually chosen from a breed that had been long in the family. Such bulls are usually dedicated to divinities and are therefore sacrificed when the occasion demands. Oxen are not suitable for such offerings.

32   Dr. Francis Mading Deng, The Dinka of the Sudan, (19...), pp. 17

When singing over his "personality ox," a man strolls with grace and revealed inner pride, his body covered and loaded with objects of beautification, a bundle of decorated and polished spears in his left hand, his left arm hanging from the angle formed by the large ivory bangle on his upper arm, his right hand holding a spear in a pointed throwing position, his head poised high and above, and his ox ahead of him waving the bushy tassels, ringing the bell, and echoing with bellows in accompaniment. His relatives delight in his performance, for his attractiveness is gratification and his name is their fame:

Certain songs, known as *keep,* are extremely long, intricate and revealing. They are usually composed for young men who have recently come of age. The notes are extremely varied and only people with excellent quality of voice would last for long. On occasions such as the memorial festival for Spearmaster, a capable young man would sing *keep* all night at the top of his voice. He would retell in the songs the origins of his clan and of his parents, praising and boasting of one descendant in one verse and castigating another in the next. If he had courage, he would position himself close to a hut or cattle camp in which a girl or family he wanted to woo was sleeping. Should his voice betray him, he would soon hear sniggering voices of laughter from his hidden audience.

Morning milking of cows took place about mid-morning and the cattle were released soon after and driven to grazing areas in the forests by young men and older boys. Younger boys then released older calves and watched them grazing near the village. The very young calves were tethered to pegs under shade trees and fresh grass was provided for those calves old enough to try it. Young men lolled beside the calves under shade trees or inside the byres. Broken ropes were repaired, and new ropes were made that time of the day. Uprooted or broken pegs were also repaired and replaced.

Festivities, such as the Spearmaster's, were always extremely busy times for women, as they had to prepare large amounts of food and quantities of beer daily for the feast. Convoys of women bringing food and beer from near and distant villages came and went all day and in the evening. These women carried back home their share of the meat of sacrificial animals slaughtered that day for the feast.

One very important daily activity of the festival was the late afternoon-early evening dance. Boys and young girls would take the opportunity of less busy periods for them to stage their own dance on the dance floor, located under three large fig trees that formed a large circle, thus shading it for much of the day. Some older girls of the nearby villages would also turn up to dance with the boys, instruct the younger girls and converse with young men who would have turned up to assist, instruct and encourage the boys.

The more serious and formal dance, however, began late in the afternoon, when young men and girls (unmarried young women) would turn up in very large numbers from near and distant villages. The festival, being essentially a Buothanyith's affair, meant that an overwhelming majority of young men and women from the section would participate in the dance. But many young people from other sections of Aguok sub-tribe, such as Agurpiny and Wuny, also turned up and participated.

On the second day of my return from Jesus' festival, I was feeling refreshed and ready for Spearmaster's. As schoolboy (*Manh Abun*), my societal role had become somewhat ambiguous: I could participate in boys' activities if I wanted to. I could also do things Dinka boys of my age would not normally do, such as helping women to prepare food, fetch water from pools and wells for cooking and so on without feeling the shame boys usually felt when doing a "woman's work."

The only initiation I had gone through thus far was the circumcision, an aesthetic affair with little, if any, social status attached to it. The removal of the six lower teeth, a must for all Jieng children, was yet to come; but, although it would mark a stage in my development, it would carry no special social status. The only initiation that would make a big difference in my social status, "the marking of the head" (*gar nhom*), was still many years in my future; and if I continued in school, it seemed likely that I would never go through such a ritual. Yet, even at that very early stage of my school days, I found myself participating in many adults' conversations. I was considered somewhat mature. As a *manh Abun*, I was both within as well as without the social order of things in the village. A misfit, some would say. When on holiday, I was, overall, left alone to decide when it was not good to be idle and thereby helped out any member of the family that might require my assistance. Since my sister, Akuch, had recently eloped, I found it necessary to help Mother as best as I could.

Although all the fields of our homestead were fully occupied, mostly by cattle herds from other clans with strange young men and boys, the cattle herders confined their movements to the fields, the shade trees in and at the vicinity of the fields. The only building the strangers entered was the byre. The herders lived on milk; but it was sometimes supplemented with other foods brought in by the women of their clans.

On the final day of the festival, however, the entire Pagong Clan of the area, spearheaded by the family of Akol Atem, was expected to do the catering for thousands of people in an open party. This needed a lot of preparation involving a lot of work, particularly for the women of the clan. Although my aunt, Atong Marach, had moved to our house to help Mother out, the two women were working flat out, and they were grateful for any assistance I could give as a self-appointed "substitute daughter."

By late afternoon Mother thought that I had done enough for the day and that I should "disappear." So, I went to the dancing ground where the dance activities of the day were about to begin. In the centre of the dancing ground was *Mangongdit* the drum, with its little complementary drum played with two pieces of sticks. Together, they sounded so melodiously loud and very inviting.

The dancing activities would begin, as usual in such festivities, with pairs of young men showing off their physique, agility and skills in attack and self-defence in an acrobatic duel called *ngaan* or *with*. Each man would don a well-groomed fur of cheetah skin, firmly tied over the buttocks and secured in front.

I watched a pair of experienced young men at *ngaan:* Each wore an ostrich feather, stuck in a metal coil whose needle-like end in turn was stuck securely in a firmly groomed clothed-hairdo. With intricate movements of feet, one of the men raked up dust from the ground with his toes as he turned his back on his opponent and, as straight as a poker, hurled himself high into the air. He then flipped himself over in mid-air to face his opponent and simultaneously fended off an attempt by his opponent to snatch the feather from his head. On landing, he moved quickly and tried in vain to snatch his opponent's cheetah's skin from his waist. His opponent, having successfully defended himself, moved in swiftly and tried to trip him with his left foot. He failed.

Slapping the opponent on top or back of the head, tripping him or snatching the feather off his head or striping him of the cheetah skin were the main aims of the attacker. Defending oneself successfully from such attacks was the main aim of the defender. Success in swiftly undoing or snatching the cheetah's fur from the waist of one's opponent would be the ultimate success for the attacker and humiliation for the opponent; but all would be taken in the spirit of *ngaan*, a game after all.

That year, I had heard a lot about "Songs of Kon Lual", first revealed to the general public in July at the annual Spring Dance (*Lor Ker*) at Dhok. Already, I could sing the entire intricate composition. But I had not seen Kon Lual himself presenting the songs. In that very formal dance, the most popular songs of the year for the Aguok sub-tribe, would surely be presented by the man himself.

There were at the dancing ground large groups of girls chatting and watching the men at *ngaan*. But there could be seen large groups of young men and girls at the staging grounds, some distance from the dancing floor. They would soon invade the dancing ground in formations of clan groupings. Each clan would be led to the dancing ground by their best dancer in a line made up of members of each clan and their guests. The last in each line would be the "eligible son of the clan", distinguished by large ivory bangles on both his upper arms. He might, in addition, wear four smaller ivory bangles, one on each elbow and wrist. Most distinguishing of all would be the conical crown, completely covered with neat black ostrich feathers. He would be holding in his left hand a collection of polished spears and in his right hand, either a large spear or a thoroughly polished stick, with the handle encased in fine leather netting. Of course, he would be wearing a fur skin of leopard, from waist to mid-legs.

The invasion of the dancing ground would take place in a leisurely run, with the leader setting pace. While each man would utter his own personal words of praise or boasting phrases, the man bringing the rear would maintain a dignified silence as he carried the burden of being the torchbearer and pride of his clan. Apart from his mother, any wife of the clan, adorned for the occasion, would install herself in front of him to sing the praises of the man himself, the family and the clan on his behalf.

The procession would run around the dancing ground twice or thrice before those who did not wish to dance dropped out, leaving only those who wanted to dance in the line. The procession would then settle down to a more rhythmic movement of the foot and body. A man, known for the clarity and attractiveness of his voice and the ability to rouse and enthuse, would move swiftly up and down the line, loudly calling a tone to which those in the line would respond enthusiastically in a chorus. Like a needle, the leader would weave his group in and out of the centre of the dancing floor to give them maximum exposure to different girl groups, usually standing at the periphery of the dance ground.

Dozens of such men's groups would simultaneously go through the same activity on the dance floor; but each would only be tuned to the songs and movements of its own group. A group's line might be moving clockwise around the dance floor in one moment and moving in the opposite direction next.

The seemingly chaotic movements, the sometimes-clashing rhythms of voices and feet from different groups, movements and voices that were not always in concert with the unceasing drumming at that stage, might all seem confusing and pointless to the uninitiated. But, if one pulled back a little and observed the spectacular from a reasonable distance, one might conclude, as *Timatiep*[33] reportedly concluded at his first experience of *awanwan* part of the dance: "It is the best organised mess I have ever seen!" Still, what was the point?

Among the Rek Jieng, it is the girls who decide in a formal dance who to dance with for the day. As a group's line passed by the girls, a girl would place on the shoulder of a man she would like to dance with a piece of soft and well-decorated leather skirt. As girls often dance in pairs or threes or even in fours with one man, there was always a shortage of these skirts, the tickets to the dance floor. Those who failed to get a skirt would not be able to dance that day and would simply be described as "eaten by the crocodile" (*aci nyang cam*). Unless one was drunk or mad, the honourable way out would be to retire gracefully for that dance, no matter how badly one wanted to dance. The main objective of *awanwan*, then, was to attract the girls to pick as many dancers as possible from amongst one's group. As competition for the limited skirts is often fierce, covert jostling is inevitable during *awanwan*.

As a girl was not expected to dance with men relatives or her

---

33   Timatiep was the ox's name for an Englishman, a former Assistant District Commissioner (ADC) of Gogrial.

men-friends[34], she would have to pick either a stranger or a relative or friend of her men-friend. Nominating a man-friend for a dance would be the signal from the girl to end the relationship.

Sooner or later, however, all the skirts would be handed out and the whole commotion would die down suddenly. While those with skirts prepared for the dance, those "eaten by the crocodile" would retire to the sideline to lick their wounded egos or console themselves by chatting up girls.

The staging of "Songs of Drum" began after *Awanwan*. The Agurpiny, with a notable presence in a Buothanyith's territory, were accorded the normal courtesy of singing one of their "Songs of Drum" first, a rounded composition of songs telling a story with a beginning, a middle and an end. A voice, from a small group of men from Agurpiny, then still sitting on the floor at the periphery of the dance floor, began a song softly and firmly. His voice was answered by a steadily rising chorus of united voices from the group around him. Men and women from Agurpiny began to make their way over to the singing group. The singing group got up and began to move in rhythm with the songs and the tone of the drum, suddenly adjusted to accompany this introductory part of the song. New arrivals inserted themselves in and joined in the singing. The moving singers soon turned into a tightly packed wall of bodies moving clockwise around the dance floor and singing at the top of their voices. Others made way for them as they wormed their way into the centre of the dancing floor, completely encircling the drum. They then settled down to tell the tale, usually of woe, by songs.

One set of "Songs of Drum" has recognisable beginning, middle and an end, just like a story. It usually takes 50 - 60 minutes to

---

34   A girl can have as many men-friends as she likes; so, would a man many girlfriends. Married women are not girls, just women. Boys initiated to manhood by the marking of the head are not boys, no matter how young they look.

complete one set and the last song in the set would send a signal to the next group to get ready with their songs. Kon Lual, of the Buothanyith Section, was next.

To compose Kon Lual's "Songs of Drum" Akuith, the great composer, must have been told these facts by Kon Lual himself:

So, the great composer set himself the task of untangling the woes in the songs that won Kon Lual fame throughout the land. Translating such songs, rich in metaphor, into a totally alien language and culture, conveys very little of the richness, the depth and spirit and soul of such songs. There is no room here for a full translation of the songs but here are a few introductory ones:

Kon: It is not that we have not cursed ourselves.

Those introductory songs took the huge, moving crowd, of singers around the dance floor three times as they inched their way to the centre and close to the drum. There followed a brief pause as the singers came to a stop around the drum. Then they knelt. Kon Lual's feather crown could be seen towering above the crowd. He cleared his voice and began the main song.

The Songs of Kon Lual were sung each day for the 15 days of the feast. These songs were for me the crowning of each day. It seemed to me that the more I listened and saw them presented live by Kon Lual himself, the more my appreciation of the complexity and beauty of the songs grew. I had no doubt then, and still do today, that the Songs of Kon Lual were the best of the year and among the best. Some day I will write them down on paper in Dinka and English for those who can read to enjoy.

The final day of the celebrations was remarkable for the quantities of alcohol and food consumed at the party. Giant empty pots, each requiring at least four strong men to lift and carry, were installed under shade trees and in the byres and then filled up with beer prepared for days and brewed overnight. Dozens of bulls, oxen, he-goats and rams were slaughtered in the name of various clan and free divinities. Meat and a variety of sorghum and millet-based dishes were available for all from early morning to late evening.

Each head of each homestead paid special attention to the needs of the youths whose cattle camps were allocated in their fields. Although the youth would not partake of the beer, they were well provided with food and meat by the mother of the homestead. This was expected of her as a matter of both generosity and duty. After all, the large quantities of dung and urine deposited in the fields by the visiting cattle would provide manure for healthy harvests for years to come.

Spontaneous singing and dancing, mostly by men with alcohol in their blood, erupted from time to time in the vicinity of the big pots and reached a crescendo later. Such dances, without accompaniment of drums or any other musical instruments, took place first in the compounds of the homesteads, under the trees and eventually extended into the fields. Combined with the sound of the cattle returning home from the grazing grounds, the din, the dust and the smoke of burning fires, produced sounds, visions and smells out of this world. Before sunset, scores of satisfied and drunk men and women were singing nonsensical songs as they staggered in all directions, presumably back to their homes.

The following morning, all the visitors cleared out of Gaikou. It was the end of public memorial for a Spearmaster, my father, and the beginning of a rather uninteresting three months holiday. I was looking forward to returning to school at the beginning of April.

Fear of Soldiers

The school year began well with a football match between Gakrial and Kuachjok. Arel Akol, the teacher, and Yono Gogor (Yohanes

Gregory) son of the richest trader in Gakrial, led the Gakrial team against Kuachjok, captained by a Fr. Tuniolli. It was a home game for us and the two leading Gakrialers played brilliantly with the crowd solidly behind them. Unfortunately, Kuajok proved too strong and Gakrial lost the game by three to nil.

Tim Atiep (or was it *Wajbek*?), then the Assistant District Commissioner of Gakrial, was supposed to lead the Gakrial Team - and it would have been the chance for me to see him. But the Englishman was never in town. My information was that he had gone to Wau, then on to Khartoum and then home to wherever he came from. There would be no more Englishmen coming to Gakrial. They were all going back home by the end of the year. "Sudan is to be ruled by Sudanese," I was told, and it sounded good.

But I had a very vague idea of what was meant by independence. I had a very vague idea of what was meant by "Sudan." In fact, whatever ideas I had about most things associated with Sudan were very vague indeed.

Still, we enthusiastically went about singing patriotic songs and building the new church,

at the same time. It all seemed a part of nation building. But serious doubts began to surface by August 1955.

It seemed that there had been an outbreak of fighting between Southern and Northern troops at a place called Torit. Through rumour and word of mouth, we came to understand that the Southern troops refused to be transferred to the North. A battle ensued. Arabs in many Southern towns were slaughtered in Equatoria Province, but a Jieng police officer called "Akot John" averted any fighting in our province, Bahr el Ghazal. The Arabs then came down from the North, after the English had negotiated peace and surrender of arms by Southern troops, and "slaughtered thousands of unarmed Southerners." We were sent home for an indefinite leave.

The independence of the Sudan after a 56-year rule by joint British and Egyptian administration in January 1956, may have been noted with joy or fear in different towns and cities of the Sudan. In our village, as I believe was the case in most villages of the South, the Independence Day passed unnoticed. Yet, there was unquiet in the air, fuelled by continued rumours of killings of Southerners by Northerners, following the Torit mutiny. There were reports of hundreds of thousands of Arab soldiers and policemen taking over in Southern towns.

These rumours increased as we returned to school in April 1956. A large military contingent from the North was reportedly conducting military exercises in Wau, the capital of the Southern province of Bahr al Ghazal. Southern chiefs and the public were reportedly invited to attend. Tanks and heavy field and machine guns were rolled out and used "against live cattle" in an open field. The bullets cut the animals into pieces and "many Jieng chiefs walked away in disgust"; but that was taken as "fear" by the soldiers.

As we sat at dinner at about 7pm that spring, there was a sudden eruption of gunfire and heavy explosions. The whole sky between Gakrial town and Village School Ayiel, was turned into day by bright flares. There was panic.

I paused long enough to see a branch of a nearby tree come down in a shower of sparkling fire; then vaulted for the bush. The gunfire seemed so close. I ran and ran. By the time I stopped, I was three miles deep in the forest west of the school. My upper lip was bleeding from a thorn scratch from a bush I failed to notice in my panic. It was dark and I was alone. My fear of lions was forgotten, as I could still hear firing and explosions coming from the direction of Gakrial. I continued my way until I emerged in a village.

I entered the first homestead and found that the owners had just gone to bed. I called. A woman came out of her hut, and I explained what I thought was going on in town. The village was far from Gakrial, but she said they had heard explosions before going to bed. I spent the night there.

In the morning, I walked back to school to find that not a single child slept in the compound. Even Uncle Abiem had disappeared with his family. Everyone was returning from wherever they had spent the night, eager to find out what exactly happened the previous evening. We were told that it was the Sudanese army that came from Wau that evening and had decided to "entertain Gakrial to a firework display!" Our teachers, we were told, should have warned us that the army was in town.

I could not believe it was totally harmless. So, I went to inspect the tree branch I saw coming down in a shower of fire. It was not there! It was a mystery because I still could see that large branch coming down in my mind's eye!

Anyway, the stories of past wars with the Arab tribes, were retold in the background of the new reality and the growing fear of the intentions of the Northern army in the South.

While top administrative posts in the South were being occupied by Northerners, Southern politicians in the north were being "treated badly by the Arabs" and their demands for a "federal status for the South" were being frustrated. Terms like "federal status" meant very little to the likes of me at the time. I returned home to the village for a lovely holiday.

Our homestead was now at Wuncuei near River Jur and I went there for the winter holidays, January to end of March, of 1957. I was really enjoying my holiday, fishing and swimming in the river for much of the day, when I heard that my mother's half-brother, Uncle Agaany Baak, a two-star sergeant in the Sudanese army, was home on holiday. I invited myself on to his tour of villages and the homes of relatives. He invited me to Wau with him at the end of his short holiday and I readily agreed.

I was very excited about the whole 60 miles journey and the chance to see Wau, "the big city" that I have heard so much about. It has always sounded so far away and out of reach. If I had known

Uncle Agaany was stationed there much earlier, I might have wanted to visit; but I didn't know where he was leave alone what he was doing.

We left Gakrial town on top of a heavily loaded lorry at about 3pm and it was about 7pm when we reached the outskirts of Grinty, an expansive military barrack just north of Wau. The lorry slowed down. Suddenly, two soldiers jumped out of the bush from each side of the road with guns pointing at the driver and demanding identification. My uncle, sitting beside me, shouted: "Angara!" The two soldiers eased up as one shouted back: "Arakangelo Baak!" They shouted coated greetings at each other in Arabic; then one of the soldiers motioned the drive to move on.

We were deposited outside the barracks and the lorry continued to Wau. We walked the rest of the way to the centre of the barracks where my uncle had his house, a large one-room building, surrounded by a high grass fence. His young wife, a local girl he had not yet brought home, welcomed us. She had recently had a baby girl.

A mosquito net was pitched over a bed under a tree in the compound for me to spend the night, indeed the rest of my nights in Wau. The weather was fine in the compound. Some nights, it was so hot that the whole family joined me under the tree.

The first morning in the army barracks was a rude awakening for me: A trumpet blasted at exactly 5am. Uncle Agaany, already dressed in a khaki uniform and on his head a brown army hat with feathers on the side, rushed out of the compound. I was up like a shot and rushed, naked, after him. He glanced back and saw me at the gate. "Stay inside!" he ordered. "I will be back for breakfast!" he shouted and disappeared into darkness. I stood inside the open entrance to the compound and peeped at booted shadows rushing towards the trumpeter. The sound of the trumpet was soon replaced by loud orders, followed by thundering of boots on stony gravel. I ran back to the bedside, got dressed and returned to the gate.

It was now daybreak, and I could see clearly as a tight group of soldiers came skipping uniformly by. Someone in the lead was shouting out a song in Arabic and they answered thunderously. They were followed by dozens of groups doing the same thing. My uncle was leading one of the groups.

He later told me at breakfast: "This is the army drilling. It happens every day except Friday. So, get used to it." I got used to it.

I also found my niche, taking over the ironing of my uncle's army uniforms from his wife, an additional job she was very pleased to hand over to me, together with the polishing of his military boots. He had two of everything: two khaki uniforms and two pairs of boots. One pair was available for washing and ironing almost daily and there was always a pair of boots to polish.

Ironing military uniforms involved judicious application of starch and use of a very hot iron, fuelled by wood charcoal. Too strong or too weak solutions could ruin the uniform and the chance for promotion. But, after a few faltering starts, I became good at it. After ironing with the starch, the shorts looked shiny and so stiff that you could stand them on their ends on a table. Other soldiers soon noticed.

Apart from my uncle, the soldier Uncle Agaany shouted to on arrival, Angara, was the first to notice my skills. He was an Arab youth in uncle's company, a pleasant and friendly fellow. I ironed his uniforms, and he paid me well. He brought in more and more customers; soon I had more than I could handle in a day. By the end of the month, I had more than 5 Sudanese pounds, a lot of money. Back home, I could buy myself two rams with it.

I went to Wau town at least once a week. There was so much to see: The zoo, the market and so many big shops full of goods I had never seen in Gakrial. Gorgor (Gregory), the owner of the biggest shop in Gakrial had a much bigger shop in Wau and he could still be the richest man even in Wau. There were so many lorries loading and unloading goods in front of his shop.

There was, however, one little saloon car, the first one I had ever seen. It was sleek and of lilac green in colour; so polished you could see your face in it. I was told it belonged to the Governor of Bahr el Ghazal Province, an Arab who replaced a Briton at independence. I was also told that there were only two such saloons in town. The second one belonged to the Deputy Governor. I was also told not to get too close to any of these two cars because armed policemen were always guarding them.

The buildings, especially the government offices along the river, were very big and smart. The house of the Governor was said to be the biggest and most beautiful in Wau. But it was hidden behind trees and impossible to approach because the gates to his house were guarded day and night by armed policemen who looked so fierce that one would sooner take a step backward than forward to have a peep.

Wau Cathedral was, however, in a class of its own. Denied a vantage point, such as the hill on which the Deputy Governor's house was built, the cathedral nevertheless towered over everything else in Wau. One could see it's dome from as far as Grinty, two to three miles away.

The biggest spectacle in town was, however, the number of the Agaar and Malual Jieng men engaged in the distribution of water to the vast ethnic suburbs (*Arab: hila*) of Wau, i.e., Hila Jenge (Dinka), Hila Balanda, Hilla Kresh, Hila Ndogo...

The Agar and the Malual invaded a few piped water points near the market with their three-gallon rectangular tins that first entered the market as containers for edible oils. Once emptied, a thick piece of wood was wedged between two opposite sides of the tin and hammered in firmly with nails. A piece of strong rope was then tied to the piece of wood; then tied to one end of a pole. With two of these tins filled with water, a man would balance the tin on his shoulder and returned to the suburbs while announcing at the top of his voice the availability of water and the going price, usually two *piasters* a tin.

Hundreds, if not thousands, were going up and down all day with these tins of water. That, I was told, was how the heavily populated suburbs got water and the Malual and Agar seasonal workers, mostly young men from the village, made their money.

I was informed that selling water in Wau was a trade dominated by young men from the Malual Dinka of Aweil District. Of late, however, the Agaar Jieng of Rumbek District, had also joined the trade in large numbers. The Malual resented it.

One day, when I was in Wau, a battle broke out between the two Jieng tribes. It began in the suburbs, but it was all over the town by late afternoon. I was in the market when three Malual young men chased an Agaar into a corner in the centre of the now deserted market. They attacked him savagely with sticks. He put up a fight, but he was soon overwhelmed. His stick was out of his hand, and he put both arms up to block the stick blows from his attackers. It was no good. Soon he was writhing on the ground as his attackers hit him all over with their sticks.

A contingent of policemen arrived on the scene as the Malual ran off, leaving their victim for the dead. The Police ignored the dying victim and went after the attackers. I went closer to the victim. His head and clothes were drenched in blood. He tried to get up, but he appeared to be in terrible shock, shaking violently all over his body. Then he went limp and stopped breathing. I walked away, not knowing what to do.

There were battles all around me. The police appeared to be totally outnumbered and had very little effect on the battle. Tear gas appeared to have very little effect on the young men who had gone wild and were demanding the blood of their opponents. While the police chased and arrested some, it seemed that there was no way of their stopping the battle before sunset.

Then the military arrived from Grinty and started shooting at those with sticks in their hands. The battles broke up. Some people threw away their clubs and pretended not to be involved in the battle. Others ran across River Juur and continued the battle on the other side. The fighting went on in pockets of the city for almost one week, despite the combatants being shot at by the police and the army. Indeed, the fighting between the two groups did not stop until the chiefs of the two communities intervened and agreed to accept the Malual's claim to a sizeable portion of the water market.

About a dozen men were reportedly killed, mostly from bullet wounds. Dozens were hospitalised and about 120 arrested.

The lessons learnt from that vicious battle between two tribes of the Jieng ethnic group were many. Although the battle appeared chaotic, it was in fact targeted. Not only were members of other races left unmolested, other Jieng tribes, such as the Rek and the Twic, were left untouched. The older members, women and children of the battling youths were also unmolested. In addition, the battle was entirely fought with sticks, not with spears, even though these weapons could have easily been deployed if needed. So, it seemed that although injury and even death were intended, it was by no means an all-out war. The Malual youth had a limited mission that they believed they could achieve with minimum bloodshed. When the Agaar youth gave up much of the water market, the Malual youth left them alone.

This method of battle caused our new administrators from Northern Sudan (Arabs) to wonder aloud: "What would happen if all the Jieng were united behind a cause in an all-out war? How can they fight like this in the middle of the provincial capital? Have they no respect for the government? Are they not afraid of the army?" Such questions could not yet be adequately answered. Later years of open hostility between North and South would supply some answers.

As for me, the two months I spent at Grinty Military barracks reduced my fear of Arab soldiers to a manageable level. My uncle was not only a soldier: he was also an officer who was saluted by all junior soldiers like Angara.

I was, however, never tempted to become one of them. Many southern boys who worked and lived in the barracks wanted to become soldiers. They did their own drills with sticks as they imitated all the activities of their masters.

"Our captain is away, and we don't do as much when he is not here," one of the boys told me.

"Who is your captain?" I asked.

"Athuai Lual. He comes from your area, and he has gone back home for holidays. He will be back in April."

I asked my uncle about Athuai and he told me he was staying in the barracks with a soldier called Bol Mahad from our area. Apparently, they both left the barracks for home the day we arrived. He did not think he was coming back because "Bol Mahad wants him to go back to school. It was time you went back to school as well."

The following day, I put my now many clothes in my new wooden box with a lock. My first box! My first keys! I felt good as I balanced it on my head going to the main road between Wau and Gakrial. I sat by the roadside from early morning to mid-afternoon before a lorry driver stopped and agreed to take five *piasters* for the journey on his lorry to Gakrial.

Elementary School Kuachjok

The lorry broke down twice and it was well after mid-night when we crawled into Kuachjok. The driver parked the lorry under trees near the only shop in the mission, got himself a blanket and went to sleep in the front seats of the lorry. The passengers made themselves as comfortable as possible under the trees in front of the shop and went to sleep. It was during that night an idea came to me: "Why not go to Kuachjok Elementary School?" I asked myself.

While the driver was messing about with the engine of the lorry, I headed for Elementary School Kuachjok. There, I sat on my box under a tree near the classrooms and waited to be noticed. Eventually a boy came over and enquired if I was a new boy at school. I told him I was, but I did not know who to talk to. He took me to a teacher called Charles Mayar Duwaar.

"What is your name?" asked the teacher. I told him my name, where I came from and what I wanted.

"Don't you know that you cannot be admitted to Kuajok Elementary School until you have finished Class 3 in Ayiel?"

I said nothing. He walked around me for a while, looking me over. Then he asked in English; "Tell me your name again in English."

"My name is…"

"What is six multiply by six?"

"Six multiply by six is thirty-six."

"Eight multiply by seven?"

I hesitated…

"Thirty-six divided by six?"

"Thirty-six divided by six is, ee …six!"

He was quiet for a while, walking up and down, thinking. Then he turned to me: "Ok, you seem to be a clever boy. I will see what I can do for you." He went away for hours before he returned to tell me that I was lucky, that a boy in Class 3 was not coming back to school and therefore I could take his place.

"You will have to work very hard to remain in Class 3. If you don't and there is no room in Class 2, you will be returned to Village School Ayiel. I was never returned to Class 2 or to Village School Ayiel.

In Class 2 though, was a new boy called Athuai Lual. Mayar Duwaar had apparently met Athuai in Wau and convinced him and Bol Mahad that he would have to go back to school instead of wasting his time at the barracks. I was as pleased to see him as he was to see me. Amazing the difference, a couple of years apart could make. Those years of fighting and rivalry were forgotten. What was remembered were the good times of climbing trees, playing cattle herding and telling stories. I doubt that Athuai ever told me how and why he left the village and ended up in Wau. Whatever school he went to before Kuachjok, his standard of education was judged to be at level 2, the class in which he began at Kuachjok.

Athuai had so much to tell me about his experiences in Wau in general and in Grinty in particular. Having just come from there, I had quite a bit to tell him myself.

However, we soon drifted apart. Athuai's obsession with the military was not matched on my part. He soon formed himself "battalions" of boys he drilled up and down the school compound at every opportunity. I never joined in, contented to watch on the side line.

Kuachjok Elementary School for boys was a much bigger school than Village School Ayiel. It ran from Class 1 to Class 4, with about 300 students in total. They came mainly from the Rek Jieng. But there was also a good number from the Northern Twic Jieng and from Ngok Kuol Arop.

If we thought the Twic accent was horrible, that of the Ngok boys sounded extremely peculiar. In due course, however, they were clearly speaking Jieng, though we thought it was heavily tinged with Arabic, which should not have been a surprise since they came from furthest north of the Jieng border with Arab tribes.

Their mode of dance was also peculiar, totally different from the vigorous stamping of the ground with both feet by the Rek. They jumped, with their arms high in the air, something similar to the Agaar dance I saw in Wau, except that the Agaar seemed to jump much higher than the Ngok. Their dance mode seemed to concentrate more on rhythm than vigour.

However, they loved singing just like the Rek. One boy, called Maluil Adaj, I found particularly funny and entertaining. One song he was fond of singing was a short one called "Raan akolwar"[35] that ran thus in Jieng:

> *Raan akolwar*
> *Le cin kier*
> *Ku le kok atum*
> *Ku ben biny thiong*
> *Cai raan ci guop ye la ngany?*
> *Kang kadiak kek jot raan ke nhial.*

I discovered many years later that Frances Mading Deng, himself a Ngok, translated this song in his book, *The Dinka of the Sudan*:
> *I saw a gentleman the other day*
> *He had coils on his lower arm*
> *And an ivory bangle on his upper arm*
> *Then he filled his spoon*
> *Gentleman, do you feel no shame?*
> *What three things the man lifted!*

He did not, however, add the chorus that Maluil was so fond of and danced to as he added it to the above song:

> *Jat nhial*
> *Jat nhial*
> *Malith ajot alung!*
> *E raan akolwar…*

Which would translate roughly thus:

---

35   Given the peculiarity of the Ngok Jieng in a Rek's ear, what I heard may not be what was said.

Lift it up
Lift it up
Malith[36] *lifts the coils!*
The man of the other day…

The Headmaster of Kuachjok Elementary School was a man called Lawrence Ndenge, a Ndogo from west of Wau. He was Jiengnised as "Deng *Macar*". "Deng" was simply derived from "Ndenge" and his personality ox, "*Macar*" (Black) from the fact that he was. He was short, on the fat side and almost as black as the Jieng boys who towered above him and whom he taught. His thick black hair was always neatly combed and divided on the left side. Apart from adding a few inches to his height, the hair made his head seemed immensely big and out of proportion with the rest of his body. But he was always smartly dressed and carried himself with immense dignity; and we admired that. He laughed a lot and joked with students.

But, alone with his wife in the heart of Jiengland and running a school entirely of Jieng boys, he had to be assertive at times with discipline and challenged any boy who displayed what he saw as "Jenge arrogance." All the same, he loved his Jieng name because he saw it as a sign of acceptance and respect. Nevertheless, boys who were particularly nasty would dismiss the headmaster derisively to his face as a "mere *dor*", a derogatory term which lumps together the non-Nilotic southern ethnic communities as "submissive".

The Jieng abhorred submissive behaviour. It was seen as cowardice or surrender of one's rights. The Jieng first saw the taking of children to school as "submissiveness" to foreign ways and as surrender of one's way of life. Only a tiny proportion of the Jieng population, the largest single ethnic community in the country, had gone to

---

36   "Malith" is presumably the singer's personality ox, taken as partner in the songs against the greedy gentleman.

school as a result. A much smaller proportion of that number had completed higher education. If school education was to advance in Jiengland, people like Lawrence Ndenge were indispensable. I wonder how many of us children recognised that fact at the time? I certainly did not.

Charles Mayar Duwaar, then a bachelor, was a Jieng dandy who loved to compose songs that portrayed his role as very important. He dressed elegantly, especially on Sundays and festivals when he marched the whole school to Church and back by the route passing by the girls' school:

And here is Charles Mayar Duwaar
He is the one that guides our hearts
And he marches us "by the left..."

So said part of a song he "composed". It was not until some years later I discovered that some of the songs he supposedly composed were parodies of other songs previously composed and sung by other people. Nevertheless, he was very popular with students and involved himself in most extracurricular activities, such as Jieng dances. It was difficult to imagine Kuajok Elementary School without Charles Mayar Duwaar at the time; so, he was indeed important. I personally liked him very much because he was responsible for my admission to Kuachjok, a far superior school in many ways compared to Village School Ayiel. He taught Arithmetic and English to Classes 3 & 2.

Fr. Umberto Passino (*Abundit*) and other priests came to school to give religious instructions that were reduced to the minimum. Those who were at the mission before independence remembered the priests being part of the school. They taught and ran the schools. But the new government of independent Sudan nationalised former Missionary schools in the South as soon as they came to power in

Khartoum and limited the role of foreign missionaries in the schools to religious instructions only.

On the other hand, the teaching of Arabic was upped by "orders of the new Education Officer of Bahr al-Ghazal, an Arab;" so it was empathised. Kuachjok Elementary School for boys received a brand-new Arabic teacher; a Jieng gentleman who was immediately nicknamed "Akol Arab" because he taught Arabic. He was the very opposite of Charles Mayar: even-tempered, unassuming, quiet and polite.

Although he was very good in teaching the subject and was generally liked and respected, it was thought by the Rek boys that he was partial to the Ngok boys, whose knowledge of Arabic was far superior to that of the Rek boys. The Ngok Jieng, being part of Kordofan, a province geographically and mainly ethnically part of Northern Sudan, appeared to us as taking to Arabic like the proverbial duck to water.

However, the Ngok boys struggled with the English Language just like the rest of us, if not more so. Many of them at least gave the impression that they found it much easier to revert to Arabic and found it painful to express themselves clearly in English. One Mariano Awet, for example, while excellent in Maths and Arabic, was known as "Mr and then" because "and then" was, curiously, the expression he unfailingly used when he was stuck for English words - which he often was.

Thought to be typical of the Ngok boys, he was constantly ending up with "the mark", a piece of coin that was used to deter third and fourth-year students from speaking Jieng or Arabic from six in the morning to six in the evening. An old practice, a prefect would hand out six of these coins to students in the evening so that they could pass them on the following day to whoever they caught speaking a language other than English. Ending the day with the coin in one's pocket meant hard labour at the weekend. There were rumours that

Arabic would soon join English in being the only two languages spoken during the mark-passing hours, a suggestion some teachers thought would defeat the purpose of getting us to learn English, since most students, if not all, would muddle along fine with colloquial Arabic. The Ngok boys would love it. In our own perverse way, looking for the Ngok boys to pass on the mark had become a feature of our days. Many of the Ngok boys may have indeed ended up with the mark simply because the Rek boys picked on them, presumably because they were so good at Arabic.

At first, the nationalisation of Mission schools appeared to be popular among students. Tonj Intermediate School and one of the two Bussere (just south of Wau) intermediate schools were said to have always been run by the colonial government and were far superior to Mission schools. Conditions were also said to be "excellent" in those schools. So, we believed that the new Sudanese Government would do better.

Kuachjok Elementary School received brand new wooden desks and chairs from Wau in 1957. Rice and Egyptian beans (*fulmassir*) and plenty of vegetable oils were added to the rations. The Mission's mill was still used to grind the sorghum for the school, but the Mission was reportedly paid for this service by the government.

A brand-new government elementary school had recently been built at Nyarkac, three miles north of Gakrial, and plans to paise-out the Kuachjok Teachers Training College and turn it into an intermediate school for boys were well underway. Overall, we were happy with the new changes the government was introducing.

Nevertheless, the more these new initiatives by Khartoum were introduced, the more rumours of ill intentions by the Northern/Arab-dominated government persisted:

"All senior administrative posts" left behind by the British/Egyptian administrators "have been taken by the North," was one of the many rumours that circulated freely in our school. And if we knew for sure that the actual numbers involved were "800 posts… but only eight would be southerners,"[37] I doubt that our fears of the intended domination of the South by the North would have been any more assuaged than affirmed.

Indeed, a "secret letter" that was reportedly written by then Prime Minister of Sudan, directed northern administrators in the South to "persecute them", "ill-treat them" and "subjugate" the Southerners "according to my orders." Those Northerners who excelled in suppressing the aspirations of the South, the letter allegedly said, would be summoned back to Khartoum to receive their well-deserved reward. Whether there was any truth or not in such allegations did not concern us. We believed it. The Arabs, it appeared to us, had not merely stepped into the English shoes, they were bent on bringing back slavery.

The mutiny by southern troops in Torit was recounted repeatedly in colours that cast the Southern soldiers as brave warriors and revolutionaries. The Northern troops response to the mutiny after the surrender and disarming of Southern troops in response to the departing British Governor General, was seen as diabolical and cowardly. "Thousands of unarmed Southerners were massacred in cold blood in Equatoria by Northern soldiers" was one of the accusations repeated. True or false we believed it. Being a "Southerner" was becoming a solid concept in our minds that were not yet clear on the limits of the Jieng territory.

Our fear of Arab intentions was not lessened by rumours that foreign Christian Missionaries going back home for holidays would not be allowed back to the South by the government. Those who thought they knew what was coming to the Christians in the South retold the story of Ajang, the giant fishermen. The Christians in the South were being deceived by Northern Moslems that they had no

---

37   F. Deng, *War of Visions*, (1995 p.94)

quarrel with them, that the departure of foreign missionaries was the logical continuation of independence. But, once the foreign missionaries had gone, the North would do what it liked with the South, for there would be no foreigners to witnesses what was going on. It all sounded logical and convincing.

Then we were told that if anyone wanted to be baptised and become a Christian, one would have to do it during the long holidays, not during school period. Why make it so difficult? Another ploy by the Moslem North! Time was running out. The sooner one became a Christian the better. I decided to be baptised during the holidays of January to March 1958.

After three weeks of intensive Bible studies, revision of catechism and Alter-service training, we were presented with saints or biblical names from which we could choose our individual saint's names. I preferred Jacob, not for his spiritual superiority over other saints but because it was fashionable at the time to choose a name that began with the first letter of one's name. Jacob, I thought, went very well with Jiel.

We were also expected to find Godfathers from among "confirmed" Christians in the mission. That was a bit difficult during the holidays, but one Valentino Hol, a carpenter, obliged. He had a lot of Godsons that winter.

I went home to Wuncuei in February, curiously disturbed by my new status as a Christians. Apart from baptism itself and the serving of Mass, there was really nothing new in all that I had learned during the short period before baptism that I did not know before. Catechism and the Dinka Bible were introduced right from the beginning of my school days. The Bible had been read repeatedly.

No, what bothered me was the fact that I was "the only one saved" in my family, for the Bible made me to understand that unless one was born again with Holy Water, one would not be able to go to Heaven. Did it mean that my father went to hell? Did it mean that my mother, brothers and sisters who were not Christians would go to hell and not to Heaven? These were weighty thoughts in my mind. As a Christian, it was my duty to inform my mother, brothers and sisters about Jesus and the fate that awaited them if they did not heed the call.

I broached the subject one dark evening when my mother and elder brother, Angui, were at home. I don't know how I did it, but I told them the whole Bible story, from creation to Jesus' ascension to Heaven and the dispersal of the Apostles to take the message to the rest of the world. I even explained what was required of anyone to become and live as a good Christian. I was always a good storyteller in the traditional sense, no doubt about that. I could feel the impact my story had on my audience as prolonged silence followed my presentation.

"So," asked my brother at last, "even those who have never done harm to anybody, those who had always been fair and good to others, will not go to Heaven? They will all go to Hell?"

"Yes," I replied, "that is what the Bible says!"

"And to become a Christian, one must marry only one wife?"

"That's correct."

"Well," he concluded, "I will think about it."

My mother said absolutely nothing.

A few days later, a man called Deng came to our house in the morning. He wore a leopard skin over his shoulder, and he carried in his hand a bright spear fitted into a long handle decorated with rings. He was clearly a Holly man, possessed by Garang divinity. He passed my brother, Angui, and I at the entrance to the byre without saying a word as he went in. My mother was around somewhere in the compound. Angui was mending a cow's rope and I was fixing a fishing hook to a line.

Deng then began to make unearthly hiccups from time to time. I looked in and found that he was sitting comfortably in the middle of the byre next to the central fireplace (*gol*), from where he scooped up with his hands ashes from burned cow dung and smeared it all over his body and over the leopard garb. I left him alone and returned to my seat next to Angui and continued with what I was doing.

But the hiccups increased and got louder and louder. They were interspersed with hymns, sung in a very deep and trembling voice that did not sound human. I was getting more and more irritated by the voice and becoming visibly angry. I kept glancing at the door of the byre and at my brother, who seemed totally at peace with himself.

As a new Christian, I felt that my faith was being challenged by the Devil and I made a standby shouting at the man to "shut up!" My brother looked at me with an anger I had never seen in his eyes before. I thought he was going to strike me with the rope he held in his hand, but he restrained himself. "Deng *Ajok* will come to this house whenever he likes, and he will stay as long as he likes without being insulted! Do you hear!"

I got the message. I had blown it. Not only had I ventured to be rude to an adult and a guest - albeit self-invited - in our house, I was bringing damnation upon our house by accosting a Holly man. With a lump in my throat, I got up and went fishing in the river.

When I returned from fishing in the evening, I found that Angui had travelled to the cattle camp at Toc Lou, a two-day walk from Wuncuei. "Why has he left so suddenly?" I asked my mother.

"Deng *Ajok* informed him that something tragic has happened at the cattle camp," said my mother. "Angui has gone to find out."

Four days later he returned with the bad news that his age-mate and close friend, Atem Akech, son of Akech Doot, was dead, bitten by a cobra at midday on the day Deng *Ajok* was in our byre. Christianity was never mentioned again in our house. Not by me anyway.

Back to school, Arabic as a language was beginning to make sense. Having gone through the initial barrier of learning new and strange-looking alphabets, problems of reading and writing from right to left, there was nothing strange in the stories contained in the first readers for children. They were about relationship among animals and between animals and humans. The stories were very much like our own back home.

Akol Arab, being a Dinka, knew the Dinka love of songs and he used this tool to sell Arabic to us. Soon we were singing in Arabic a variety of songs, including the National Anthem, which we heard and learned for the first time from him.

But there was this song about a cock that tickled our ethnic chauvinism to no end:

> *Before daybreak comes*
> *My Cock crows early*
> *He crows and runs*
> *Saying: "ki-ki-kiki!"*
> *When heard by cocks of all villages*
> *They crow with him*
> *Saying: "ki-ki-kiki!"*
> *And when I tell him:*
> *"Be quiet!*
> *That's enough my Cock!"*
> *He crows and crows*
> *Saying: "Ki-ki-kiki!"*

"How can any man be proud of a mere cock?" said one of us after the class.

"Have Arabs no bulls to be proud of?" asked another.

"Arabs are just *duor*. They have no cattle," said a third "well-informed" fellow from Kuach

"No," said Maluil Adaj, "The Bagara Arabs have a lot of cattle. That is why they are called 'Bagara', people of the cattle."

This was followed by a brief silence as all eyes turned to Maluil to gauge the truth or lie of what he had just said from his face. Maluil seized the moment:

"Yes, the Bagara have a lot of cattle because they come to our country in the dry season. They ride their cattle like donkeys."

"What? You mean they sit on their bulls and ride them like donkeys?"

"Yes," said Maluil, "that's what they do!"

Well, if the character of the Arab was dented by the song about a mere cock, riding the noble cow like a donkey tore it to shreds.

"Did I not say they were just *duor* - even if they keep cattle they don't know how to look after them!"

All the same, Arabic was getting very interesting indeed. Akol Arab made it so. We even did a biblical play about King Solomon's wisdom in Arabic. I played the woman who wanted the child cut into two.

King Solomon was a wise man; but nothing was strange about that. People like Chief Wek Agoth were always demonstrating their seemingly infinite wisdom at court. He was a living legend that would pass into the folklore over many generations. Many stories of wisdom he was never responsible for would be attributed to him just like the Fox.

King Solomon would be Fox in our village folklore. The case of Lion and Hyena for example, when the two beasts visited distant friends and met on their way back home. Lion had a bull given him by his friend. Hyena had a pregnant cow given him by his friend. They spent a night together in a clearing in the forest. In the morning, there was a calf lying next to Lion's bull. Of course, Hyena's cow had given birth to the calf during the night, but Lion claimed the calf was born by his bull.

"You have no idea what God is capable of!" Lion argued.

The case was brought to a court presided over by Elephant. The way Lion looked at those giving their opinions ensured that everyone in the court argued in favour of Lion. But Elephant insisted he would like to hear Fox's opinion on the case before passing judgement. Fox was not at the court. When sent for, he told the messenger he was very busy. Elephant and Lion did not like this, and more messengers were sent with orders to bring him to court by force.

At that instance, Fox arrived, balancing a pot of hot water on his shoulder. Everyone breathed a sigh, but Fox proceeded to walk past the court. Elephant and the Lion shouted at him to stop, but he paused just to say:

"This is a matter of life and death. I must hurry otherwise my father will die. He needs hot water for a bath!"

"That is ridiculous," said Elephant, "I don't see why your father has to take a bath - and with hot water too!"

"Yea," said Lion, "I don't see the point either. The rascal is up to something."

"You see," said Fox, "my father gave birth last night!"

"Don't be such a fool!" shouted Lion amid laughter. "How can your father, a male, give birth to a baby? Ha, ha, ha! ..."

His laughter faded away as he realised all the other animals were looking at him. He realised he had just condemned himself. He got up, took his bull and left Hyena with the calf. Thus, wisdom prevailed over brute force.

But General Ibrahim Aboud did not think so. He deposed an elected government in a military coup in November 1958. At first, we thought the military amusing. Their reported cryptic announcement of the location of the coup, for example, reportedly went like this:

"This is a river (Blue Nile) and this is a river (White Nile). I am in the middle of the river (The Nile). The military has seized the country! Who opposes it will be hanged!"

The next thing we heard was that the "constitution" was suspended. We had a very vague idea of what was meant by "constitution" and we even had less understanding of the significance of its suspension. Parliament was closed. So what? We had no idea what those parliamentarians were up to anyway. If the members were detained, it was because they opposed the military.

But it was a different matter when it was reported that "the discussions for the federal status for the South were no longer on the cards." We had no precise idea how the South would benefit from such a status, but it sounded good. It was then reported that Arab military governors were replacing civilian governors in the South. Rumours circulating in the winter of 1959 that southern members of the armed forces were being transferred to the north and that more and more northern soldiers and the police were taking over, brought to light once more the Torit mutiny and its consequences.

Back home and the cattle camps, it was known that a soldier called "Abouddit" was now ruling the country; but really, who cared? What mattered was that they were left alone to mind their cattle and live in peace. What happened in faraway places like Khartoum - and even Torit - was none of their concern. At home, only Antioko Athuai and I seemed to understand and feared a lot more about the coup. Somehow, we looked forward to going back to school to discuss our experiences with other school colleagues.

Back to school in April, the Catholic Bishop of Bhar al-Ghazal visited Kuachjok Catholic Mission for Easter and for confirmation of Christians baptised the previous year. I was one of them; so was Athuai.

The bishop was received with great pomp. Mayar Duwaar was in his element. He revived old songs praising the bishop and composed new ones. He marched us to the T-junction where the mission's road joined the main Gakrial-Wau road to await the bishop. All the other schools and members of the mission were out there as well.

Amazingly, the bishop was late for only one hour! He alighted from his vehicle at the T-junction, blessed the crowd and walked the one-mile distance to the Church in the blazing sun, acknowledging cheers left and right from the crowd along the route with the Sign of the Cross.

The bishop returned to Wau after two glorious days of prayers and feasting. But he left a sharpshooter priest to kill a male hippo for meat for the schools. This was an old practice by the missionaries that had been stopped by the government since independence. The bishop had apparently managed to obtain a license from Wau to shoot one hippo for the schools.

The whole elementary school for boys trooped off with the priest the following morning to the river. One section of the river was full of hippos but identifying a male from a female just by looking at their noses and ears above water was not as easy as it was supposed to be.

After waiting for an hour, however, a gigantic crocodile surfaced and surveyed the crowd. One did not need a licence for a crocodile because the river was full of them, and they were dangerous. The priest aimed and fired. The crocodile disappeared under water. He boasted he never missed, but the beast was surely not dead.

While waiting, a large hippo raised his thick neck and tore angrily through water. "That's a male!" said the priest and fired. The hippo dived with the other hippos. When they surfaced, it was difficult to tell which was which. We waited.

Meanwhile, someone spotted the crocodile down the stream, moving towards the shallow end. We ran after it. It dived but then, surfaced very quickly. It rolled repeatedly. Eventually it stopped with its white underneath to the sky. The priest said it was dead and that we should pull it out of the water.

Some big boys and men from the village got into the water up to their necks. They tied the crocodile's feet with the thick ropes we brought for the hippo. We pulled at it but when only half of its body was above the water, we could not move it any further. We had not realised how big it was. The villagers said they knew it was very big because it had been killing and eating domestic animals and people for years along that section of the river. No matter: We cut it up where it was and removed chunks of meat. Then we made a barbecue of it under the trees near the river. We gave some meat to the villagers and carried the rest back to the school.

The priest insisted that he had hit the hippo with the single bullet he fired and that he would die during the night, but we didn't believe him. Anyway, we were satisfied with the crocodile's meat and did not worry too much about the hippo.

The following day, however, a villager came to inform us that the hippo was dead; that they had cut it up and had taken their share and should we not go and collect our share?

The visit of the bishop and the shooting of both the crocodile and the hippo were undoubtedly the highlights of the year. It seemed that the more these Italian Missionaries distanced themselves from schools as directed by the government, the more desirable was their presence.

The 1959 school year was a very busy period for me because it was the final year before the next stage called "Intermediate School". The former Teachers Training College at Kuachjok had been successfully paced out and turned into Kuachjok Intermediate School. The first batch was admitted in April 1959 and the second lot was due in April 1960, after passing the December 1959 entry examinations.

The intermediate school entry examinations were very tough precisely because, out of hundreds of students taking the exams in the district, only 40 would gain entry to the only intermediate school in the area. Some students would find places in the Wau Technical School. A few would join the Catholic Seminary at Bussere; but for the vast majority, that would be the end of school education.

While I continued to work hard, Antiok Athuai and I decided to develop a neglected plot behind Class 1 and Class 2 buildings. We went to an abandoned cattle-camp nearby and transported in wheelbarrows cow dung for manure. We planted maize, beans and ladyfingers. We then planted colourful flowers at the edges of the plot. We weeded it almost every week. By July, everything in the plot was flouring like mad. We loved it.

So did the Province Education Officer, PEO, (an Arab), who visited Kuajok. While walking with Deng *Machar* (the headmaster) around the school, he saw the garden. He liked it so much that Antiok and I were called out of lessons to the plot to meet the PEO. Deng *Machar* himself came for us and he proudly presented us to the PEO. He asked why we did it. We told him the beans and the maize would be good to eat and the ladyfingers would be sold for money. He congratulated us by shaking hands and told the headmaster that we were the sort of students he would like to see in schools.

We were bowled over by his recognition of our efforts. We never thought any teacher, including Deng *Machar,* ever noticed it. If they did, we were not aware of it. We could not wipe the smiles off our faces as we returned to our separate classes. Arabs, we thought, were not bad people after all.

During the last holidays, it had become clear to me that Antiok, who was a class behind me, had serious problems with his maths, English, general science - in fact everything. During my last year at the elementary school, we spent a lot of time together because we worked on the plot. I helped him with his work as best as I could. But he and I knew that unless he worked harder the chances of his passing the Intermediate School Examinations, due for him in a year's time, were very slim indeed.

I passed the examinations quite easily at the end of 1959. Antiok, despite his own doubts, passed the examinations in December 1960 and joined me at Kuachjok Intermediate School.

Intermediate School Kuachjok

Kuachjok Intermediate School was located close to the T-junction of the Gakrial-Wau road and the main Mission road leading directly east to the Church. It consisted mainly of four large buildings of stone and brick wall.

Three of these buildings, set back in a U-shape from the main roads, had thatched roofs and served as the dormitories. They were named after the three main southern tributaries to the White Nile: Bhar al-Ghazal, Sobat and Zeraf. I was in Sobat.

The fourth building was T-shaped, had a corrugated iron roof and stood closer to the main Mission's road. It housed the classrooms, the teachers' preparation room and the office of the headmaster.

For my first two years at the intermediate school, the headmaster was a Mr Gasfred Kamis Redi, a red-skinned Balanda from west of Wau. He was short, small-built, lightweight and athletic. He taught geography, English and gymnastics and he loved football. Gasfred always looked starved, though we all knew he was as fit as a fiddle.

He was very good in all the subjects he taught because he demonstrated or illustrated almost everything. It is difficult to forget, for example, the improvised River Nile we dug up under a group of trees, the Egyptian farms we flooded in the wet season and planted with imaginary crops after we turned off the tap and the floods receded from the fields. Or who would forget how the earth, spinning on its axis, made day and night after Gasfred had spun a globe against a lit and stationary candle for the sun, with pins stuck on the globe to represent people at different times of the day? Or how the orbital and tilting movements of the earth made the seasons in a year? He seemed to enjoy teaching the subject too because he swore "damn bell" each time it rang for the end of lesson.

One of us asked Gasfred one day how it is that people on the other side of the earth don't fall off. Gasfred looked for an ant and put it on a globe and we observed it crawling all over it "You see," said Gasfred, "no matter where the ant is it is not going to fall off the globe because it is too small. You are too small to fall off the face of the earth."

He was alone in Kuachjok and we knew very little about his past life. Some people said he was previously married with no children. There was also a suggestion that he had a brother that went mad. This last suggestion could have arisen from the fact that Gasfred himself rarely smiled, let alone laughed. Apart from occasional trips to Wau, the headmaster appeared to have no life outside the school. He walked about and contemplated a lot. Some thought he was going mad.

Gasfred had a dry sense of humour that was often rudely matched by some students. A very tall boy called Machok (*chok* means hunger), for example, was standing one day under a tree with his shirttail lose over his shorts. This was against the rules. Gasfred looked critically at him, then said, "Machok, are you hungry or silly?"

Machok did not respond.

Gasfred paused, then said, "Machok, come here."

Machok moved agonisingly slowly towards the headmaster.

"Machok, how long is it going to take you to get here? One hour? A week? One year?"

"Provided I am coming," was the sullen reply from Machok.

Those were the times when Gasfred fretted aloud about the strong-headed Jieng boys: "Why don't you get your own people to teach you!" Out of our hearing, however, he was known to be immensely proud of the school and boasted about the brightness of "my boys". Even when the first batch of students were still at the beginning of the third year, Gasfred was already boasting that half of them could pass the then widely contested Rumbek Secondary School Entrance Examinations. He was that confident. Unfortunately, he was not able to see even the first batch through third year because he was soon transferred.

Othuon Kiir, a Shilluk, took over from Gasfred as the headmaster. Apart from the fact that he was ethnically Nilotic and therefore shared some ethnic affinities with us, there was nothing remarkable about

Othuon. If anything, it was his name, Othuon, which Madutdit discovered it was the Shilluk name for hyena (Angui in Jieng).

Stephen Madut Bak, or Madutdit, or *Chorti* (Arabic for police) as he was variously called, was a pioneer student of Nyarkac Primary School and one of the first batch at Kuachjok Intermediate School. I do not know why he was nicknamed *Chorti*. As for Madutdit, *dit* usually refers to "senior" or a peculiarity. The only peculiarity about Madut that could have attracted the adjective to his name was his big head, which was proportionately larger than normal; but I don't know.

Stephen's big head was however sharper than most and he was often top of his class. Though he was a year ahead of me, he and I got on very well and I benefited greatly from his knowledge of mathematics, a subject in which he excelled.

He had a quiet sense of humour too. For example: When they were in the Third Year, at the intermediate school, they went on strike for a month because of "too much sand in the food". One of his classmates, a boy called Akok, refused to join them. After the strike, Akok fell sick with diarrhoea, bordering on dysentery. Stephen was far from sympathetic: "You ate more than your fair share of sand, Akok, that's why. You should have gone on strike."

He also called the headmaster, Othuon, "*Murafayin*" (Arabic for hyena) because it sounded more derogatory than the other names for hyena. So, when things were not going well in school, Stephen would contend that "we shouldn't expect anything good from a "*Murafayin*".

Our maths teacher was from Equatoria, probably a Latuka from Torit area. His name was called Francis. We never knew his surname because somebody had nicknamed him "Drake", we didn't know why. So, he was known as Francis Drake. He was very good at teaching the subject and encouraged us to work through the 1001 Examples by Laurence Durrell.

Gai Cikom Ayiei, a Jieng, taught us English, shared with Gasfred and later with Uthuon. He was colourless.

On the other hand, Father Rocco Malardi, an Italian, was very lively, bubbly and talked a lot without being intelligible. He came to our class once a week to give religious instructions in English, which was a laugh because his understanding of the language was very poor. Often, he said things upside down: "In Italy we meat eat once a month", that sort of thing. I will never know how he ever got away with what we thought were well thought out theological questions such as this:

"Father Rocco," one of us would ask, "if God is All Wise, knows the Past, the Present and the Future; if He is all Good and forgiving, why would he create someone knowing that he would live and die as a sinner that will go to hell?"

I suppose he disarmed such loaded questions with his only Arabic expression he knew and used for almost anything from greeting to exclamation: *"Ya salaam alaikum,"* a mixture of *"ya salaam"* (an expression of surprise) and *"salaam aleikum"* (a greeting that means "peace be with you"). Anyway, we liked him a lot.

Fouzi, an Egyptian, taught us Arabic. He was on the fat side. He was also unfit as he sweated and puffed a lot after a short walk from his house to the school. He did not know our Arabic, the colloquial Northern Sudanese sneer at and refer to as *"Arabi Junub"* (Southern Arabic) or *"Arabi Juba"*, (the southern main city). His colloquial was Egyptian, which we did not understand. So, he stuck to the classical, which we understood even less.

His approach to the teaching of Arabic was highly classical, fit for would be Arabic scholars. He demanded very high standards from us but only very few could meet his expectations. Unlike Akol Arab, he did not sing or use the local folklore or biblical characters to promote Arabic. Fouzi, though a pleasant enough chap, was largely a disincentive to the learning of Arabic in our school.

Fouzi had a wife, a formidable Egyptian woman of about the same height, size and weight as her husband. She taught Arabic at the girls' elementary school further down the road. She carried a large umbrella over her head to protect herself from both heat and rain. She never came to our school. She and her husband were two of the only three Arabs there were in Kuachjok.

The third Arab was a young fellow who had recently joined the staff of the boys' elementary school. He was our sort of Arab (Sudanese) because, unlike Fouzi and his wife who looked almost white, he was bronze, brown in colour with curly black hair. He lived next to the Fouzis near the T-junction and walked to work and back.

He was thought to be eccentric because he sang aloud and concentrated in his singing that he often walked unintentionally across the road into the hedge. Head thrown back, fingers snapping sharp rhythmic clicks, his voice could have easily been mistaken for Mohammed Wardi's, then the most popular male singer on the only radio station then available in the country, *Radio Omdurman*. Fouzi, in one of his rare sparks of humour, nicknamed him "Radio Jadid" (new radio); and "Radio Jadid" he was to us. I never came to know his real name. A handsome fellow, he lived alone and hardly talked to anyone. He never came to our school, which was close to his house.

There were, however, rumours that he was homosexual. Those who "knew" the Arabs spread the highly prejudiced gossip that "homosexuality was a very common practice among the Arabs." The Jieng abhor the very idea.

While the Arabic language and the culture that goes with it struggled for recognition and acceptance in the intermediate school, the English language and the culture that goes with it had achieved their own momentum. The library was well stocked with English classic adventure books for boys, like *Tom Brown's School Days, Lorna Doune, The Prisoner of Zenda, Treasure Island, Around the World in Eighty Days, The Journey to the Centre of the Earth, Robinson Crusoe…* and many, many more.

Although we could not yet appreciate a book like *Animal Farm* for what it was intended - as a ridicule of Soviet Communism/ Dictatorship - we nevertheless enjoyed the book for its simplistic yet imaginative animal characters.

The boys closest to me in our class were Jacob Buok and Beda Ayai. We studied together and the three of us were among the top ten in our class. We were also among the small group in our class that was expected by the headmaster to sit for the Rumbek Secondary School Examinations a year in advance. We three enjoyed playing football, but another boy called Archangelo Ayai, an excellent footballer, loved to bully me on the football field.

As he was often one of the captains to pick from the crowd those, they would like to play their sides, he consistently ignored me. When I was picked by his opponent to play against him, he developed the habit of kicking the ball at me with all his might - and he could kick very hard too. One day he kicked the ball right into my chest and sent me sprawling on the ground. Other people came to my aid, and I was carried off the pitch. Archangelo boasted later that he intended to kill me; that if I challenged him again on the field, he would kick the ball into my face.

My friends and I racked our heads about what to do with Archangelo's bullying. Beda was convinced that Archangelo was a coward, that I should challenge him to a fight off the field. Another friend of mind called Placido Lual Manok, who knew Archangelo well, agreed with Beda. Jacob Buok was not too sure and feared that I might end up the worse for it.

It was Antiok Athuai who eventually came up with an idea that worked, just. "You know, he does not know you. I am going to tell him about the fight you had with Anai in the village. If he knows that you will not give up a fight once committed, he will give up bullying you." Antiok told him the story and I let it be known that I was fed up with his bullying. If he didn't stop, I would fight him; the message was relayed to him by Placido, himself a very good footballer. Three days later Archangelo relented and picked me for his side, and we got on well thereafter.

A mentor to both Jacob Buok and I was Fabio Deng Akol, a relative of Buok. The two of them traced their lineage back to the small Jurchol (the Luo) ethnic community near Wau. Traditionally the Jurchol owned no cattle; but they were good at iron craft and made hoes and spears they traded with the Jieng. They were also good hunters and made nets for trapping wild game and birds like the guineafowl. They were good at fishing as well; but they were known mainly for their skill in hunting hippos.

According to Jacob Buok and Fabio Deng, one of their descendants left Jurchol Land because of a feud and went to settle among the Jieng. Through hard work he became rich in cattle among the Jieng. In due time his family became Jieng for all intent and purposes. But in the songs of the young men of the tribe, they still expressed pride in what their descendants were back in the land of the Jurchol and boasted about their established status among the Jieng:

> *Father Deng Akol has made me proud*
> *I have two hornless Majoks.*[38]
> *The two for a gentleman!*
> *So, one is the River of the Panuel*
> *And one is Ayak*
> *Ayak, daughter of Panuel*
> *She was brought from home far away*
> *And when she arrived*
> *She was married by great Buok Akuei*
> *And he lacks no cattle*
> *Cattle is plentiful,*

---

38   A bull or ox of "majok" colour (black & white in a certain pattern) the most valued among the Dinka.

Cattle is plentiful
There is a byre of 'thok' (collective for goats and sheep),
And there is the 'wut' of cattle.

It was the net we set
We trapped with guineafowl nets
Guineafowl nets made at the home the Jurchol!
It was the feud
That made the sons of Akuen Chum leave
And to leave behind their trap-nets
And Nyanker the Hen remained behind!
With Nyanker the Hen we made invocations
Our bodies were blessed
And people became healthy because of Chicken,
Chicken eeh
Nyanker the Hen
Nyanker the Hen
It was slaughtered in the afternoon,
Our trap-nets have remained behind.

And Deng Akoldit Tong sons of Buok Akuei
They hunt the lion they don't see![39]
They fit their harpoons,
To hunt a lion they don't see!
The Dinka watch in awe:
"They are hunting a lion they don't see!"
Father Deng Akol has made me proud I have two Majoks...

Both Buok *Manyiel* and Deng *Magotdit* loved singing those songs and I got to know and grew to love them in due course.

---

39   Hippos under water cannot be seen by the hunters.

The Brewing Conflict

We thought we had our own "Animal Farm", run by General Ibrahim Aboud. His appointment of a single Southerner as "Minister of Animal Resources" was interpreted as confirmation that the North always saw the South as nothing but a source of wealth for itself: First ivory, then slaves. Animals and Southerners, they were all the same! No matter how far-fetched and simplistic this view of North-South relations appears now, many of the decrees issued by the military government of the time sounded very much to us like a return to something like the old days of slave trade; thus, influencing our way of reasoning.

Parliament was dissolved and talks of a new constitution disappeared with the future of the South in a united Sudan. Indeed, it was believed that the coup was not a coup at all but a hand-over by an elected government to the military in order to avoid giving the South the federal status it deserved. True or false, it did not matter. We believed ill intentions from the North, particularly from the military.

Sure, enough many politicians, northerners and southerners alike, were arrested and detained when the coup took place. But while all northern politicians were reportedly released, southern politicians who asked for federal status either remained in jail in Khartoum or were barred from travelling to the South.

Building of new Churches in the South needed licenses that were never issued. More and more foreign missionaries, including our own Fr. Umberto, went on home-leave and never returned. The nationalisation of Christian missionary schools 1957 in the south was welcomed at first, but later actions by the government made it look like persecution of the Christians.

The government's decision in February 1960 that Friday instead of Sunday should be the official resting day in the South was the last nail in the coffin of the then fading North-South unity. It resulted in widespread school strikes throughout the South. Southern leaders of the Church received more than 10 years for daring to question the order. Some student leaders were jailed for 10 years by the military government.

If anyone in the South had any doubts about the Northerner-Arab-dominated military government's intentions, that vanished with the "Mission Societies Act 1962." Although details of the act were not as yet known to us, we understood, quite correctly, that Christian Missionaries were no longer allowed to preach or worship or convert anyone under eighteen years of age without special permission from the government and parents/guardians. Suspicious of the government, we concluded that permits would never be given. The prohibitions were far ranging:

Under Section 10, formation of clubs, the establishment of societies, organisations and social activities, collection of money, famine and flood relief, the holding of land and the publication and the distribution of papers, pamphlets or books were all subjected to ministerial regulations.[40]

While new Islamic schools were being encouraged, old Christians schools in the South, which meant virtually all schools before independence, were being neglected and falling apart. Our own school was one of them. It was overcrowded as accommodation got smaller and smaller year by year. The three dormitories added a new batch of students each year from the opening of the school in April 1959 to April 1962, after which the Fourth-Year students were expected to move on.

By April 1962, however, the Fourth-Year students had seen the student population doubled, then tripled and finally reached four times the original size. Any room between beds got smaller and

---

40 See Francis M. Deng's *Dynamics of Identification: A Basis for National Integration in the Sudan*, (1973, pp. 39-40).

smaller each year until it disappeared altogether. Student's property was stored under the beds. No new accommodation was added or planned in all those years. Despite a weekly general clean up and inspections, general hygiene had become a serious problem, with flue and colds spreading rapidly and regularly.

School desks, chairs, gymnastic equipment - indeed all school property - was getting worn out and broken with no replacements - although our parents had begun paying school fees for intermediate school attendance.

For food we had sorghum, rice, Egyptian beans and lentils. Meat and fish were rare. Apart from vegetable oils, there were no green vegetables or fruits. Although the rations were adequate, the cereals were full of weevils and sand. Diarrhoea and dysentery had become common among students.

There was, therefore, plenty for the South to be angry about. Our elders and the overwhelmingly illiterate rural population back home were not shocked to see that things were not well between North and South. They did not hope for wisdom and fairness from the majority North. They joined forces once with the Mahdists to get rid of then Turco-Egyptian's slave trade, only to be turned upon later by their "allies", the Mahdists, who proved to be among the most destructive slave traders. For the new Sudan, they only hoped to be left alone to run their own lives; and that the deteriorating relationship between North and South would not turn into a shooting war. These hopes were now waning.

As believers of traditional African religions, restrictions of Christian Missionary's activities were of little concern to our parents and leaders back in the village. But persecution and imprisonment of their Christian educated children was something else: it reminded them of the old days of the slave trade that was suppressed by the British not so far back in history. There were many of them still alive who had lived through those very dark days.

As for us school-educated Christian Southerners, we knew that the actions of the government were not just aimed at the foreign missionaries. They were aimed at us Missionary-educated Southerners. We believed that the policy of the government was to persecute, and if possable eliminate, Christian-educated Southerners in the hope of bringing up new generations of Arab-cultured Southern Moslems. If such were the aims, and various policies of the government left no ground for doubt, armed resistance seemed the only alternative left for the South.

By mid 1962, there were, at first, talks of the existence of an organised Southern armed resistance, formed by the remnants of the 1955 Torit mutineers who fled to the neighbouring countries of Uganda and Congo. Then there were talks of an organised political wing called "Sudan African National Union, SANU". Names began to circulate: William Deng, Fr. Saturino and Joseph Oduho suddenly became instant heroes in our school for a book which none of us had yet seen: *The Problem of Southern Sudan*, which they jointly wrote and published in East Africa. I suppose all schools in Southern Sudan were like us primed up for rebellion.

Rumours were also rife that heavily armed Southern guerrillas were roaming the countryside. Indeed, some students at Kuachjok Intermediate School swore - "confidentially" of course - to everyone that they had personally seen and even talked to "freedom fighters". It all seemed credible at the time and it sure was what we wanted to hear.

I remember I expressed mild doubt one day about these rumours and something someone had "confidentially" told my then close friend, Placido Lual Manok. I cannot remember the exact words, but our "confidential conversation" went something like this:

Placido: This is between you and me, right?
Jacob: What is between you and me?
Placido: Agreed, right?
Jacob: Right.

Placido: Right. Radio Jadid is not coming back from Wau. He fears the fighters, and he is not coming back.

Jacob: How do you know he's not coming back?

Placido: We have ways of knowing. Just take it from me that he is not coming back. I told you because I trust you. You remember what I told you about the fighters? They are here; I have seen them myself. They have big guns, machineguns that sit up like squirrels in the bush. They come to collect food sometimes from our house. Soon I will let you meet them, but keep it to yourself, you understand!

I told him I understood.

Rumbek Secondary, the highest academic institution then in the South, went on strike first. Many of the students were rounded up by the police and detained, while others escaped to the safety of remote cattle camps and villages. Others escaped to neighbouring countries in search of education and to swell the rank of "freedom fighters" and refugee camps.

Intermediate schools followed next with Tonj and the two Busseres leading the way in Bhar al Ghazal. They all advanced different grievances for going on strike, never the real reason, which was that they feared being victims of Arab soldiers in the event of their being attacked by Southern guerrillas.

Students from schools already on strike who had homes near our school called on us daily to evacuate the school. One Kostantino Muong of Rumbek Secondary School, then a renowned "super brain", was a constant visitor. A confidential letter from the President of the Sudan, addressed to the military governors in the Southern provinces, he said, was in the possession of some of his colleagues. The full contents of the letter, he empathised, were yet confidential and could not be made known to the public for fear of panic. However, we were to know that the letter instructed the Northern soldiers to "teach the Southerners a lesson they will never forget if they rise against the North."

"You of course know what this means, don't you?" Kostantino put the question to a group of us one evening. We had ideas but none were volunteered.

Kostantino continued: "It means that if attacked by the Southern Freedom Fighters, the Arabs can wipe out the Christians in the South; that means all educated Southerners including students. What could be easier to wipe out than a boarding school!"

We got the message, and it was not long after that Kuachjok Intermediate School went on strike. The headmaster tried his best to convince the Fourth-Year students and the Third-Year students who were tipped to prepare and sit the Rumbek exams in advance, that it was not in our interest to go on strike so close to the examination date. "You don't know what you are getting yourselves into," he pleaded. "Get back to your classes, I tell you!"

But we were no longer in the mood to listen and postpone what we believed was inevitable. We sang something close to war songs as we marched through Kuachjok. Both the boys' and girls' elementary schools joined the strike.

Radio Jadid did not return from Wau; so, we decided to pay a "courtesy visit" to our Egyptian friends, Mr and Mrs Fouzi, "just to let them know they have nothing to worry about," said one of the leaders. But we discovered that the Egyptian couple had gone that morning to Wau, why and how, we did not know. Maybe they thought there could be violence, clearly not our intention.

Anyway, we chanted so loudly that even the headmaster left for Gakrial. He returned in the afternoon with armed policemen led by an Arab officer. As we marched, still singing war songs, towards the headmaster's house to present our petition of excuses for the strike, the officer lined up his forces in our path. A pistol hanged on the side of his right pocket. He stepped forward about five paces while his forces stood at attention behind him. We marched on. When we were about 50 yards from the police line, the officer raised his right hand and ordered us to stop. We marched on. At 30 yards, he turned his back on us and ordered his forces to get ready and aim. He turned to order us to stop; but we already had. He ordered us to turn back and return to school. We turned back and returned to school to collect our belongings. Those who lived nearby went home that evening. Those who lived far from school, like Antiok and I, spent the night at the school and departed for our various homes in the morning. We had no idea what would happen next.

Antiok and I had a great holiday together. First, we went to our house at Wuncuei near the river and did some fishing. There was plenty of tilapia, Nile-perch, tigerfish, catfish and many other varieties. Some parts of the river were so crowded with tilapia that we sometimes threw in a hook without a bait and hooked a fish. We roasted and ate as much as we could stomach and took the rest home. We spent over two weeks there.

We then went about seven miles up north to Nyinakoi to see my sister, Akuch, and her young children. We spent three days there and then moved on to Gok, some eight miles north-west of Nyinakoi, to visit Amiir Angaany, Father's sixth wife. She had moved there from Gaikou after my father's death. We spent two days with her, her son, Malou and his young wife.

We then moved on down south towards Gakrial to Kuruec, Antiok's and mother's home. We spent about ten days there; then moved on down to Gaikou, where the bulk of the Akol family still lived. We spent five days there before we returned to Gakrial, just to get news of what was happening concerning the strikes and any news about the country. We found information posted at the local council administrative headquarters, telling all students on strike to return to their schools immediately. All complaints, said the notice, would be dealt with to our satisfaction by the PEO himself.

The notice had been up for five days. So we proceeded on foot, our only mode of travel, to Kuachjok, arriving there in the evening.

That evening, we found out that three students in my class had already been suspended from school for their role in the strike. I had reason to believe that I would be suspended.

In the morning, we went to see the headmaster to find out where we stood. Antiok was called in first. The headmaster told him to lie on his stomach on the brick floor. He then gave him - I can't recall how many - lashes on his buttocks. I could hear the terrible "swish" sound of leather in the air and the "thud" on the khaki shorts from where I was.

Antiok came out with both his hands stroking his buttocks. His face was twisted with pain.

"Next!" came the voice of the headmaster. I entered. He did not look up at me. Instead, he was looking through a file in front of him. Then he abstracted a piece of paper. He then signed it, put it in an envelope, then looked up for the first time. He then handed the envelope to me unclosed. "That is a letter for your guardian," he said. "You are suspended from school until further notice. You may spend the night here if you like but you must leave the school tomorrow."

Antiok was waiting to know what happened to me, but I guess he already knew because he did not hear the whip.

"What are you going to do now?" Antiok wanted to know.

"Go home, what else?" I replied curtly. We said nothing as we walked back to the dormitories.

Antiok and I really got on very well during the strike period away from school. Although both of us had known for a long time that Antiok's understanding of maths was still very poor, we never had time together to see how I could help him because I was good at the subject and a year ahead of him. During the strike, I walked him through basic geometry and mathematical problems such as finding "the area grazed by a horse tied to a peg at (a) the corner (b) the centre and (c) the side of a fenced square field by a rope of so many feet". We drew the said field on the sand and tied up the said horse at various locations. The result: a quarter, a semicircle and a circle of definite radius (the length of the rope) was grazed in each case. Finding the area was a simple matter of slotting the numbers in appropriate formulae. I even started Antiok on the simple algebra he was due to start in the following school year. For the first time in his life, he said, he was really looking forward to returning to school.

"What are you going to do?" Antiok asked me again later in the evening.

"Well, I am going home for a while and wait out the suspension. I don't know how long the schools will remain open in the South. In any case, we are only two weeks away from the end of the school year and I can't see how they can do the Rumbek Entrance Examinations in such a short time. The likelihood is that the exams will be postponed until next year. I may decide to go to Port Sudan to see my uncle. I can go to school there." This was a serious suggestion.

Uncle Archangelo Agaany was transferred to Khartoum soon after my first and last visit to Wau. We lost touch until he came home for a holiday in 1961. I borrowed a bicycle, asked for a week's absence from school and followed him home. I had three enjoyable days with him, visiting various homes of relatives and making Gakrial town our occasional home base.

Not only did he have a brand-new bicycle, but he was also always dressed in the bright white uniforms of the Sudanese Navy. While in the North, he was one of the few Southerners selected to go to Yugoslavia for training for the Sudanese Navy. He was now based in Port Sudan. When I departed, he presented me with a watch he said he had bought for me in Yugoslavia. I loved it.

"I am coming with you," said Antiok, "Bol Mahad (the one he stayed with in Wau) is also in the North. I am going to find him."

"Don't be silly!" I tried to discourage him. "I did not say I am going to Port Sudan for sure. I may be called back next week. Where will you be then? You will have spoiled your chances because they will not take you back."

"I don't care," he said. "This school will be closed soon anyway because there is going to be war in the South. I am going back home with you in the morning."

We returned to Gakrial in the morning, then proceeded together to our homes. We explained that we had been suspended from school and that we were going to the North and that we would go to school there. We said goodbye to everyone, believing that it could be a year or two at worst before we could return. Little did we know it would be well over a decade before we returned home. Some of the relatives we lovingly embraced and whom we loved so much we would never see again. So were the majority of our schoolmates: We would never see them again. This was the beginning of *The Long Way to Tipperary*, though we did not recognise it yet.

Ayai, Archangelo: He joined the Anya-Nya (Southern Sudan's guerrilla movement of the 60s) and died in action.
Ayai, Beda: He ended up in the Soviet Union as a student. He returned to Sudan in the 70s as an engineer. He became Minister in the Government of Warrap State, capital Kuachjok, following the Comprehensive Peace Agreement (CPA) which led to independence of South Sudan.
Buok, Jacob: He went into exile and eventually ended up in Liberia as a medical doctor. He later migrated to USA.
Deng, Fabio: He joined the Anya-Nya, (Southern Sudan's guerrilla movement of the 60s) and died in action in Lirangu. I learned recently from Dr Raphael Abiem, then a boy on a liberation mission to Congo in mid-1960s, that Fabio was one of the officers who loss their lives in a night attack at Anya-Nya base at Lirangu.
Lual, Placido: He became a policeman.
Madut, Stephen: He joined the Anya-Nya army and reached the rank of Col. Following peace agreement in 1972, he was integrated into the national army at that rank. After the murder of Col. Manuel Abuur, a former officer in the Anya-Nya and close friend of his,

Stephen became mentally disturbed in what was said to be "delayed shellshock". Treatment in Khartoum was not successful, and Stephen became paranoid and believed in "Arabs plan to eliminate former Anya- Nya officers". He was taken to London where he recovered after a long period of treatment. By then the war had broken out anew between North and South and Stephen became the UK representative for the new Southern rebels' "Sudan People Liberation Movement/Army, SPLM/A."

Athuai Antiok: He died in London soon after the Comprehensive Peace Agreement. He is survived by two daughters and a son.

PART THREE: THE REFUGEE

"For a people who had grown up thinking of themselves and their country as second to none, the indignities of refugee life brought lamentation and feeling of isolation... but the boys showed remarkable resilience and little evidence of the impact of the trauma normally expected under similar circumstances."

-Francis Mading Deng
in the forward to this book.

Way to Congo (DRC)

Antiok and I met Valantino Akol Wol in Gakrial by chance. We were reading official notices posted on the wall outside his office when he called us in. From Awon Mou, he was one of the very few high-ranking southerners in the local government in Gakrial. Though we knew of him we had never met or spoken to him before.

He introduced himself and told us he knew who we were. He also knew that I had been suspended from school but did not know why Antiok was not in school. We told him we were planning to go to Port Sudan.

"How are you going to go there?" he asked.

We said we were going to go to Wau, then to Juba, asking for lifts on lorries. Then we would find a way of getting on a steamer from Juba to Khartoum, then by train to Port Sudan.

"You realise Port Sudan is thousands of miles away? Do you realise that this could take you years and that you may never make it to the North?"

We found his doubts discouraging; so, we said nothing.

"Come to my house later in the afternoon," he said, "there is someone I would like you to meet."

We got there just after 2pm. The entrance in the grass fence around his house was opened, so we went in. From the inside the house came voices of men singing the Guot Malual's song (see part two) and laughing very loudly. The door was opened, so we clapped our hands to announce our presence. A man's voice within invited us in. Valantino was there with two other men, all seated on easy chairs and drinking *aregi* as they sang. Valantino indicated with his hands that we should sit down. When the song was over, Valantino introduced us to the two men. One of the men was Joseph Bel Kuol. They went back to singing more of Guot *Ngokdit*'s songs until a woman entered from the kitchen with food and more drinks.

The woman, I recognised, was Anyuat Mou, the daughter of our Chief Muon Aken. The last time I had seen her was under a tree at their house at Adiem, a village between Gakrial and Wuncuei, our new home near the river. My elder brother, Angui and I were returning home from Gakrial when Angui decided to call on Anyuat. We sat under the tree and Angui cleared his throat very loudly to announce that "there is a man standing", a normal Jieng way of announcing one's presence when visiting a girl in her house. Anyuat came with water. Then I was introduced to her. It was obvious that she and my brother knew each other very well because much of their conversation was coded in terms I did not understand. My first impression of her was that she was very attractive and had a very pleasant voice. I volunteered to my brother later that if he wanted to marry her, I would be very supportive.

Seeing her in Valantino's house reminded me of the fact that their marriage was in fact a high profiled affair, with Akol Wol's family paying many cattle to the family of the chief. Anyuat said simply that she knew I was the son of Akol Atem and that we had met before, that she knew our home at Wuncuei and that we were welcome.

The third man left after drinks and the afternoon meal. Valantino then paused and said in a "by-the-way" manner: "The situation is very bad throughout the South at the moment. Many students are being rounded up by the military and are disappearing. Most of the Southern politicians recently released by the government have been quietly rearrested. Some are on the run. Dominic Muorwel is hiding somewhere here in Bhar al Ghazal."

Dominic Muorwel, we all knew, was a member of the National Assembly and a known proponent of federal status for the South. He was arrested and detained in Khartoum by the military soon after the coup. We did not know he had been released, leave alone his presence in the South.

What Valantino accomplished in a few sentences was the attainment of our full confidence in what he was saying. His seeming casualness in passing on to us sensitive information that could lose him his job or get him arrested left no doubt that he was taking us into his full confidence and that he trusted us. To us, he demonstrated a superior knowledge of what was going on throughout the country. We listened attentively as he continued.

"Maybe you are the lucky ones because war is about to break

out between us and the Arabs. Those students who are lucky to get out now may be able to go to school in East Africa. Our politicians, including William Deng Nhial, are there to find schools for boys like you. It is going to be very difficult later in March and April for anyone to get out because the Arabs want to seal all our Southern borders."

"Since I returned from England, I have not spent more than three days in one place," said Joseph. "It was better when I was in Khartoum but here in the South, I am on the blacklist. I can be arrested and detained any time."

"Jacob Jiel, as a strike leader on suspension, is already on the blacklist. And so are you by now, Athuai, for deserting with Jiel," said Valantino.

From our point of view, this new information put matters in a different perspective: Our own liberty, if not yet our lives, were at stake.

"We will leave for Wau in the next two days," said Joseph, "I have a few things to sort out."

The few things Joseph referred to include the girl problem that was quickly disposed of by Chief Wek Agoth. We said goodbye to Valantino. We could never have guessed that we would never see him again.

We got a ride on a lorry to Wau, where we kept a low profile in the house of a teacher. While Antiok and I had very little to do, Joseph was frantically gathering information about the road ahead, the security situation, transportation and the actual exit point out of Sudan to Congo.

Publicly though, we broadcast that we were on our way to Juba on our way to Khartoum. Heading in a southern direction instead of heading directly north to Khartoum was plausible because of the availability of steamer transport from Juba.

As additional protection against arrest and imprisonment, we kept in our little wooden boxes some Arabic books we had been reading at school. We also kept our Arabic exercise books, along with those of other subjects, excluding Christian literature. We believed that if arrested by Arab soldiers or police, having Arabic books would verify our claim that we were heading north. What was more, I had the photograph of my uncle in his Sudanese Navy uniform to prove my destination: Port Sudan.

We left Wau on a lorry heading for Juba via Yambio in January 1963. Our departure from Sudan was Yubu, a trading post in western Equatoria Province, which lies between the town of Tambura and Yambio and at the borders of Sudan, the Central Africa Republic and Congo. If it went well with transport and security on the way, we expected it would take two to three days to get to Yubu and then out to Congo.

As soon as we left Wau heading south, we were out of the Jieng territory. Any Jieng travelling south of Wau, we were warned, was subject to questioning by the police or military to explain where they were going and why. Failure to satisfy those authorities would result in immediate arrest and detention. Our agreement was to say, if asked, that Antiok and I were not in company with Joseph. If questioned, we would only answer questions about ourselves and say little or nothing at all about Joseph's destination. All we should say would be that we knew he was going back to Khartoum.

There were three other Muonyjieng on the lorry. One young man we had seen before in Wau with Joseph. He was a student at Rumbek Secondary School. The other two we did not know yet.

We stopped late at night at Bo River Post, about 55 miles south of Wau, at the border between Bahr al Ghazal and Equatoria. We stayed in the house of a Captain Magot, a retired member of the Sudanese armed forces. We never knew in which section of the armed forces he was a captain: the police or the military. What we learned was that he was very brave and a very good marksman. We were told that he owned a variety of rifles that the Arabs dared not take from him. He had given the government his word that he was for peace and if pushed too far he could go into the bush and started a war all by himself. "He is better left alone" seemed to be the policy adopted by the government; but I doubt such a policy, if it existed, was adhered to for long.

We left early in the morning for Tambura. Joseph climbed down from the lorry and spoke to someone under a mango tree when the lorry stopped at about 11.30am at a market place a few miles north of Tambura. He then beckoned us to come down and told Antiok, Jacob Ayiu (we met on the lorry) and I not to go into Tambura town. He said there was the likelihood that we would be arrested, all of us. He told us to go to a Catholic Mission east of Tambura and wait there for a message from him. If no message came, we should try to find our way to Yubu that night and then out to Congo. He and the other two boys were going to meet a contact in Tambura to get up to date news and fresh directions.

At the Mission, a worker told us to wait under a tree; that he would inform one of the two Italian Sisters that still lived there. He soon returned and told us to follow him into the bush and showed us a thatched shed where he said we should wait for one of the sisters.

A Sister came one hour later with a small tin of peanuts in her hand. She looked incredibly white, as if she had not seen the sun for days. She also looked very tired and sad. She greeted us in Jieng. We expressed surprise because we did not expect to find someone in Zandeland who spoke Jieng. She gave us the nuts, then spoke haltingly in English:

"The situation here is very bad. The only remaining priest of the Mission was taken to Juba two weeks ago for questioning by the soldiers. We don't think he will come back. There are only two Sisters left here me and another. We are very frightened of the future. It is not easy for you either because Jieng people are hunted down here and arrested by the military. Stay where you are for the moment. I will let you know if there is information from your colleagues in town."

She got up, went to the door and stopped, looked at us with those sad eyes, then said with a light smile on her lips: "Dominic Muorwel was here two days ago. I hope he is safe now." She returned to their compound.

We did not know whether to believe that the famous parliamentarian was still hiding around Tambura, arrested or over the border in Congo or Central Africa Republic. It did not lessen our growing fears.

We received a message from Joseph at about five in the evening. We were to go through the bush and waited for them at a road junction a few miles south of Tambura. So we left the Mission at about 6pm for the junction. Not only did we have our own boxes to carry, we also had an extra box each, property of our colleagues in town, "because we may have to run for it," Joseph had said. Now we had about five miles to walk to the junction. The only saving grace was that much of the contents of those boxes were clothes and few books. We carried the heavier boxes on our heads and the lighter ones in our hands.

We found the junction at 7pm. It was very dark as we waited silently by the roadside for about fifty minutes. Our nerves were tuned to the slightest movements as we waited. Any sudden noise from bats or rats set our hair on hedge. Instructions from Joseph were that if by 7.30pm they had not shown up, we should assume that all was not well with them. If they did not show up, it would be because they were either arrested or had run away. We should therefore proceed to Yubu and find our way out to Congo. They would meet us there if not arrested. So, we picked up the boxes again and headed south towards Yubu.

We were so exhausted by 2am that we decided we would lie down under a big tree we could see beside the road just ahead of us. But when we got there, both Antiok and Jacob Ayiu suddenly hurried on along without explanation. I wanted to know why we did not stop under the tree, but they shushed me. After some distance from the tree, they both insisted that they had seen a lion near the tree. They could not believe I did not see it. They were so serious and so frightened I could not doubt what they said they saw. Energy returned miraculously and we slogged on.

Not until 5.30am did we meet anyone on the road. From then on, the number of travellers increased hour by hour. Most travellers were on foot, a few on bicycles. A lorry came hurtling along from the south. We dashed into the bush and stayed there until we could not hear the engine.

As the sun rose to mid-morning and the number of people on the road increased, we began to worry that someone would tell the police or military that there were Jieng boys on the road and we could be arrested. We were also worried that perhaps we had passed the exit route to Congo during the night. We panicked, left the main road and followed a track leading west. Our hope was that the path would lead us out of Sudan into Central African Republic or Congo. From there we would find our way to any border town in those countries.

However, the road led into a thick tropical forest with giant trees we had never seen in our part of the world. The path itself turned out to be an elephant path. Antiok and I had never seen an elephant, either in the wild or in the zoo. The zoo in Wau had no elephants in it. Elephants in our area were by that time found only in the Toc, the swamps where herders went in the dry season. I have no idea if Ayiu had ever seen one. But their unmistakable footprints were clearly on the wet floor of the forest. No other animal would have such giant footprints. Their droppings were suddenly everywhere. We were suddenly worried and feared the worst if we continued that path. We decided to retrace our steps and returned to the main road.

We walked for another five miles on the main road when a man on a bicycle stopped and greeted us in colloquial Arabic. "You are going to Congo? I know because many of our brothers have gone there. They are running away from Arabs. I am Congolese and I just came from there."

We did not know whether to trust him or not, so I said, "We are not going to Congo. We are going to Juba. A lorry left us behind last night. We are looking for Yubu market to buy something to eat then wait there for any lorry going to Juba or Yambio."

"Yubu is about seven miles down the road. Anyway, if you are going to Congo, don't go there. Many Arab soldiers from Yambio or Tambura always go there. They arrest Jenge people coming this way because they say they are going to Congo to join the guerrillas. There is a footpath about three miles on the right side of the road. Turn into that. You will find a stream about a mile down the path. Cross that and you are in the Central African Republic. Go six miles on that path and you will come to a main road. Turn left on that road and you will soon cross into Congo. Stay on that road. By tomorrow afternoon you will arrive in Doruma and you will find many of your brothers there."

We looked at each other, not knowing what to say next. "Thank you very much," I said at last, and we started to walk away.

"You will need Congolese money, like this." He pulled out of his back pocket a wad of Congolese Francs notes. "Here," he gave us Fr.100 each and said he had more if we wanted to exchange it with Sudanese pounds. He would exchange one Sudanese pound for Fr.50 Congolese. It seemed fair. He also seemed convinced that we were going to Congo anyway and there was no point continuing to deny it. Nevertheless, we haggled for the price to come down to One Sudanese pound for 100 Congolese Francs. We handed him all the amount of Sudanese money we had and took the Congolese money. We left, feeling satisfied with our first money exchange deal, only to discover later that we had been cheated by a ratio of one to ten.

But he was right about the path, the stream and the main road. We turned left and walked for about a mile, then collapsed under a tree and went to sleep.

Akol, Valantino: Following the resurgence of the civil war in 1983, Valantino was killed in Sudan while on his way to exile in Ethiopia.

Garaged in Paulis (now Isiro)

We woke up late in the afternoon feeling refreshed. But we were very hungry, having eaten nothing since we left Tambura the previous evening. We would have to walk on along the road and hoped to find a market to buy food. But, first, there was a ritual we had to perform before moving on. We took out all the Arabic books we had and tore them into pieces, then dumped them in the bush. As far as we were concerned, we were done with the Arabic language and Arabs and all that it entailed. If only life could be that simple!

We moved on south, following the road through thick tropical forest. Soon we came to a village, with houses built on both sides of the road. The houses were set well back from the main road in banana plantations. The paths leading to the houses were swept clean. Some people had set up wooden platforms by the roadside. On the platforms were displayed big yellow bananas and boiled and raw cassava as well as boiled sweet potatoes. We assumed correctly that they were for sale. We stood beside one and a woman came out of the house to serve us. She greeted us in Arabic and said "Doruma?" pointing down the road. We said "yes", we were going to Doruma and she nodded.

She was a small, red-skinned woman, a Zande, a people our geography lessons had taught us lived on both sides of Sudan-Congo border. We all three towered over her as she looked up at our faces with bemusement. We were much blacker and taller too and we wondered which of our strange features weighed heavily on her.

"*Mlai, mlai, mlai!*" she said, raising a hand above her head to indicate height. We gathered she was impressed by our height.

We took a whole bunch of bananas and gave her 5 francs. She wanted ten more. We gave her five more. She took it but gave us some cooked cassava and sweet potatoes free. "*Mlai, mlai, mlai!*" she shouted and giggled as a group of other small women and men came out of the house. We asked for water to drink, which she gladly supplied.

We moved on. We ate the bananas as we walked. All along the road was village after village, separated here and there by small streams.

Now and again, the road turned dangerously close to the Sudanese border. Somehow, we still felt that we were not yet out of the woods. There was no sign of any Congolese administrative presence along the route. If the Sudanese police or soldiers knew we were on our way to Doruma, they would guess we were somewhere on that road, and they could cross over and get us.

Anyway, we walked on. Congolese men and women came out of their houses and banana fields to greet us, some in Southern Arabic while others shouted as they waved: "B*ote, bote! Malamu yee!*" which, along with "*mlai*", were the first Lingala words we learned.

We retired to one of the houses along the road at about 9pm. We were welcomed and given food to eat and water to drink. The banana, the cassava and the sweet potato, Gasfred had taught us, were the staples of the Congolese people along the border with Sudan. We were not surprised that what we were given to eat was not different from what we bought earlier along the road. We stored it for the following day. We then spread on the floor of the compound a blanket each and went to sleep. The owners retired inside their house.

We left before sunrise and arrived at Doruma at about 11am. Joseph and his group were already there, having arrived the previous evening. It was really a relief to see them. They were also delighted to see us because they feared the police who turned up at the junction as they arrived at 6.45pm had either arrested us or killed us while we were attempting to escape. They were also over the moon about the arrival of their boxes.

"Dominic Muorwel", Joseph informed us, "was here last week. He is gone on to Paulis".

There were about 35 recently arrived Southern Sudanese in Doruma. they were mostly students from Rumbek Secondary School and of various intermediate schools in Bhar al Ghazal. More and more refugees were arriving each day from Sudan. After five days in Doruma, the number we left behind to follow us the following week was as big as the one we found there when we arrived. They were almost all Jieng.

The Congolese authorities were uneasy about the increasing number of Sudanese refugees so close to the border. They wanted us to move on south to Paulis as soon as possible. A bus travelled the 150 miles or so between Doruma and Paulis at least once a week. We sold our spare clothes and blankets to raise cash for the bus fare to Paulis. Some Congolese wanted to buy the watch given to me by my uncle, but I refused, no matter how much they offered.

The bus took all day to reach Paulis and we were then deposited outside a large building, which turned out to be an old garage, now occupied by about 80 Sudanese refugees.

We were expected by the Sudanese refugees already in Paulis because it had become regular for the weekly bus service from Doruma to have Sudanese refugee passengers on it. But they had no idea how many were on the bus each week. Since the first group arrived late in 1962 and had been garaged there by the local authorities, there had been a dribble of refugees coming from Doruma each week. Recently however, the number of arrivals from Doruma had increased considerably, reflecting a deteriorating security situation in Southern Sudan. Our group of 40 was the largest number yet to arrive.

The refugees in the garage were all anxious to hear the latest news from Sudan. What was going on? How did we get out and so on. Joseph and the other two had a more thrilling story to tell than us because they were chased and shot at by the police who wanted to arrest them near the junction we agreed to meet at. Our group escaped detection probably because there was some mix-up in the information the police received.

But a group of four students that arrived at Doruma two days after us, had a more blood curdling story to tell: There were five of them. Arrested at Tambura, they were put on a lorry to Juba under the supervision of two armed policemen. Although their hands were manacled, they managed to free themselves and overpower the policemen, they knifed one in the throat and bolted for the bush. One of the policemen shot and probably killed their fifth companion. They never stopped to find out whether the policeman and their colleague were still alive or dead.

Such stories of daring escapes became more common to the residents of the garage as the year progressed.

It was a large garage, with corrugated iron-roof and a cement floor. Cement had come off the floor in places. If one was allocated a space with such holes, the solution was to find cardboard to cover up the holes and spread a blanket over them. A Catholic Mission in Paulis donated a blanket to each new arrival. With now over 130 refugees sleeping on the floor, the garage was already overcrowded, and more refugees were expected.

Ministering to the occupants of the garage was a demanding task for those who took it on. We were all leaders and politicians with small 'l' and small 'p'. But the only leader and politician that deserved both capital letters was Dominic Muorwel or "Muorweldit," as we generally called him. Although the local Congolese would have thought him a tall man, he was of average height by Jieng standards. He looked frail, probably the result of many years in prison.

I never saw Muorweldit arguing with anyone. This I think was due to several reasons: A former seminarian, he was generally disciplined, quiet and meditative. He was never liberal at airing his views, almost secretive and always very polite to everyone. Some called his behaviour "submissive", simply because he lacked the general aggressive edge of the Nilotic. There was no doubt that fire was bubbling under his seeming calm.

Our benefactors, the Congolese officials and foreign missionaries, loved him. He was our acknowledged leader and they demanded to discuss with him any matters concerning us, such as food and accommodation. They showed him great respect. How did he earn it?

One day, I was in company with Elia Duang, "Muorwel's deputy", when Muorweldit asked Elia to accompany him to a local government's ministry. They said I could come along if I wanted to, and I was delighted to be in company with the great man. We were going to see the minister responsible for refugees because we were "hungry and restless".

When the assistant to the minister saw Muorweldit, he almost spilled his tea as he hurriedly stood up to welcome him. "Please sit down, Monsieur Dominique, please sit down! I will tell the Minister you are here."

Muorweldit thanked him effusively for his kindness and then directed us to sit down. The Minister himself returned with the secretary. Muorweldit, who had remained standing, almost tripped over himself as he bowed his head and held his right hand out to the minister in greeting. I was dumfounded! I had never seen a Jieng do that before for any authority other than a Spearmaster. Men feared Chief Wek Agoth, for instance, but no one would bow to him!

Muorweldit was, however, received in like-manner by the minister. After a long discussion about seemingly irrelevant issues, Muorweldit apologetically broached the issue of food for the refugees, adding, "I am very sorry to have to bother you with such trivial matters my brother." The minister rose to the bait and promised to find rice "if at all available in my city. If I find no food for my brothers in my city, I will go to my village and confiscate all the bananas!" He laughed loudly. Muorweldit laughed shyly while Duang and I joined them with guarded laughter.

"You see," boasted the Minister, "I am from here, a Mangweto! We know these Arabs who are persecuting our brothers in Southern Sudan! We know them. We used to fight with them long ago and they know us very well because we killed them and ate them! That's the lesson they know. Eat them!" He laughed loudly again. Muorweldit and Duang laughed along with him.

I went contemplative. Jieng children were always warned that if they did not behave themselves, they would be handed over to a "*dor*". During the wars of the "*Turuk*" (Turks) and "Mahad Bok" (Mahadi), so went the story, the Arabs were always followed by the "*dor*" whose only aim was to capture babies and children. They would then put them into the pounding pestles, alive and headfirst and then pound them to mincemeat before they ate them. Not that I any longer believed in such stories, but this *dor* sounded and looked like he could do just that.

The Mangweto of northern Congo bounded (I don't know if they still do) the heads of their babies - with what I don't know - leaving the top of the head unbound; thus, restricting the sideways and allowing the upwards expansion of the head. The result: corn-heads! It made them look taller and fiercer than they really were. But hearing the man talk of eating people, even when they happened to be Arabs, did not inspire confidence in our safety.

Still, Muorweldit knew better: we received a large consignment of rice that afternoon. It was for me a lasting lesson in cunning humility, a trait of successful politicians and diplomat. I bet many of us will associate Muorweldit with the bad days when we were hungry, the days we went without food. Few will recall him for the days we received food and other essentials from the Congolese and the Missionaries. If he "humiliated himself", as some thought he did, by appearing submissive in front of the Congolese and Missionaries, it was that his 'boys' might have food to eat. That was leadership.

Muorweldit was one day sent for by the Congolese authorities in Kinshasa. I never saw him again.

Elia Duang, or *Maguangdit*,[41] was tall and gaunt in a horizontal way; thus his ox-nickname, *Maguangdit*, which he did not seem to mind. He was, nevertheless, one of those truly tall Jieng of whom a Mangweto woman dismissed as "A waste of two children in one. Why did your mother do that?" she asked of Duang.

Maguangdit, a Twic of Gakrial and student from Rumbek Secondary School, was intelligent, fast-talking and argumentative. He was direct, never beat about the bush. If you did not agree with what he said, you could take it or leave it. As our new leader during Muorweldit's absence, he confronted our benefactors with a lot of bravado befitting a Jieng warrior, an approach most of us appreciated but earned us less and less bread.

More refugees were arriving, and the Garage was teeming with refugees. Soon there was almost starvation and an open rebellion. Many refugees were disappearing from the garage, and we assumed that they either found their way out to other Congolese towns or had gone back to the bus to join the guerrillas. Both suppositions were correct. Still, the overcrowding in the garage was becoming unbearable.

---

41   When the horn of a young oxen is about three inches long, they are shaped with a hot spear and left to grow to any desired shape: backward, forward (*maguang*), sideways (*mageer/magar*) or inward (*madul*) or any other combination. There is an incredible art in the Jieng's training of the horns of their oxen, often imitated in the various shapes of arms when dancing.

One day we all packed up whatever belongings we had and headed on a road leading south of Paulis. Our aim was to walk to Uganda. The road went south, then turned north-east and eventually eastward toward Uganda. It all looked straightforward on the map but, we would have clocked up thousands of miles before arriving at the Ugandan border. But we didn't know that, and we did not seem to care anymore. We were desperate and determined to get out of Congo.

However, when we settled down on the roadside to rest in late afternoon, a large contingent of Congolese police and military caught up with us. They barred the road south and ordered us to turn back or else. "Else" we understood meant they would shoot at us. No one doubted that, least of all those who swore they "knew" the Congolese were cannibals. We thought it wise not to challenge them. We got back to the Garage after midnight, and we settled in as best as we could.

Antiok and I, two other young boys and a much older one called Manuel Abur *Matuong*, Abur Nhial, ate from the same plate. Abur was from Rumbek Secondary School, where he was regarded as "university material," long before he was due to take the university entrance examinations. But Rumbek Secondary School went on strike. He and others evaded arrest and went into exile.

Abur *Matuong*, or "*Matuongdit*", was a natural leader and an excellent mentor. He was incredibly even-tempered, never raised his voice and listened patiently even when everyone around him argued vehemently. When he spoke, it was rarely easy to dispute the logic of his arguments. As a result, his opinion was always sought after.

As food was often scarce and in small quantities, Abur would often tell a joke and excuse himself from continuing to eat, thus leaving us younger boys to finish the food. I know this was not unique in such situations. In fact, the mixing of younger and older boys was intended to provide such care and leadership. But the regularity and grace with which Abur went about it was outstandingly unique.

The five of us also slept next to each other. Abur, though he always listened to our own folktales, always had something new and significant to say before we went to sleep. He knew all about the Southern politicians who were imprisoned back home. He knew who was abroad and where. He told us about William Deng Nhial, Joseph Oduoh and Father Saturino. They were in Uganda, he told us. He also knew about guerrilla fighters and that he wanted to join them. He said we were too young to even think about joining the freedom fighters. "You should continue your education." He was always willing to teach anyone of us who was willing to learn. There was no subject we wanted to learn that he could not teach.

When we asked *Matuongdit* about the schools we were told were available for us in the neighbouring countries, he told us that this was only possible in East Africa where English was the official language and language of instruction like Southern Sudan. "You will have to find your own way to Uganda if you want to go to school," he told us. "As for me, I am going to fight Arabs."

Meanwhile, he was growing thinner and thinner. We began to worry a lot about him and refused to eat when he retired from eating halfway through the tiny meals we received unless he finished the food with us.

But Abur *Matuong* disappeared one day, and we were later informed that he returned home to Southern Sudan. But we knew in our hearts that he had joined the "Southern Sudan Liberation Army", better known as "*Anya-Nya*", snake's poison.

Back to the Garage, I discovered that I had a nephew called Riny *Makoor*, son of Chief Giir Thiik and only son of Ajok Baak, Mother's half-sister. I met him briefly once at Grandmother's. I was a small boy then and he was a big "child of *Abun*." I paid little attention to him as he did to me. Anyway, he was much older than I was, and we would have had little in common to talk about.

However, at the Garage so far away from home, we were the

closest of relatives and we had so much in common to talk about. The reason we hadn't met thus far was that neither he nor I knew that the other was out of Sudan and in Congo. He arrived at the Garage a month before me. By the time I got there he had moved out to work in a coffee plantation in a place called Nala, some eleven kilometres north of Paulis (Isiro).

Our togetherness was, however, short-lived because Riiny *Makoor* had returned to the Garage to say goodbye to friends and colleagues - and now to a nephew. "I am going back to the bush to fight the Arabs," he announced. He was a hefty young man full of life and energy. Unlike my friend, Abur *Matuongdit*, my nephew looked fit enough to take on an army single-handed.

Before leaving for Sudan, however, Riny told me that I could go to Nala and claim his place at the coffee farm where he was working as a labourer. I hastened there and indeed got the job. His bed was still there in a room shared with two other Sudanese refugees. One of them was a Jieng young man called Ambrose, a former student of Bussere Seminary School. The other (non-Jieng) was a young man called Felix, a former student of Rumbek Secondary School. They hotly argued about anything and everything; no subject was too small or too big for either of them to have strong opinions about.

The only things about which they never seemed to argue were women. Felix had a Congolese woman called Monica, who visited him once every Sunday. He would spend the whole morning grooming himself before Monica arrived promptly at noon. Ambrose and I always waited to greet Monica before leaving the house for them. I don't know why. When we returned about three hours later, Monica was ready to leave. Felix would accompany her out of the village before returning to the room to argue with Ambrose. I never knew if Monica was married or not.

Ambrose, on the other hand, was sleeping with two women neighbours, one on each side of our house. They were both married to fellow (Congolese) workers at the coffee plantation. It always happened after we received our wages and when their husbands were not around. I assumed that Ambrose was paying them for their services and the husbands probably knew about it. I remembered warning Ambrose about the consequences if their husbands discovered, but he said it was all watertight. Whatever he meant, both Felix and I made ourselves scarce when it became obvious that Ambrose wanted us out of the way. The women always came to him for the liaison, never in their own houses.

We woke up at 6 am and walked to the farm, about a kilometre away from the worker's compound. It was a very large plantation, the full width and breadth I had no idea of or cared to know. It was owned by a Belgian but, given the chaos leading to the attempted secession of Katanga and the death of the first Congolese leader, Patrice Lumumba, in 1961, who owned what in Congo at that time was a matter of conjecture. What was clear was that the farm had been abandoned or neglected for at least two years and it was being rehabilitated with our labour.

The workers assembled on cleared ground on the coffee farm. The farm manager, Epherimo was his name, carried out the roll call and issued various tools to various groups. While one group uprooted coffee bushes, another group cleared them away to make bonfires with when dry. While one group planted coffee seedlings, another group was busy elsewhere weeding older plants. There were so many things to do.

We had a lunch break at noon. Sometimes we had bananas but often we went to the nearby bush and dug up the wild cassava that grew there and roasted it over fire. It tasted better than boiled cassava.

I was paid 1,500 Congolese francs a week, (about £2), enough to live on. However, we contributed to the Garage 500 francs weekly towards the feeding of our brothers.

The rubber shoes I came with from Sudan were wearing out at

the toes. Someone suggested I did not have to spoil my shoes in the mud while working. So, I took them off and worked barefooted like most of my fellow labourers.

But a worm the Congolese called "*tuktugi*" imbedded itself under the skin of bare feet and toenails and enlarged itself to a big round thing in a couple of days. A victim was first alerted by a slight hitch, then forced to search for the cause as the swelling and itch became unbearable. After work, we washed our feet and searched for the worm which, when mature, was easily visible under a bluish skin patch. We dug the parasites out of our feet and burnt or squashed them.

However, some of the holes they left behind either developed into wounds or became easy targets for new infestations. Epherimo laughed at me one day, saying, "Yakobo, if you don't watch it the *tuktugi* will turn your feet inside out and make you walk like a duck. See the workers around here? They walk like ducks. It is *tuktugi* which ate their feet that way when they were your age!" He roared with laughter. I did not see anything funny about duck feet and I resumed the wearing of my old shoes; but they soon developed holes in them. When the worms began to find their way into my feet again, I threw the shoes away and went to Paulis in search of new ones, cheap but effective.

It was when I was in Paulis I let Antiok talk me into an idea he said would make us a lot of money. He needed about 2,500 francs to buy dry fish from big merchants and then sell it in the local market. It sounded good. Three weeks later I had saved enough for Antiok to start his business. "You will get it back in less than two weeks," he promised and returned to Paulis. I continued working at Nala.

A week later, I got a message that Antiok was not in Paulis. From the information, it seemed that he had decided to use the money I gave him to get as far away as possible from Paulis. There was nothing I could do about it. So, I continued working for five more weeks, then went to Paulis for a break. Antiok was there, having that day returned from wherever he disappeared to with my money. He was looking well.

"Well, how are you?" I enquired after his health.

"I am very well," he said, "and what about you?"

"I am well," I said.

We were silent for an awkward moment; then I said: "What happened to you? Where have you been? What happened to the money I gave you?"

"I was trying to go to Stanleyville (now Kisangani) to buy fish. I was told it was cheap there." It made sense. The big river, River Congo, was said to be full of fish and Stanleyville was right on it.

"So did you get the fish?"

"No. I was stuck at Wamba Mission. The missionaries there told me it was a foolish idea. They told me that fish in Stanleyville was very expensive. They said I could get robbed or killed on the way. So, I stayed in Wamba and the money finished and I could not get transport. So, I worked at a printing press there at the Mission to get some money for transport back to Paulis. I am sorry."

It was not at all convincing, but what to do? "I am going to go to East Africa and go to school there," I said knowing that Antiok would come.

"But they will not allow you to leave Paulis," said Antiok. "You remember last time they returned us before we reached Wamba."

"But you reached Wamba and no one stopped you," I argued.

"I was alone, and the missionaries did not agree with my going further anyway," said Antiok.

"Because you were not going to look for education and you were alone anyway. You say they are looking for workers at the printing press. So, we can go there and work for them and then convince them about why we have to go to East Africa."

"Yes," said Antiok uncertainly.

"It is now August and we have been in and out of The Garage since February," I said. "If we don't get out now, we will never go to school." I pressed my determination to leave: "If we were in Sudan I would now be at Rumbek (assuming I sat the secondary school entrance exams a year in advance and passed them with very high grades)."

"No, you would not," said Antiok.

"Why not?" was he doubting my ability to pass? I wondered.

"Because all the schools in Southern Sudan are closed."

"I know that. I am only supposing they were not."

It was settled anyway. I had about 3,000 Congolese francs. We would try to use it in emergency situations and saved it as long as possible. We were now good at Lingala, a commonly spoken language in Northern Congo. We could work and beg for food and transport all the way to east Africa, we agreed. Anything but the Garage was acceptable. In the following morning, we would just clear out without telling anyone. After all, many of our colleagues were getting out of the Garage that way.

Abur, Manuel: By the end of the war in 1972, Manuel Abur was a colonel in the Anya-Nya army and was, as per agreement, incorporated at that rank into the Sudanese army. I met Col. Abur briefly in Juba in the mid-70s on his way to Wau. A contingent from his former command in the Anya-Nya, led by a Captain Aguet, had just vacated their barracks in Wau and had gone into the nearby bush. They were no longer in support of the Addis Ababa Agreement. Still, they gave the impression that they could be persuaded because they were still talking to the Regional Government. Abur offered to negotiate, and he went "unarmed" to talk to the rebels. But Aguet "chained him, tortured and killed him in cold blood", then ran away. The Regional Government saw the killing of Abur as the biggest challenge yet to its authority. No expense was spared to bring Aguet to justice. He was traced to Bangui where the Central African Republic authorities arrested him and returned him to Sudan after a Southern Sudanese minister had gone there to identify him. He was then "court-martialled and executed in Wau".

Bel, Joseph: I cannot recall what happened to Joseph Bel when we arrived in Paulis. Some accounts were that he proceeded to Leopoldville (Kinsahsa) shortly after our arrival at the Garage. But I know that he was back in Southern Sudan in the 70s and was married to my boyhood girlfriend, Nyibol. "Good luck to him" I said. Being about my age then, there was never any chance Nyibol and I had a future together. By the time I would be ready for a family, she would have had many children of her own. Men married women much younger than themselves. That's the way it was most likely the way it still is in Sudan.

Giir, Riny: He was one of the early casualties of the war. I do not know exactly where in Africa I first learned of his death. Apparently, a handful of
Freedom fighters led by Riiny invaded Gakrial town and tried to capture it. They failed, they were chased and Riiny was eventually wounded, captured at Karkou between Gakrial and Kuachjok and executed or died of his wounds in captivity.

Muorwel, Dominic: When a North-South peace agreement was signed and the war ended in 1972, Muorweldit and a few other Southern politicians refused to join in, arguing that they could not trust a union between North and South and they maintained their demand for a separate South Sudan. He died in the Central African Republic's capital, Bangui, in the 70s, still believing that "the so-called peace" would not last. His predictions came true in 1983, when war between the two regions resumed in a more destructive form.

Way to Bunia

The white missionaries at Wamba gave us work at their printing press, binding exercise books for their schools. But we soon let them know that we were determined to go to East Africa in search of education. They neither encouraged nor discouraged us.

We left Wamba three days later when a lorry driver passing through Wamba agreed to take us to Stanleyville (now Kisangani) at a very small fee. We informed the Brother who ran the printing press and he gave us an exercise book each for our three days of work and wished us good luck.

I had an old map on which a road out of Stanleyville to Rwanda seemed the most direct route to East Africa and therefore the route we intended to take.

We reached Nia-Nia, a post at the junction where the road from Bunia joins the Paulis-Stanleyville Road. The driver stopped in front of a shop and prepared to sleep in the front of the lorry. It was raining heavily and was very dark, with the thick tropical forest pressing in on us. There was no electric light at the post. A few oil lamps flickered here and there, indicating houses.

We were, suddenly, surrounded by soldiers. They were shouting and pointing their guns at us and nudging us towards a building in which a paraffin lamp was burning. They told us to keep our hands up while one of them picked up our bags. They kept telling us to keep our hands up above our heads inside the building and it looked like we were in for a very rough night.

"Who are you?" one of them barked at us in Lingala, "and where are you going this time of the night? Who are you? Eh? Eh?"

"These are Sudani," said another. "Where are you going, you Sudani! Sudani, where are your identity cards? Give me, give me your identity cards, quickly!"

But we had none. One soldier was about to search my pockets

when another soldier, a senior by the look of him, emerged from another room. He carried in his left hand a paraffin lamp and a stick in his right hand. A pistol hunged on the right side of his khaki shorts. The soldiers in the room saluted and stood at attention.

"These are Sudani people, sir," one of them reported, pointing at us. "They have no travel permits and…"

"You Sudani?"

"Good evening brother officer," I greeted him in Lingala in a firm voice that concealed fear. "We are Sudanese, and we are going to East Africa to go to…"

"You are Arabs?"

"No, we are not Arabs! We are Sudanese! We are African people from Southern Sudan, and we are running away from Arabs. Brother Patrice Lumumba said Congo is opened for African people. That's…"

Although Lumumba died in prison under controversial circumstances in Katanga in 1961, his memory was still fresh in the mind of many Congolese who saw him as the "Father of the Nation." This regard for Lumumba was particularly still strong in northern Congo. I had come to appreciate this fact when I was working in the coffee plantation in Nala. Congolese there danced to rhythms of songs praising Lumumba's "victory over the Belgians" and that he had freed Congo from foreign domination. "*Patrice Lumumba aliki sana…*" (Patrice Lumumba has truly won…) was one of the songs sung even by very young children. My reference to the Arabs as the persecutors and the mention of Lumumba as the liberator of Africa hit a chord with the officer.

"Put your guns down!" the officer shouted at his men. "Don't you know these are our brothers from Southern Sudan!" he said as if he had known this fact all along and was pretending when he wanted to know who we were.

"They are our brothers, and they are being persecuted by the

Arabs! Sit down! Sit down! You!" he ordered one of his men, "go get some food and drinks for our brothers here. They must be hungry."

In a space of fifteen minutes or so, we were arrested, bullied, welcomed and entertained. We ate well, slept well and were fed early in the morning before our "soldier brothers" waved us off. What was more, they wanted to know if the lorry driver had taken any money from us. We told them the driver was a good man, that he had not taken any money from us.

The officer looked at the driver suspiciously, then told him: "These are refugees from Sudan. They are our brothers. Arabs are persecuting them. You take no money from them! Alright?" The driver nodded fearfully, glancing at us from time to time.

We were not being charitable to or protective of the driver. His was the only lorry available to Stanleyville and we wanted to get away from the soldiers. No matter how seemingly friendly they appeared to be we knew they could turn nasty at a misplaced word or action.

The driver stopped near the centre of Stanleyville and told all the passengers to disembark. "This is the end of the journey," he announced. We disembarked and he drove off towards the city centre. We followed him and soon saw him parked in front of a big shop in the city centre. Goods were being unloaded from the lorry, supervised by a very fat *Kawaja*, who looked like our Gorgor in Gakrial. He was probably the owner of the lorry and the goods on which we had been sitting.

We were impressed by the size, height of buildings and general beauty of Stanleyville. It was much bigger and more beautiful than Wau. There were long and wide avenues of well-kept arcades of shops full of varieties of merchandise. Big houses in the centre of the city and along the River Congo had manicured gardens and flowering hedges of plants we had never seen before. Rich Congolese, Government people, white people and "Arabs" (any Asian we saw) lived in those houses.

Many roads were tarred and the port on the River Congo was busy with steamers and many boats. Having not seen the River Nile in our own country, River Congo was by far the biggest river we had ever seen. Its impressive body of water flowed gently towards the sunset.

The city was built on the north-bank of the river. Upstream was a white water-break where the river bent on its way to the city. Our geography teacher had told us about cataracts on the River Nile that prevented steamers from going much further beyond Khartoum. This was clearly a cataract, and no steamer could go beyond that.

We bought bananas and sat by the riverbank, eating and wondering what to do next. But a man walked up to us and greeted us in Arabic. "I am from Lebanon," he introduced himself and said in English: "You are Sudanese from Southern Sudan. We know the problems you are facing in Paulis. Some of your people came through here and we helped them to move on to Leopoldville or East Africa. Come with me to my house. It is just over there." We were overwhelmed by his generosity and by our good luck. So, we followed him without questions.

It was a very large house and indeed close by. The man told us to wait in a large and well-furnished sitting room and disappeared behind a door. Then we heard hushed voices behind the door and we looked at each other, picked up our bags and disappeared through the main door. We were thinking the same thing: How could we have been so stupid! These were not Lebanese but Sudanese Arabs. Their business we believed was to capture Southern Sudanese refugees and returned them to Sudan by force! Never again would we allow ourselves to fall in to such a trap, we promised ourselves and looked for assistance elsewhere.

We went to a Catholic Mission in the centre of the city that was easily identified by a magnificent Cathedral. Why had we not done so immediately we arrived in the city? Perhaps it was because we were greatly disappointed by the Catholic Brother in Wamba who paid our labour in notebooks and not in the money we so badly needed.

But we were lucky this time because a priest at the centre listened attentively to our story, told in Lingala because his English was as bad as our French was, which meant negligible. There was a time when we thought that all *Turuks* understood English; that was way back in Gakrial. We had since come to know that Africa was full of different *Turuks* who did not speak English: There were Italians, French, Belgians and many others. This priest we assumed was Belgian. He listened silently and did not appear at all surprised or doubtful of our story. He told us to sit under a tree in the compound and went into a building. Then he returned with another priest with a heavy face and a long, thick brown beard. He reminded us of Fr. Umberto *Abundit* without the smile back in Kuachjok.

"Where do you want to go? East Africa?" he asked in heavily accented English.

"Yes," I replied. "We want to go to school there."

"And how are you going to get there? Have you any money?"

"No, we will walk and ask for lifts on the way. And also, if anyone can help us with money on the way that would be good."

"You don't know what you are talking about. Do you know how far it is? Do you know how dangerous it is? There is fighting going on all over Congo. You will be better off returning to the refugee camp in Paulis."

"No, we are not going back, Father. There is nothing there for us and there are schools to go to in Uganda."

"Who told you that?"

We did not answer.

"There are no schools there. Anyway, the road to East Africa is not through Stanleyville. You will have to go up north to Bunia and then to Uganda."

They gave us food, put us up in a student's hostel and put us on a lorry going to the Ituri town of Mambasa in the morning. "Go to the catholic Mission in Mambasa. They will help you find transport to Bunia," said the priest who first met us at the Mission. We went back on the road we came to Nia-Nia.

We stopped briefly at Nia-Nia for document check. Our "brothers" the soldiers welcomed us. While the chief fed us, his subordinates were making deals with the driver and other passengers to compensate for their almost non-existent salaries. Bunia, he told us, was a lovely city. He was born there, and we would love it. He was great; but he kept looking longingly at my watch. So, we were happy all the same to be on our way.

We had also feared that the Missionaries in Stanleyville might have played a trick on us, that the driver might have been instructed to hand us over to the Congolese soldiers at Nia-Nia so to return us to Paulis. Our fears were not founded, and we settled atop the lorry to enjoy the trip and discover new territories and new people.

The route, like the one from Paulis to Stanleyville, was through tropical forest. Born and brought up in the savannah of Southern Sudan, where one could see miles and miles of open country, the tropical forest was like a prison. Our eyes were restricted even from seeing much of the sky above. The bright light from the tropical sun dissipated in the thick leaves of giant tropical trees. Yet, the relentless rain seemed to find its way through the leaves and poured into the lorry like water from buckets. There was a waterproof canvas cover for the top of the lorry, but the driver had tied it firmly around the sacks containing coffee beans, beans and salt to protect them from passengers and rain. We were allowed to sit on the waterproof canvas, thus leaving us unprotected from elements.

We arrived at Mambasa late at night and spent the night on the lorry. We picked up our bags and located the Catholic Mission recommended early in the morning. It was a small place with a straggly church building, not better looking than our own Church at

Ayiel. It did not look like a place that would have anything to spare for transient refugees. The priest we were supposed to see was not there and no one who could help was available either. "He has gone to Bunia," a worker told us. "I don't know when he's coming back."

Mambasa was the capital town of Ituri Sub-District, something like Gakrial back home. So we went to the administrative offices of the town and presented a well-constructed letter explaining who we were, where we were coming from, where we were going and why and what specific help we needed from the authorities.

We saw an authoritative-looking young man standing in the administrative compound surrounded by hangers-on. So, we edged close enough to catch his attention, which soon happened. Not only were we much taller and bigger than the average boys of our age then in Mambasa, but we were also much darker. We handed him the letter we had addressed to "Monsieur le Commissar" and written in Lingala. He glanced at it and handed it back to me. "I have no transport or money for transport to Bunia", he told us and turned to one of his administrative police officers: "See that these boys have something to eat and put them on any lorry going to Bunia." He returned to his office.

We were surprised by his fast-reading ability, the way he captured the gist of the letter and the quick decisions so made. Coming to the government, we agreed, was a lot more fruitful than waiting around for the priest to come back from Bunia.

We were given food to eat, slept in a shed near the church at the Mission and looked out for any vehicle on its way to Bunia. Three days later, only two lorries had come by, but they "are all full and the driver will not take you without pay," the policeman told us each time. Somehow, he was always the first to talk to the drivers before we had any chance to try ourselves. Then he hung around and interrupted any attempts we made to talk to the drivers. We suspected he wanted to be the one making the negotiations for us in the hope of receiving "something small" in the end from us.

The fourth day was full of unusual activities. It began with the sound of drums coming from deep in the forest. The drumming and singing gained momentum with the rising sun. Then small bands of very small people with decorated faces and mostly dressed in bark cloths and leaves emerged from the forest. They were the famous "Pigmies of the Ituri Forest" we had learned about in geography lessons.

However, those geography lessons did not prepare us for the actual physical appearance of the Pigmies. Until then, we had thought they would look like "Abraham Ayoom," a hunchback colleague back at Kuachjok. Nothing could have been further from the truth: Ayoom, though short, was solid and powerful. Challenging Ayoom to wrestling or provoking him to a fight was only done at one's own risk. Not only was he hard to grab, but he was also always as fast and as strong as a ram. And when Ayoom rammed his head into one's knee or belly there was no chance of resisting the fall.

But these Pigmies were something else. Everything about them could be summed up in one word: SMALL: Size, height - name it, it was small. They sang with voices like children's as they moved in circles in processions. They rarely smiled, if at all and their small faces were determined but sad.

But they had stamina, despite their anaemic appearance. All morning they sang, going around and around in circles. The guest of honour they were welcoming to their district was the Governor of Bunia. He arrived late in the afternoon in a convoy of four-wheel vehicles. The din from the Pigmies rose to a sharper pitch. We watched in amazement the stamina of those tiny people.

But we did not forget the reason we were in Mambasa, which was to proceed to Bunia and on to East Africa. We have come to believe that the police officer had not tried his best to put us on board those lorries that he said were full. We have been contemplating the possibility of dipping into our dwindling reserve of cash from my wages in Nala to persuade him to try a little harder.

However, a man from the Governor's team appeared to be interested in the tall and dark strangers who were obviously not natives of the Ituri Forest. We edged closer to him and handed him the letter to "Monsieur le Commissar." He read the letter carefully, then said: "How long have you been here?"

"Four days!" we both said in tones that conveyed they had been terrible days.

He looked at us again and shook his head sympathetically. No doubt the eight months or so we had been away from home, not just the last four days, must have been telling on us. "Come here," he called one of his assistants. "Make sure these boys get transport to Bunia this evening. Make sure they have something to eat and put them up at Foyer des Eleves. Bring them to my office tomorrow morning." He turned to us and introduced himself: "I am Allain Chabanenge, Chef de Cabinet at Bunia."

We were beside ourselves with happiness. Not only were we assured of transportation to Bunia, but we were also assured of food and accommodation at the end of the journey. Never had we been so sure of what to find in the next hour, leave alone at the end of a long journey.

We left for Bunia on a pickup vehicle late in the afternoon. Before long, we emerged from the dark shadows of Ituri Forest into more open countryside. The land was hilly with scattered forests here and there. Although this was nowhere close to the flat and open countryside of the Jieng, it was like areas between Wau and Tambura. We could see the wide-open sky and at sunset the stars. To our right, a range of dark mountains loomed above the eastern horizon.

"Bunia is not far from Uganda," I said to Antiok.

"No, it is not," Antiok agreed and added, "it is not very far from Sudan either. We have been travelling north since we left Stanleyville."

"North-east from Nia-Nia," I corrected him. "Bunia must be

200 to 300 miles south of the Sudan border. Anyway, we are not going to Sudan."

We were silent for a moment. I don't know what Antiok was thinking. My thoughts were back on the day we left Gakrial, the day we left Wau and on the road to Tambura, the night walk and the way across the border to Congo. The shredding of Arabic books. The walk to Doruma and the bus trip to Paulis. The grinding months in the Garage and the coffee plantation and then to Stanleyville and then, eight months later, on our way to Bunia, close to Uganda. "It all seems like an eternity," I concluded dreamily, "and yet it seems like it was only yesterday we were in Sudan."

"What?" asked Antiok.

"What?" I was fully awake. "Oh, it's nothing. It is just that we have been on the road for so long. Do you think we will find a school to go to in Uganda?"

"I don't know," said Antiok. "They told us in Gakrial and in Paulis that there are schools for Sudanese in East Africa."

"But the priest in Stanleyville said there were none."

"I don't know," he said. It was getting late, and we were feeling exhausted.

Stanleyville/Kisangani: Many years later I read "A BEND IN THE RIVER" (1979) by V.S. Naipaul. He does not name the city at the bend in the river but anyone who has been to Stanleyville would know that city. But what has happened to the city? "The country, like others in Africa, had had its troubles after independence. The town in the interior, at the bend of the great river, had almost ceased to exist; was more than half destroyed. What had been the European suburbs near the rapids had been burned down, and bush had grown over the ruins; it was hard to distinguish what had been gardens from what had been streets. The official and the commercial centre near the dock and customs house survived, and some residential streets in the centre."

On Revisit: I returned to former Stanleyville, now Kisangani, 36 years later as an aid-worker/journalist. The city, like this part of the country, owed no allegiance to the government in the capital, Kinshasa, as it was now occupied by Ugandan troops and Congolese rebels. The commander and his bodyguards occupied the big house overlooking the river that was still there and flowing as majestically and relentlessly as ever. But the destruction looked worse than described by Naipaul. The commercial buildings, though still standing, were bullet-marked, shell-shocked and dilapidated. The school and the hostel which we spent the night in so many years back had returned to the bush. But The Mission was still there, and a few European Missionaries were still there. A European colleague and I were this time accommodated and fed at the Mission at a modest fee. But a week after our departure a bomb dropped on the city by a high-flying Antenov aircraft hit part of the Mission. It was claimed that the bomber had come from Sudan and not from Kinshasa. Sudan denied it. Perhaps we will never know.

Bunia

The Student Hostel was an isolated residential building just south of Bunia. There were about three students already there. Antiok and I shared a large bedroom with two beds in it. On each bed were one cotton mattress, two ironed cotton bedsheets and a blanket. There was electricity and a flush toilette. The whole house looked very clean and comfortable; just like the hostel we stayed in for the night in Stanleyville. We slept very soundly.

A cook woke us up in the morning and gave us a breakfast of milk-tea, scrambled eggs and bread. He then directed us to the office of Monsieur Allen, Chef de Cabinet. We could see the government offices high on a hill, not very far from the hostel.

"Le Chef de Cabinet is in a Cabinet meeting," his assistant, the man he introduced us to in Mambasa, told us. "Can you wait for him?" We nodded in agreement. We had nothing to do. We had all the time in the world.

The Chef came out of the meeting at about 2 in the afternoon. He greeted us and told us to wait in the sitting room and went into his office.

Allain Chabanenge was unlike the tropical forest Congolese we had seen. He was almost six feet tall and was neither fat nor thin. In short, he was a very well-built gentleman in his early forties. He was dressed in what later became known as a "Kaunda Suit": trousers with a matching collared shirt worn over them. He had tucked a dark-red scarf under the collar of his shirt and around his neck. He looked as important as he certainly was. With a low bow, his assistant opened every door he entered or exited.

"A Jieng," I remarked for Antiok's benefit, "cannot do his assistant's job."

"No," he agreed. "Only a *dor* can do it." There was no sign of condescension in his voice or a trace of doubt in my acceptance of what he had said. It was only a statement of an accepted fact: a Jieng's worldview.

There was movement inside the boss's office and the assistant rushed from his desk to open the door for his boss. The Chef entered the room, looking very pleased with the world around him. "Come, boys. Let's go for something to eat. There is a Sudanese I would like you to meet."

We were a bit apprehensive about meeting this Sudanese. I don't know why. But the Chef de Cabinet was transparently honest and seemed genuinely kind. Anyway, we had no option but to go for food and meet this man. Our future in Bunia and the way to Uganda depended on this kind man, a very important member of the Government in the province.

His assistant opened the doors all the way to the front of the building where a smart black Volvo was waiting. We followed close behind him and through the doors. The assistant did not seem to mind holding doors open for us as well. The driver jumped out of his seat and opened the left back door for us to enter. The assistant opened the other door to let in his boss. He then jumped in next to the driver as we settled into the soft leather seats.

Apart from the Governor's car in Wau, we had not seen a car as smart as that big Volvo before, not even in the one day we spent in Stanleyville. Thinking about it later, there could have been such smart vehicles in Paulis but I had not seen one. But seeing one is different from sitting in one. The car swayed gently and the bumps in on the dirt parts of the roads felt like soft cradles. I thought our host had noticed our appreciation of the vehicle, but he did not show it.

"The man we are going to see is called Abondio. He has been in Bunia for three months now. He knows Uganda very well - the conditions there. He will tell you more about it."

We stopped at a smart restaurant on the main street of Bunia. The assistant and the driver opened the doors for us and stood there as we entered the restaurant. They stayed in the car.

There were a lot of people, including a few *Kawajas/Turuk* families and other smartly dressed city people in the restaurant. They all turned to look at us. Certainly, many of them, if not all, knew about our host and his position in Bunia because their stares were polite and respectful. Some of the people at the tables nodded their heads in our direction. Our host nodded back with dignity and allowed a waiter to lead us to a table in a corner.

There was already a man seated at our table. He got up and greeted our host in Kiswahili. Then, without introduction, greeted us in Arabic. So, this was the Sudanese we were to meet.

Abondio was his name, in his early 30s. He was tall and dark, probably an Equatorian from one of the Niolotic tribes we had heard about and who live at the Sudan-Uganda border. An Acholi? A

Kakwa? Abondio introduced himself, listened to our story patiently, then said:

"You are mad going to Uganda. There is nothing there but suffering. Sudanese refugees are starving in the camps in Uganda. There are no schools and people are running away from the camps. How many Sudanese refugees you said you left behind in Paulis?"

"About 200," I told him, upping the number a bit, then added, "but the number was increasing every week."

"That's nothing. There are half a million refugees already in Uganda and more people are arriving every day. Fighting is bad in Sudan now. You can never go to school in Uganda!"

Our host paid the bill and took us back to the Student Hostel. He left Abondio with us. "Perhaps you want to find out more about Uganda from Abondio. Come to my office tomorrow. I will be there. We will then talk about what you want to do: go back to Paulis, stay here or go to Uganda."

Abondio then told us his story: He was arrested inside Congo over a year back by the Anya-Nya and accused of spying for the Government of Sudan. He was tortured and then handed over to local Congolese authorities at the border, who also tortured and treated him very badly. He showed us healing wounds on his back, stomach, thighs and on the back of his head as evidence of his suffering at the hands of the "liberators" and the local Congolese authorities.

"Are you a spy?" I asked rather tactlessly.

"Me! Never! I am not a spy!" He seemed genuinely shocked by the question. So, I dropped that direct line of questioning. "What happened to you then? How come you are in Bunia?"

"The Congolese kept me in prison at the border for five months then I was sick. They transferred me to Bunia for medical treatment because they thought I was mentally sick. I am well now."

Antiok and I were silent, totally convinced of Abondio's story. How shocking! How can the liberators do that to a Southern

Sudanese? Still, Abondio's posture and manner of speaking suggested something unsettling. Perhaps he was mentally unstable?

"Did they put you in prison here at Bunia?" I ventured a question just to break the ice.

"Yes, I was in prison all the time even when they treated me. They took me to hospital in chains and then brought me back to the prison. I am well now though."

"How did you get out of prison?" asked Antiok

"Le Chef de Cabinet. He found me in hospital and after talking to me he ordered my release. He is a good man. He is a very good Christian. He believes I am not a spy because I am not."

We went to the office of the big man in the morning, but we did not see him until after 2pm because of meetings. No matter, we were well looked after by his assistant who treated us to tea and biscuits.

"Well," asked our host as soon as he entered, "have you decided what to do?"

"Yes," I told him, "We are going to go Tanganyika instead."

"Why Tanganyika?" he seemed a little surprised.

"Because it is very far away," I explained.

"It is very far away, that's true. So?"

"We think that because it is very far from Sudan there are not many Sudanese there. If there are not many Sudanese, there we may find a school to take us."

He was quiet for a moment chewing over what I had just said. "Maybe you have a point. In fact, I think it is a very good idea. You can go to Bukavu then to Uvira and out to Tanganyika by boat. It can be done but it is a long and dangerous journey. There is fighting going on in Rwanda and Burundi. Come to my office tomorrow. I want to consult some people about it."

We were pleased with this turn of events. We told Abondio what we had decided and what Le Chef de Cabinet thought about it. He also agreed that we had a better chance of going to school in

Tanganyika than in Uganda and Kenya, "but the journey!" he added. "Tanzania is a long way away. How are you going to get there?"

"Le Chef de Cabinet thinks it is possible. He will help us," Antiok told him. "Why don't you come with us?"

"No, I don't want to leave here, and I have things to do," he said and looked about himself as if he did not want us to discuss the matter any further. "Good luck with the Chef de Cabinet," he said and left.

But Le Chef de Cabinet was not in his office when we called there in the morning. His office was locked; no one was there to tell us anything. We hung around, hoping that he was merely late, but he did not turn up. His assistant did not turn up and there was no one to tell us his whereabouts. We looked for his Volvo in the hope of finding the driver to tell us where his boss was. The car was not there either.

A policeman wanted to know what we were looking for. We asked for our host, but he was surprised we had any business with Le Chef de Cabinet. Anyway, he said he did not come to the office that morning and did not know where he could be. He kept an eye on us and followed us each time we moved in the corridors. He told us at about 2.30pm to go away because the offices were closed for the day.

We were just about to return to the hostel when a man came out of the office next to the Chef's and called us: "Are you not the Sudanese boys who have been coming to see Le Chef de Cabinet?"

What a relief! We turned to him and said together: "Yes we are."

"Ha!" sighed the man, "he left this morning for Leopoldville (later Kinshasa). He was urgently sent for by the President."

We were speechless for a moment, then I asked him, "Do you know when he is coming back?"

"No. Tomorrow? Next week? Next year? I don't know. It is up to the President." The man got on his bike and rode off.

We returned to the hostel, wondering what to do next. The little money we had was dwindling fast. But we consoled ourselves with the hope that the big man must have left someone with a message for us. When in the evening no one had contacted us, we consoled ourselves with the hope that he would soon be back. Abondio had not come to see us, and we did not know where he lived.

We went to the office on the hill every working day for the next two weeks in the hope of seeing our host, but no luck.

One day, someone in the Ministry of Social Affairs told us that we had only two days in the hostel. "There is no more money for the Government to pay the rent," he said. "The owner wants all students out."

"What will happen to us?" asked Antiok.

"I don't know," said the man with a shake of the shoulders. "There is no money either to pay the cook. We will give you some rice and some vegetable oil for you to cook. That's all I can do for you."

Two days later we were still in the hostel with nowhere to go. The landlord sent someone to throw us out and lock the doors. But we returned to the house as soon as he left and spread the two old blankets, we had brought from Paulis on the sandy compound and spent the night there.

In the morning, we picked up our bags and moved to the government offices in the hope of seeing our host or someone who could help us. But there was no message from our host and no government official was any longer interested in our case. The Social Affairs Department official who issued us with rice now told us that "there is no more. Come tomorrow." And then a policeman guarding the offices told us to go away from the offices or else.

We wandered in the town, wondering what to do. Then, after buying fried sweet potatoes, we returned to the compound of the hostel, ate the potatoes and retired for the night in the compound. This went on for another ten days and we began to lose hope of getting help from anyone. We did not look for help from the Church in town because we believed they would not help us go to Tanganyika. The likelihood was that they would think we were crazy and would tell us to return to Paulis, stay around in Bunia or go to Uganda. If only Le Chef de Cabinet would come! But he did not come. We therefore resolved to go to Tanganyika even if we had to walk the whole way.

Way to Bukavu

We started very early in the morning on the road heading south-west towards Ituri Forest. We were on this road five weeks back heading in the opposite direction. If all went well, we hoped to spend the night in the town of Irumu, just north of the junction where the road forked: One route continued south-west into Ituri Forest and on to Mambasa. The other route lead southwards, avoiding the Ituri Forest to the west and skirting the foothills of the Blue Mountain Range to the east.

The Blue Mountains are the northern extension of the Ruwenzori Mountains or Mountains of the Moon. On the eastern side of the mountains is the "Great Rift Valley in which the great lakes of the continent are located." Gasfred Kamis Redi was always very proud of stressing the majesty of the Mountains of the Moon and the beauty of the Rift Valley as if he had seen all those things with his own eyes. Maybe he did. As for us, the old map I had suggested that we would be walking along the west-side of these mountains for weeks before the road crossed the lowest summit of the range and then over and down into the Rift Valley and the lakes.

Our luck was good. An old lorry caught up with us as soon as we got out of Bunia. The driver told us he was on his way to Butembo. That was a good distant down our road, but he was charging a huge amount of money which we could not afford even if we gave him all the money we had. We looked at him dejectedly and begged him to charge less. He reduced the fare by half, but we still found it too high. He revved up the engine and rolled forward slowly while still demanding the fare. We offered him a quarter of half of the original fare. He revved up the engine even louder and moved off, still slowly. I took out half of the half of the original fare from my pocket and held it out to him. He took it, put it in his pocket in disgust and waved us up onto the lorry.

We enjoyed the beautiful scenery, with the forest to the right and Blue Mountains to the left. But the lorry soon broke down. The driver repaired it, but it broke down again after 7 miles. This went on all day. Sometimes it was the engine overheating with steam hissing out on the side of the bonnet. He would stop to cool down the engine by opening the bonnet and letting fresh air in. At other times it was a flat tyre and we made ourselves useful by being available for anything he needed handed to him.

Someone on the lorry had informed us that the driver was in fact going to Goma, a town in the Rift Valley and on the northern shore of Lake Kivu. If we got there, that would be almost halfway to Tanganyika, we told each other. From there we planned to find a boat to the city of Bukavu on the southern shore of the lake and then on to Uvira on Lake Tanganyika.

"What do you want to go to Goma for?" asked the driver in a mixture of Lingala and Kiswahili. Here, in the region of the Mountains of the Moon, the two languages, one from the Congolese interior and the other from East Africa, met each other and developed into a peculiar language of their own.

"We are Sudanese students, you see," I explained as best as I could in my northern Congo Lingala. "We want to go to Tanganyika to look for education. We are refugees and we have no money."

He broke off the conversation at that point. It seemed that people without money were of little use to him. But we persisted in helping him each time the lorry broke down. He understood perfectly well why we were sucking up to him. "Alright," he said at last, "how much money do you have?"

"Fifty francs," I told him with a straight face. It was not exactly true but really, we had very little money left. The days of waiting for Chef de Cabinet in Bunia had eaten into our little reserve of cash.

"You give me your watch," he said.

I walked away. This was the watch given me by my uncle and I never wanted to part with it. I came back to him and told him: "No, I am not giving you, my watch. You can leave us behind if you like."

He walked away, pulling on his cigarette and breathing out smoke with the skill of an experienced smoker. "Ok," he said decisively, "I will take the same amount you gave me for Butembo. Goma is very far". I looked down at my feet and said nothing. He left us standing there and climbed back into the lorry.

The next thing we heard was the revving of the engine and we scrambled up onto the lorry as it moved off. Did he want to leave us in the bush halfway to Butembo? We would never know.

We arrived in Butembo at midnight and parked in front of a shop. There was no electricity in the town. The sky was coldly ablaze with billions of stars. It was very cold because Butembo was at the foothills of the mountain range. We spread one blanket on the floor to lie on and covered ourselves with the other.

The driver woke us up three hours later with the roar of the engine. We picked up our things quickly and went to him. He had switched on the light above him. He did not look at us, but I knew he was waiting. I took out 30 francs and offered it to him. He looked at it and turned away. I added another 20, offered it to him and threw up my arms in desperation, an expression that left no doubt in his mind that I had no more to offer. He took the money, pocketed it and waved us up onto the lorry.

We reached the summit of the range just before sunrise and hurtled down the mountainside. Suddenly there it was in front us:

The expansive beauty of the Rift Valley at sunrise! Immediately left was Lake Mobutu (Lake Edward) and beyond that was Lake Idi Amin (Lake Albert). Further right was Lake Kivu. A silvery stream just below us shimmered brightly in the morning sunrays. Birds of various colours and sizes filled the morning sky over the valley. They were all there: herons, storks, pelicans, ducks and many more. Ibis calls pierced through the noise of the lorry's engine.

We reached the floor of the valley and the driver stopped to smoke before crossing the stream. Birdcalls were magnified by the silence of the engine. Just to the left along the stream was to me the most beautiful sight I had ever seen: a herd of long-horned brown cattle grazing peacefully alongside three grown hippos with a baby we immediately nickname "hippopotamus". On the opposite side of the stream was a group of gazelles and two buffaloes. The more we looked the wilder animals we saw. Apart from the lorry and its passengers there were, curiously, no other people about.

"Who owns these cattle," asked Antiok.

"Over there," one of our fellow passengers pointed towards the hills to the right, "you see those houses over there?" Pointed out, we could just about pick out two tiny stone huts nestling on the side of the mountain. "The owners of the cattle live there", he concluded.

We moved on towards Goma. The valley was lush green with fresh grass and scattered bushes. There was plenty of wildlife along much of the route with human settlements here and there in banana plantations. A few volcanic mountains stood out prominently in the valley. Some were said to be active. We had never seen a volcano before.

We drove into the centre of Goma, the second largest city in Kivu Province. It had beautiful suburbs built on dark rocky soil and ash from volcano deposits.

Left alone in the centre of the city, we began a search for a Church building, close to which there must be a foreign mission with white missionaries. Experience had taught us that the white missionaries were often interested in our case, sympathetic and in a position to help. While most Congolese so far away from the Sudan border might not understand or care to know what was going on in Sudan, we felt confident that foreign missionaries would be aware of what was going on and therefore more sympathetic. We soon located a Catholic Mission Centre.

The centre was enclosed by a high circular wall with many buildings inside. A high metal gate opened into an inner courtyard with gardens of exotic flowers and trimmed grass lawns. A veranda shaded the front of all the doors facing the centre of the circular compound. Some doors were opened while others were shut. Next to each door was a wooden bench that could seat three strangers and five friends. We supposed that was where visitors waited before being called in. A few people moved about in the corridors and between rooms. Many visitors were exiting through the gate as it was getting late in the afternoon.

However, there was a couple sitting on a bench in front of a door. One was a white priest by the way he was dressed and the other a strikingly African woman. She was light brown in colour and had a very long neck. Few Congolese women we had seen thus far had those features. If she were much darker, she could pass for a Jieng woman. We were later to discover that such features were predominantly found in Rwanda, whose border town of Gisenyi was almost a twin-town of Goma; but we did not know that yet.

"What do we do now?" asked Antiok.

"I don't know," I replied, looking in the direction of the priest and the woman. "Maybe we can talk to that priest over there."

The priest and the woman were engrossed in conversation and smiled. We supposed they knew each other very well; yet it looked very strange. Never had we seen a catholic priest so engrossed in conversation with a woman, save perhaps in a confession.

We were suddenly conscious of the way we looked. Our clothes, though still in one piece, were filthy. Our heads were covered with dust picked up from the dirt roads. Nevertheless, we approached the couple. We had to speak to this priest before sunset. The priest and the woman were so engrossed in each other's company that they did not see us until we stood next to the bench. Perhaps they smelled rather than saw us as they suddenly looked up with irritation in their faces.

"What do you want!" the priest yelled at us.

It was not a question that sought to know but to scold. I remembered the time in Kuachjok Elementary School when a friend and I jumped over a fence into the Mission's fruit garden and attempted to help ourselves to very juicy mangoes under the tree. One of the priests there barked and hurled stones at us as we scrambled over the fence. He had reason to be so angry. But we were shocked by the hostility in the eyes of that priest at Goma Mission. I stumbled for words, trying to introduce myself; but he was not having it. He waved us away with his hand and with the single French word-phrase we were familiar with: "Allez! Allez!" He then got up and disappeared behind a door. Left alone, the woman got up and walked out through the main gate. We walked out behind her.

We went to the lakeside where a passenger boat was expected to leave for Bukavu at 8pm. We tried to negotiate down the price, but it was impossible. So, we paid the full fair with almost all the money we had and waited by the ticket office until boarding time at 7pm. We moved on to Bukavu.

Goma: I returned to Goma in November 1996 as an aid-worker/journalist. Although the town had grown like Stanleyville/Kisangani, it had equally been ruined by various wars. The rebels lead by Laurent Kabila and oppose to Mobutu were in the town. The Mission and the beautiful suburbs on the lakeside were either no longer there or not beautiful anymore. Almost all buildings in the town were pockmarked with bullets. Many had their roofs blown off. The walls and corrugated iron roofs were brown with dust or black and green with decay.

Fears had increased about the activities of one of the volcanic mountains not very far from Goma. Japanese experts were recently called in, but their findings were not well publicised.

I tried to go to the airport, but I was stopped by two heavily armed rebels and told to turn back. One of them recognised me as Sudanese and he spoke to me in very good southern Sudanese Arabic. He knew Sudan very well, he said, and had been as far as Khartoum. What was he doing in a Congolese rebel's army or, rather, what was he doing in Sudan? He would not tell.

Goma had been and still was home to millions of refugees since the Rwanda genocide of 1994. Thousands of refugees died there of cholera within a week of crossing over from Rwanda. About a million moved out of the refugee camps when Congolese rebels supported by Rwanda invaded the town early in 1996. The million or so refugees that remained in the camps were threatened with forceful eviction back to Rwanda. "UN and aid agencies are helpless to prevent this," I said then to an Australian TV reporter interviewing me on the main road to the refugee camp west of Goma. We could hear sporadic gunfire coming from the direction of the camps. At a military barrier, we were not allowed to go further west along the road to the refugee camps "for your own security", so a soldier told us.

We returned to Rwanda in the evening but the following day the refugee camps were attack from the north and west which forced the refugees out of the camp through the only exit then left to them: back to Rwanda. The "Exodus" title of my eyewitness report started in the afternoon and continued throughout the night and all the following day.

This Goma was a far cry from the beautiful city of October

1963. But more disaster awaited the town in the shadows of volcanic mountains: In January 2002, Mt Nyiragongo erupted and sent thick red-hot lava through the centre of the town on its way to Lake Kivu, thus burning and smothering everything in its path. No doubt a new Goma will spring up again in the ashes of the old one to await another destruction.

Bukavu

We reached Bukavu early in the morning. With the experience of the day before still fresh in our minds, we decide to seek help from the government. Luckily the department of "Social Affairs" office was located near the port, and we found it quite easily. We waited outside the office until they opened at about 8.30am.

We introduced ourselves at the reception in Lingala. The receptionist did not understand. We tried English but that was no use either. She spoke back to us in Kiswahili or French, languages we did not understand. But she remembered that a student on work experience from the University of Elizabethville (Lubumbashi) had been boasting about his "excellent English." "Un moment," she said and disappeared behind a door and reappearing with a smiling young man in tow.

"How do you do my brothers?" he said, stretching out his right hand in greeting. We were speechless while we shook hands. We had not until then met a Congolese who spoke such good English. "You speak English, don't you?"

"Yes, yes! Indeed, we do," I replied.

"Come, come. Come with me."

We picked up our bags and followed him to his office. While we told him our story, he listened sympathetic and with concern about our condition. "You want something to eat? You must be hungry." We nodded in agreement. He gave the receptionist some money and told her to go to a nearby market to buy some food for us. She soon returned with some fried bananas, sweet potatoes and dried-fish soup cooked in palm oil and cassava leaves. We had by then got used to the Congolese food and tasted delicious.

He told us about the beauty of Elizabethville and his university there as we ate. He told us there was no other city as beautiful as that city in Congo, not even Leopoldville. We told him we wanted to go to Tanganyika, but he told us that it was impossible without passports. We had a vague idea about "passports", but we did not really know who to obtain them from. "You cannot get passports because you are foreigners," he told us. "Go to Elizabethville. I know a lot of people who can help you go to school there."

"How do we go to Elizabethville?" asked Antiok. I looked at him with concern. He knew we wanted to go to Tanganyika, not another Congolese city.

"By boat," said the young man. "You take a boat from Uvira on Lake Tanganyika, you stop at Bujumbura, capital of Burundi, and you stop at Kigoma in Tanzania. Then you proceed to Albertville (Kalemie?) and you take the train to Elizabethville. It is easy and I know a lot of people there who will take care of you."

"But we have no money for the ticket," said Antiok.

"No problem. We can issue you with a student's travel warrant from this ministry. The national corporation buses and boats are obliged to transport students on warrants and claim their money from the ministry of education later.

An idea came to me: while at Kigoma we could miss the boat purposely and then surrender to the Tanganyika authorities. Nyerere was one of the great African leaders we were very proud of way back in Kuachjok Intermediate School. We rhymed the names of African leaders off the top of our heads: "Kwame Nkrumah of Ghana, Julius Nyerere of Tanzania, Jomo Kenyatta of Kenya, Milton Obote of Uganda, Patrice Lumumba of Congo". Curiously for boys who saw

Arabs as our enemies, "Abdel Nasir of Egypt" was always considered as a great African leader. They were all our great heroes, especially Nkrumah and Nyerere. To be so close to Nyerere's country and not be able to go there would be a great disappointment.

"We will go to Elizabethville," I announced, "thank you very much." It was Antiok's time to be alarmed; but I shut him up with a look.

"Well," said the young man, "give me your names. We will take you to a studio for photographs and I will prepare your travel documents. It will take two days."

We then went with him to a photo studio nearby, then on to a student hostel to eat and stay there for the night. We couldn't believe our luck. Bukavu, it seemed, was working out extremely well for us, much better than Bunia. Everybody appeared to be smiling. A very friendly people indeed, so it seemed.

But Antiok was not comfortable with the idea of going on to Elizabethville. He suspected I had a plan and he wanted to know before we retired for the night.

"Actually," I said, "I don't mind learning French if there is a school to go to. Our friend said there would be no problem in finding a school in Elizabethville."

"But I don't want to learn French!" Antiok protested.

"There is something else we can do," I told him, and he wanted to know. "We don't get on the boat again when we stop at Kigoma, then we surrender to the Tanganyikan authorities as refugees after the boat has gone."

Antiok was quiet for a while, then said: "What if they don't allow us off the boat?"

I had not thought of that.

"They can also wait for the boat to return then put us back on it and then back to Congo," said Antiok.

"Well," I said, "how else do you expect us to get into Tanganyika? We will just have to try and hope for the best."

Two days later, we were on an *Otaraco* (a corporation bus) on our way south to Uvira on the north-western shore of Lake Tanganyika, supposedly on our way to the Katangese city of Elizabethville where Lumumba was killed, and his body disappeared.

We arrived at Uvira late in the afternoon and went straight to the port. We were shown the boat but there was no official to talk to. There were many would be passengers milling about. Some appeared to have come from up the country and carried large baskets loaded with goods - mostly food items. They all seemed to have settled down for the night under trees close to the boat. Some women had started fires and were cooking.

We found ourselves a spot and spread one blanket on the floor while we covered ourselves with the other. So, close it seemed to our goal. In two days, we would be in Tanganyika where English was spoken and there was a possibility of our finding a school. We were very tired and fell asleep as soon as we put our heads down.

However, the next day began with really bad news: All the little money we had was stolen during the night while we slept. What would we do for food on the way to Tanganyika? As if that was not enough, the captain of the boat refused to accept the students' travel warrants: "The government never pays. Give me money and I will take you." We implored and begged him, but it was no good. I offered my watch, which I thought was expensive, but he laughed at it. "I wouldn't take it even if you gave it to me free!"

We refused to give up hope until the boat had pulled out of the port and headed east towards Bujumbura. We were suddenly exhausted, tired and dejected.

But we soon recovered and headed into the town, looking out for someone who might be able to help. Soon we saw a Church building and we headed for it.

It was indeed a Catholic Mission but there seemed to be nobody about. So, we sat down by the Church and waited until a worker saw us. We tried to explain what we were looking for, but we did not understand each other's language. So, he indicated with his hands that we follow him.

He pointed at a garage, which we entered and found someone working under a lorry. We made our presence known by talking to each other. A white man, dressed in dirty overalls, emerged from under the lorry and looked enquiringly at us. He looked like those Catholic Brothers who worked for the Catholic Mission in Kuachjok. We addressed him in English, but he clearly did not understand the language. "English no, no understand English," he said and disappeared under the car. We were encouraged. At least he was not unfriendly. We sat down under a tree in the compound and waited for him.

He came by about noon and indicated that we should wait where we were. He went into a building and returned with bread, a can of tinned fish and some water. He gave it to us and somehow managed to convey that someone who knew English had gone to Bujumbura and that we should wait for him.

The English-speaking priest returned in the evening. He listened to our story silently. It seemed that he knew what was going on in Sudan and he seemed sympathetic. He was also amazed at the distances we had covered from Paulis to Bukavu. There was a Simba rebellion going on in the north and there were mercenaries looting towns all over, he said. They were on their way to Stanleyville and possibly to Paulis. We had not heard of the word "mercenaries" before but the news that these looters were heading for Paulis sent a chill through us. What would happen to our colleagues there?

Anyway, the good priest took us in to eat at the same table with them and wanted to know what we were going to do. We told him we would go back to Bukavu and ask the government for cash instead of travel warrants. They put us up for the night and then put us on a lorry back to Bukavu in the morning.

"Come back if you have trouble with the government," the priest told us, "Then we will see what we can do."

Our student friend was surprised to see us back. "What are you doing in Bukavu? What happened?"

We told him everything.

"Well," he said after the end of our story, "we will just have to give you money." He told us that he would talk to the Minister of Social Affairs and ask for money for transport and all that we needed for the journey to Elizabethville. "He is my relative. It may take two to three days, but you will get the money and be on your way."

He took us to "*Foyer des Enfants*". The "*Foyer des Eleves*" where we had stayed for two days was no longer available. He did not tell us why.

"This *foyer* is a play school for children. They start at 10am and close at 4pm. You can stay here tonight. I will find a suitable accommodation for you tomorrow." He gave us a key and some money to buy food from a nearby market.

The *foyer* consisted of a large hall with a cement floor. It was completely empty and appeared to have just been washed clean. Some places were still wet and smelled like soap. There were three side doors. The first led to a kitchen, in which there were a couple of aluminium cooking pots and a few dishes. The second door led to a toilet. The third was locked. We supposed the children's playthings were stored behind that door.

We spread our blankets on the cement floor and went to sleep very early. We felt so tired and disappointed with the way things had turned out.

We got up early in the morning, packed our bags and headed for the Ministry of Social Affairs. The nearest route to the city centre was a footpath that led steeply down to a gully in which ran a small stream following northward to Lake Kivu. The path then rose steeply from the gully and led to the city centre.

It rained almost all night and the footpath appeared muddy, slippery and dangerous. Only surefooted youngsters would dare the path on such a day. Most people were taking the longer tarred road route north and then over a bridge across the stream closer to the lake. We took this route because it took us closer to the lakeside where the Ministry of Social Affairs was located.

Our student friend found us waiting outside the office. He told us to wait nearby, and he did not return until about 2pm. But he seemed very happy, and we assumed that things had gone very well for us. They had.

"Money has been approved for you," he announced and handed me an official-looking document, with a large Ministry of Social Affairs stamped at the bottom of the page. There were three signatures, including that of the minister himself. I looked at the approved figure and smiled. It was a substantial sum that would buy the tickets to Elizabethville and leave enough over for food and other essentials like clothes. I showed it to Antiok and he smiled broadly with delight. We thanked our friend very sincerely.

"It is nothing," he said, "It is nothing. You will have to go to the treasurer tomorrow with this document to receive your money. I will show you where it is now, then take you back to *Foyer des Enfants*. I am sorry I have not had time to find a better place for you today. We will find one tomorrow."

We packed our things again in the morning and headed for the town. This time we took the footpath because it was the direct route to the Treasurer's office, just on the other side of the gully. We were there long before the Treasurer's staff arrived to open the offices and many hours before the Treasurer himself showed up.

Our document was duly stamped as "received" at the reception and then passed on to other minions of the big man with the cash. We waited, expecting to be called in any time. We were called in around noon and told to go away and "come tomorrow." There was no explanation.

We walked to the Ministry of Social Affairs to inform our student friend of progress, only to find that "he returned to Elizabethville this afternoon." Why suddenly and without telling us we will never know.

We still had the key to *Foyer des Anfants* and we returned there early. The children and their mothers were still there. So, we sat outside and waited.

A White priest walked up to us. For the first time we noticed a Church nearby. "You are from Sudan?" This was more like a statement than a question. But we confirmed our identity. He spoke good English and we told him our story. He was not surprised. In fact, he had known about our story from our friend the student, to whom he gave the key to the foyer. *Foyer des Anfants,* we now understood, belonged to the Catholic Church nearby. We could stay there if we liked but we must "vacate for mothers and children during the day. Pack your things and leave them in the kitchen. There is some rice and vegetable oil in the kitchen for you. Are you Catholics? "

We nodded in confirmation. "Well, there is the Church. The services are in Latin and the local language," he said and wished us good night.

We returned to the office of the Treasurer in the morning. We were told by the end of the day that the Treasury was empty, that salaries for the month had not arrived from Leopoldville and the staff had not yet been paid for October. No one was worried yet. It was not the first time it happened. So, we were told to check daily.

We spent the next two weeks between the foyer and the Treasury. With nothing else to do, it all seemed like an eternity. We went to the Church of course on Sundays. The priest called on us now and again just to see if we had rice, salt and vegetable oil. Sometimes he left a portion of tiny dry fish in the kitchen for us to cook.

One day, he came very early in the morning and informed us that "John Kennedy has been assassinated. Come to the Church. We are all going to pray for his soul!" We were visibly shocked by this news, and we hurried behind him to pray for the soul of the President of the United States of America.

I think I know why we felt so shocked by his assassination. Way back in Kuachjok Intermediate School we gathered around the big school radio every evening to listen to the "BBC World Service" recounting of the day's exchanges between Kennedy and Khrushchev during the Cuban missile's crisis. The threat of the atom and the nuclear bombs was very real to us.

"What can you do if you see an atomic bomb coming?" one fearful student asked Gasfred, the headmaster, who often joined us in listening to the BBC. "Kneel down and pray," that was his answer.

Kennedy to us was a good man who, with all the power at his command, refused to use it because he did not want to be responsible for the destruction of the whole world, which included us. In refusing to attack the Soviet missiles next door to America, Kennedy spoke directly to us: he was a good and wise man who cared. His soul deserved praying for and we prayed vehemently.

Praying for Kennedy did not, however, give us the cash we needed from the Congolese treasury. December and Christmas found us in Bukavu.

By mid-January, we were so desperate that we explored ways of returning to Uvira in the hope that our priest friend there might assist us. But we had no money to pay for transport to Uvira and we could not think of anyone to help us. Sometime soon we would have to move on foot towards Uvira and hoped for a lift on the way.

One afternoon we took a walk through the city to eastern Bukavu and took the main road heading out east, just to investigate any alternative route out of Bukavu to Uvira. We soon came to a border post between Congo and Rwanda. We had not realised how close the border was to Bukavu. We could see the Rwandan flag by the gate on the other side of the border. Two Congolese soldiers picked up their guns and looked in our direction. We turned and walked back into Bukavu.

As we walked back, we saw an imposing building with many floors. A sign nearby said it was a college for boys. By impulse, we crossed the road and went in through a tall iron-gate. Once inside, we did not know what to do next. So, we hung around idly.

Suddenly there was noise all around us. Boys of about our age and older poured out of the building and out of the gate into the streets. The college was closing for the day. But quite a good number of students and teachers lingered along the corridors. We saw a white priest talking to someone near a door and we approached and waited at a respectable distance until they had finished talking and began to walk away.

The priest saw us and realised we were strangers and came to talk to us. He understood little English, but he listened patiently to our story. He then told us to write a letter to the principal of the college telling him our story and to bring the letter the following day.

We returned to the foyer, dug out one of the exercise books and composed the letter. As always there was no dispute as to who should write the letter. Being a class ahead of Antiok, plus the fact that I evidently enjoyed reading and writing, lead us to take it for granted that I would always be both the spokesman and thus the writer on this seemingly endless expedition. But there was no electricity for the evening; so, I spent the night composing and tearing up the letter in my head.

But in the morning, I filled four pages of a foolscap exercise book with our story, and we returned to the college. We realised we did not know the name of the priest we had met the day before. So, we hung around for a long time until the priest showed up. We gave him the letter. He took it and told us to follow him. Then he told us to wait by a door, knocked on it and entered after a voice inside answered. He came out a few minutes later with another priest he introduced as the "Principal" of the college. The principal spoke English well and he told us to "see me tomorrow afternoon."

He told us the following afternoon that he had no places at the college for us and that we should not even think about it because we did not know French, the language of instructions at the college. "Have you seen the UNHCR?"

We did not understand what he was talking about.

"The United Nations High Commission for Refugees, that's what it means. Have you been to their office?"

We did not even know such an office existed in Bukavu.

"Well," said the principal, "here is a letter of introduction. Take it to their office tomorrow morning and see if they can do something for you."

We went away disappointed that we could not be admitted to the college but glad about the new information. We sought out the location of the office of the UNHCR before returning to the foyer for the night.

It rained heavily during the night and the footpath was very muddy and slippery. We removed our shoes, as we always did when the path was muddy and slippery, and slid down very carefully, holding to the mud walls of any buildings along the path to steady ourselves.

I was well ahead when I heard a thud and a shriek behind me. I glanced back to see Antiok on his bum and sliding speedily towards me. He ploughed into me, and down we went into the gully next to the stream. It happened so fast. Antiok scratched the back of his head. Above us next to a hut was a scruffy-looking fellow shaking his fist at us and swearing in a strange language. He kept pointing at the wall of his house, indicating that we had destroyed it by holding on to it while sliding down. He threatened to come down; so, we crumbled up to the other side of the ridge as fast as possible and disappeared towards the centre of the city.

We found a big swelling on the back of Antiok's head. The angry man, it appeared, had hit him on the head with a blunt object we did not know what, possibly a stone. Antiok said it was painful but not serious. We went to the lakeside near the UNHCR office and cleaned ourselves of the mud as best as possible. Then we returned to find the office of the UNHCR was still locked, just as well because our clothes, though reasonably free of mud, were soaking wet. We walked around for a bit until our cloths were dry. Then we returned to the UNHCR office.

The office was in one of many buildings in Bukavu built on a steep slope away from the main road down to the lakefront. People working or living in these buildings parked their cars along the main road and walked down many stone steps. I fished out the envelope containing the introductory letter from the college principal to the UNHCR before we climbed down the steps. It was in a reasonable state but needed a bit of airing to dry off the damp. So, we waited at the top of the steps leading to the office.

As we waited, a white woman approached the stairs. She was wearing a beautiful cotton dress covered with red and white spots. She had beautifully shaped legs. Her long blond hair was filed up on the top of her head and that seemed to exaggerate the slenderness of her neck. She wore dark sunglasses and appeared to be in her late twenties. We stood aside and let her pass. She did not even glance at us as she descended. Seen from behind, she even looked smarter.

"That's one pretty woman," I said to Antiok.

"She's beautiful," said Antiok as he glanced back at me. He was surprised at me because it was the first time since we left Sudan, he had heard me pay any compliment to a woman. We stayed up the steps for a while before we realised that maybe she worked for the UNHCR, and it was time we went down anyway. We climbed down the stairs to find the office wide open. We knocked at the door anyway.

"Come in," answered a woman's voice in French from within. She walked out of an inner room as we entered. It was the woman who we had just complimented. Her face without glasses was even more attractive. "What can I do for you?" she said in French.

"We don't speak French," I replied in English.

"But you speak English?" she said in English.

"Yes," I said and handed her the envelope containing the introduction letter from the principal. She opened the letter while still standing and removed a note and two pages of what I recognised to be my handwriting. She read the note very quickly and then concentrated on my letter. She paused at the bottom of the first page and looked at us critically. She then turned the page over and continued reading more intently. She paused again and indicated that we should sit down on two straight chairs at a desk. She then walked around the table, still reading, to the opposite side of the desk and sat down slowly, still reading. She turned the third page and read on, then over. She placed the letter on the table and looked at us critically gain.

"You mean to say that you have come all the way from Sudan?" There was no doubt in her question, just amazement and sympathy.

"Yes, madam, " I replied.

"I am Maria Joseph. Just call me Maria. I am the assistant to the UNHCR representative in Bukavu. You have been here since October, why did you not come to see us?"

"Because we did not know you were here until yesterday," I told her.

"And where are you staying now?" We told her.

"Let's go there." She got up and we followed her out. We got into a four-wheel drive vehicle, and she drove us back to the *foyer*.

The children and their mothers were playing outside in the shade of a tree. We went in and she looked around, shaking her head now and then. "And you have been sleeping on this floor since October?" We did not see why she found it so strange, but we said "yes" to her question. She went into the kitchen and looked around. "And this is the rice you have been eating?" We nodded. "What else?" she asked and added: "Look, I have seen enough! No wonder you are so thin! Pick up your things and come with me. You are not staying here anymore." We picked up our things and followed her to the car.

She took us to a beautiful bungalow with many rooms. She showed us around. There was a large sitting room and a shower with hot and cold water.

"This is the kitchen, with a cooker and a refrigerator but don't worry about that. There is a cook. He will also wash your clothes and you can iron them yourselves - though you look like you don't have any other clothes."

We assured her that we did not have much, and she noted it down on a pad.

We had a room each with a bed, a mattress, two freshly ironed bed sheets and a blanket because it was often cold at night. "The cook will change your bed sheets once a week," she said.

She then introduced us to the cook who had just returned from the market. On discovering that we had just come from northern Congo, he greeted us in Lingala. He himself, he said, came as a young man from Stanleyville.

Maria Joseph told us that there were three other refugees from Rwanda staying at the hostel temporarily. They attended a college nearby. "They should be back in the evening," she said.

She then gave us what seemed like a lot of Congolese francs "for pocket money. Also buy yourselves some clothes and clean up a little. Come back to the office tomorrow at noon. I would like you to meet my boss and see what we can do for you."

She went to the cook and gave him a string of instructions. We did not understand but it sounded like she wanted him to take good care of us. She then went back to her car and waved at us as she drove away.

Left alone, we were suddenly speechless. It seemed like a nightmare replaced by a dream. The cook brought us back to earth as he called us to the table for tea and biscuits half-coated with chocolate. We devoured the biscuits before drinking tea. We were that hungry.

We showered, wrapped a towel each around our waists and washed all the clothes we had. We each had a faded khaki uniform (a pair of shorts and a shirt) from Kuachjok and another pair of shorts and a shirt bought with my wages from the coffee plantation. Each also had two pairs of underpants and two vests.

In towels, we sat on the cool veranda of the bungalow and watched our clothes dry on a line in the back garden. Except for the khaki uniforms, all the other clothes had holes in them and showed critical signs of disintegration. The underwear and vests were not only in tatters, but the dirt in them also seemed immune to soap. They looked terribly spotty with dark marks all over. Now that we had money they could be happily discarded.

The clothes dried within an hour. We gathered them in and ironed them on the veranda with an electric iron, the first time we had used such an instrument. It felt so clean and smooth, but it did nothing to improve the dirty look of the underwear lot. If anything, it highlighted the underlying grime. We put them in a dustbin.

We counted the cash left behind by Maria Joseph. It would have taken me at least five weeks in the coffee plantation to earn this "pocket money!" How could things change in a single day? The very cloudy morning had now turned into a bright afternoon. We put on our freshly ironed and clean-smelling clothes, without the underpants, and strolled into downtown Bukavu in late afternoon. We felt good with cash in our pockets. We bought some underpants and a few other clothes and returned to the hostel for an excellent dinner of fried steak and rise.

We reported to Maria Joseph in the morning in our old uniforms now washed and ironed. She was impressed: "What a transformation! You look great. You will have to eat a little more though. You look terribly bony. What did you eat this morning?"

We told her but she continued with more questions about what we had eaten previously for lunch and dinner. At last, she changed the subject to that of her boss: "He went to Bujumbura this morning. We have an emergency there. What are your plans now? What would you like to do?"

"We would like to go to school," I told her.

"That's good, but you know you can't go to school here without French?"

"Yes, but we can learn," I said.

"I know you can. What about your idea of going to Tanganyika, have you abandoned that?"

"Of course not," I said. The reason we had not brought up Tanganyika was that we despaired at the thought of the difficulties and the suffering we had gone through thus far in our attempts to get there.

"Well," said Maria, "I have friends here who have connections in Tanganyika. I will see what they can do for you. Meanwhile, what would you like to do?"

"Have you any books in English that we can read?" I asked.

"Yes," she said, "and I can do better than that. Come with me. I will introduce you to the American Library."

She walked with us to the library, which was very close to the UNHCR office.

Apart from Kuachjok Intermediate School's little collection of books, which we thought was extensive, we had never seen a real library before. Two big rooms full of books from floor to ceiling! I could lose myself here, I told myself. I think Maria Joseph and the lady librarian, an African American lady, had just gathered that. "Well," said the librarian in a very strange English accent - first time meeting an American - "you can come here any time during the day and stay as long as you like from 9am to 5pm. This section here is English. Plenty for you to read."

For the next three weeks, our lives seemed to rotate between our residence and the library. Maria Joseph saw us almost every day, either in the library or in the house. She seemed very pleased with our progressing health and interest in learning. Sometimes she indicated that she was expecting to hear something soon from her friends about Tanganyika, but sometimes she seemed to despair.

When we mentioned the Congolese Ministry of Social Affairs and the money, they said we could get cash from the treasurer. She confirmed what we already knew to be the truth: "You will never get any money out of them," she said. "They can't even pay their staff. Forget it." So, we dropped it.

"I don't know what will happen to you if you don't go to school. I would very much like to see you go to school in East Africa where you will not have to worry too much about learning a new language of instruction. You seemed to have had a very good education back home because of the level you say reached."

We could only smile at her appreciation because we believed we had had a very competitive educational background that had pushed our grades above normal. Anyway, the more we knew her the more we became fond of her. Her concern for us had won our full confidence in her. We felt we could tell her anything. We also liked to think that she personally liked us; that we were not just business, but her little project.

As days went by, Antiok's interest in reading began to wane. Often, I went alone because Antiok thought "it is too early" or "I have something to do. I will come tomorrow." Often, I returned to the house and Antiok was not there. He came in sometimes at about 9 pm and sometimes even later. When I asked him where he had been he would say he had been exploring.

One evening he returned to the house in a terrible rush and in his underpants.

"What happened to your clothes?" I asked. He mumbled

something and rushed to his room. I followed him in. "What happened to your clothes?" I asked again while standing at the door. He was busy putting on a pair of shorts and a shirt, so I waited.

"That woman! She took my clothes!"

"What woman?" I was completely puzzled. I had no idea what he was talking about.

"The woman in the kiosk," he said.

That rang a bell. There was a kiosk nearby. Often, we stopped there to buy Fanta or Coca-Cola. A little woman in the kiosk sold them and she smiled a lot at Antiok.

I looked at Antiok. Back home we would be men, not boys, and chasing unmarried girls was indeed a challenging exercise for all young men, no matter how limited their chances of ever sleeping with them, leave alone getting married to them. But certain rules, based on the consequences of being caught having sex governed the relationship between young people. In towns, our own included, those rules had broken down considerably and the line between prostitution, lust and real love became very thin indeed. My immediate assumption and reaction to Antiok's revelation was that he had been sleeping with prostitutes.

"You have been sleeping with prostitutes? What if you get disease?"

"I did not know she was a prostitute!" he protested.

"So, what happened?"

"She wanted money, and I didn't have any. So, she took my clothes and hid them. She will not give them back to me unless I pay her."

"What happened to your pocket money?"

"I don't have any left. Any way those clothes are very old, and I don't want to give her money for them. Let her keep them."

That was true. He was wearing the clothes he had bought in Paulis with my money. They were not as tough and of as good material as the Sudanese khaki because they were already falling apart. I let it drop but it gave me an idea how Antiok had been spending his days and evenings and why he was always short of money.

One day, Maria Joseph arrived at the house early in the morning. I heard the tyres of her vehicle on the gravel outside and I met her at the door. She was bubbling with infectious excitement: "Look, look, Yakob! See what I have got!" She held up a piece of paper. "It is a letter from a college in Tanganyika. You have been accepted. Isn't that brilliant!"

I took the letter from her and read it. Antiok was looking over my shoulder. "I can't believe it!" I said, "thank you very much!"

She hugged both of us with tears in her eyes. "There is nothing I can't do to see you boys back in school."

"So, when are we going?" asked Antiok enthusiastically. I wondered why but I thought he wanted to get away from the wrath of the woman he had jilted; but I said nothing of the sort in the presence of this good woman.

"Ha," said Maria Joseph, "you just wait till you hear my brilliant plan." She called the cook and asked for tea as we settled down on the veranda. "You see, tomorrow my boss and I are going to Bujumbura. We have agreed that we will take you as our servants over the border, then we will leave you in Bujumbura with people at the Catholic Mission there. Their Mission runs the school in northern Tanganyika near the border with Burundi. They will take you over the border without any problem. Isn't that brilliant?"

There was no doubt in our minds that her plan was excellent. So, we got ourselves geared up for the trip in the morning to Bujumbura.

However, Maria Joseph arrived very early in the morning. I had just come out of the shower and Antiok was still in it. I met her at the door. One look at her face told me everything: Things had not worked out as planned. "I am sorry, Yakob, very, very sorry! My boss says we cannot take you because the UNHCR could be accused of transporting refugees illegally over international borders. He is right of course. How stupid of me not to have thought about that!"

I was speechless. So, I looked down at my feet, completely overwhelmed by disappointment. It made Maria Joseph feel even worse. With tears in her eyes, she hugged me as we stood in the open door, shedding tears on each other's shoulders. Antiok came out of the shower, saw us at the door and wondered what was going on. By the time he had dressed and came out, Maria Joseph was gone, trusting me to explain things to Antiok as best as I could.

"I trust you!" that's what she said when she departed. "Explain things to Antiok. Don't do anything stupid. You must trust me too. I will sort things out when I return from Bujumbura tomorrow."

"What is going on?" asked Antiok guardedly as he saw me sitting with my head between my hands.

"We are not going to Tanganyika," I told him what Maria Joseph had told me.

"So, what are we going to do?"

"We wait for Maria Joseph to come back. She will sort it out. That's what she said."

"Maybe we should just go to Tanganyika ourselves and look for that school," he suggested.

"How?"

"We walk. Maybe someone will give us a lift on the way."

I took a few seconds to think about this; then I retrieved the old Congo map from my room. It included parts of East Africa, including the whole of Rwanda, Burundi and north-west Tanganyika. "We could take this route to Rwanda and then to Tanganyika or go through Burundi to north-western Tanganyika," I traced the route with my finger. "That's where the school is."

We were already packed, so we hit the road, following the road we had taken when the soldiers on the Congolese side of the border had taken interest in our approach. We reasoned that since we were evidently not Congolese, they would not stop us from leaving their country.

We were a bit worried though about Rwanda. Since we had moved to the bungalow, we had heard a lot more about the war in Rwanda. Hutus were killing Tutsis and the latter were crossing over to Congo. The refugees who shared the house with us were Tutsis. They were tall and lanky, just like the Jieng; but they were very brown like the girl we saw in Goma with the priest. Their war seemed unlike ours. Theirs was tribe against tribe. Ours was Africans against Arabs. Two different wars altogether.

Yet Rwanda was a stones-throw from Bukavu. Since we had moved to this house so close to the border, we heard gunfire every night coming from across the border we were now heading to. The Rwandan town on the other side of the border was called Cyan Gugu. We thought it was a lovely name, probably a lovely town too because we could see beautiful houses on the cliff over the border from the Congolese side. People over there walked casually on a road along the lake, just like they did in late afternoon on the Congolese side of the border. It looked so peaceful.

At the Congolese side of the border, however, the border guards laughed at what they thought was our idea of crossing to Rwanda without documents. On discovering that the UNHCR was responsible for us in Bukavu, they phoned them, and someone there instructed them to detain us until someone came to collect us. So, we stayed at the border all day until 5.45pm when someone came from the UNHCR and took us back to the house.

The white man who picked us up told us that "Maria Joseph will come to see you at about noon tomorrow. She will be back then from Bujumbura." He drove away.

We still had the keys to the house and our rooms, having forgotten to leave them behind in the morning. The cook and the Rwandans were nowhere to be seen. Just as well because we did not want to have to explain to anyone who would like to know about our day. We also wanted to review the events of the day and make plans for our next move.

We wondered about the white man who had picked us up from the border. Who was he? Our relations with the UNHCR had always been conducted entirely with Maria Joseph. As far as we were concerned the UNHCR in Bukavu was Maria Joseph. We had never had any reason to look for anyone else in that office. She had everything: charms, understanding and care. We trusted her 100%. In doing so we had perhaps overrated her ability to move mountains. Now it seemed that there was somebody called "Boss" that we had never met but could derail her best plans. Well, we had come thus far, and no one was going to stop us from reaching Tanganyika; our resolved was absolute.

In the morning, neither the cook nor the Rwandans were anywhere to be seen. The absence of the Rwandans was understandable. They usually disappeared to college early in the morning and came back late. They also disappeared at weekends. They lived their own lives and we ours. Rarely did we communicate since there was no common language.

We wondered about the cook though; but then, this was a weekend and maybe he had gone home to the country to see his people, his family. He told us once he had a family in the village. People like him always had a family somewhere, usually in the village where it was cheaper to live. Live chickens had been turning up recently in our back garden and the cook slaughtered them one by one during the week for our meat. Tough meat but delicious to eat in fried onions and salt. We believed he brought the chicken from his village because they always turned up after the weekend the cook was not around. It was cheaper to buy them from the village than in the city market.

Maria Joseph arrived back from Bujumbura much earlier than was expected. She came to see us at the house after a brief stop in her house and had probably updated on our Friday escapade. She found us sitting on the veranda.

"So, you slept in the house? How did you get in?"

We looked at each other, wondering what she was talking about.

"We have keys," I told her. "How was your trip to Bujumbura?" I asked, though I was not really interested.

"It went very well," she said and then looked away towards the hills on the other side of the border.

"Look Yakob, Antiok, I am sorry about what happened yesterday morning with my boss. I understand your getting upset with me and I totally understand why you tried to leave Congo. You have been in Bukavu for a long time, and I can understand your frustration. In the end of course it will be what you decide to do that will make a difference but give me a chance to try again. You must be patient with me." She concluded with a bright smile. We smiled back. "Friends again?" she asked still smiling charmingly. We nodded.

Maria Joseph then explained to us that the landlord wanted the house evacuated on Friday. The UNHCR had requested another week, but the man ignored the request and kicked everyone out just before we returned last night. Luckily for us we were not in the house and so we were missed. Luckily still we forgot to leave the keys behind.

"I have friends you can stay with for a few days, maybe a week. By then I will have sorted out something. Pack your things and I will take you there."

It was a Catholic Mission residence. As usual the mission buildings were encircled with a brick wall while the buildings inside faced an inner courtyard. There were three residents in that compound, all of them from Switzerland as we later found out. Perhaps that was where Maria Joseph came from, but we never really bothered to find that out for sure. There was no need to know.

The priests knew very little English, but they appeared to welcome us all the same. It seemed that Maria Joseph had done a good a job of explaining our case to the priests and they appeared to have no interest in knowing more about us. We ate with them in the evening, and we said very little to each other. They seemed aloof and cold.

Antiok and I shared a room, and we discussed a lot of things. We had learnt at least one important thing on this journey: being useful. So, in the morning we offered to cut the grass and weed the flower border in the compound. Suddenly the priests' attitudes warmed up a bit.

Five days later, Maria Joseph turned up unannounced for dinner. It was the first time since we met that we had not seen her for so long. We were very pleased to see her, and we babbled away with questions about our future. But she was guarded with her answers, either because there was something important, she wanted to reveal later or because there was nothing important to tell us. Or perhaps it was because the priests were present?

After dinner, Maria Joseph announced: "There is a school between Bukavu and Uvira. This Mission," she said indicating the two priests at the table, "runs it for Rwandan refugees. It is a good school and I believe you boys can learn French very quickly there and will be able to follow instructions. What do you think?"

We were silent for a minute or so, thinking it over. No one was rushing us. Coffee was being served. Meanwhile I looked at Antiok for inspiration, but he registered a blank expression on his face. I must say I liked the idea of going to school, no matter what school. I also thought that we could learn French very quickly if forced to do so by lack of other languages to resort to. "Well," I said to Maria Joseph but looking at Antiok, "it is better to be in school than stay around here, don't you think?"

Antiok nodded his head in agreement.

"That's settled then," said Maria Joseph. "One of the Fathers here will take you to the school tomorrow morning. I will of course continue to find ways of getting you to the school in northern Tanganyika."

Before departing, she embraced us and said goodbye. "I will see you soon," she said and exited very quickly. That was the last time we saw Maria Joseph. We left for the Rwanda refugee school early in the morning.

The school for Rwandan refugees, in fact a school for Tutsis, was situated about six miles from the main Bukavu-Uvira road, almost half way between the two towns. The students and teachers were all Tutsis and entirely male. There were no women at the school or anywhere that I could see. There was nothing strange about that. All the Sudanese refugees I had met thus far in Congo were males. The reason was that at the early stage of the war in Southern Sudan, only educated Southern Christians, who were mostly males, were targeted. I did not know the reason for the absence of women among the Rwandan refugees. Perhaps they were somewhere nearby.

The school was new and appeared to have been recently carved out of the bush. It was built with local materials: wood, stone, mud and straw grass. It looked isolated amongst many hills and surrounded by virgin bush.

For breakfast, lunch and dinner we ate kidney beans and rice, kidney beans and rice and kidney beans and rice. Perhaps there would be a variety by the end of the season. We woke up early in the morning and started clearing and planting the new farms with beans and groundnuts, stalks of cassava and sweet potatoes. Then we ate kidney beans and rice for breakfast and went to classes.

Antiok and I learned French in a separate room while the Rwandan students attend normal classes. We did not know whether this was an intermediate or secondary school; but that did not matter yet because our French was still very poor.

Two of the teachers who took turns to teach us French spoke good English and they told us a bit more about themselves and the reasons they were refugees. I was very impressed by the teachers' dedication to their children and cause. Many of them, we were informed, were university graduates who could find jobs anywhere around the world; but had decided to stay in the refugee camp to teach their children.

The teachers were very friendly and very patient with us. After ten days of learning French, I began to feel as if I was getting somewhere. The language that sounded so strange in my ears began to make sense. The gibberish words heard in passing over the previous twelve months began to make sense and sounded attractive. I was beginning to like the French language. For the first time I was beginning to feel that I could get on with my education there in Congo and I made that known to Antiok.

But Antiok had other ideas: "Do you remember what the priest in Uvira told us when we were there?"

I remembered very well. He told us to come back if we found no help in Bukavu. "Come back and I will see what I can do," he had said.

"I think we should go and see if he can help us go to Tanganyika. I don't like French."

"What if we go there and he is not there or unable to help us and we have left this school, what then?"

"I don't know," said Antiok.

We discussed the matter further. In the end we came up with a compromise: Antiok was to go to Uvira to see the priest. I would remain behind to explain why Antiok had gone to Uvira. So, he left very early in the morning for the main road and hitched a lift on a lorry. He came back the following afternoon and told me what the priest had said: "Come."

We said goodbye to our Rwandan friends after twelve days in their school. We left a "thank you" note for Maria Joseph and the Swiss priests and walked to the main road to look for transport to Uvira.

The priest was as good as his word. The following morning, we boarded a steamer from Uvira with a ticket to Albertville. Only then could we be allowed to travel to the ports of Bujumbura in Burundi and Kigoma in Tanganyika.

"One last piece of advice," said the priest as we boarded, "stay on the boat at Bujumbura. Do not disembark. From afar you look like Tutsis. They shoot first over there and ask questions later."

Bukavu: I returned to the border from the Rwandan side in 1997 when Laurent Kabila, with the help of Rwanda and Burundi Tutsis, had heightened his rebellion against Mobutu. As an aid-worker/journalist, I had come on the dangerous and often barred-to-journalists road between the towns of Kibuye on the north-eastern shore of Lake Kivu and Cyangugu on the south-eastern shore. We heard the night before from the governor of Kibuye blood-curling stories of massacres in1994 of Tutsis and Hutu moderates by Hutu extremists in both Kibuye and Cyangugu. The tea plantations along the eastern shore of Lake Kivu and along the route between the two towns was still infested with "Hutu rebels", he warned, "but we will make sure you get to the displaced people's camps along the road."

Cyangugu looked grim. Most houses there had bullet and shell holes, some old some fresh. Some destruction might have dated back to the 1960s when I was in Bukavu on the other side of the border. Much of the recent damage was from fire directed at the town from over the border in Bukavu. Like when I could not get across to Cyangugu from Bukavu in 1964, I could not get over to Bukavu from Cyangugu in 1997. There was civil war 1964 in Rwanda. There was civil war in Congo in 1997. Two different wars; but were they really?

Uvira: I returned to Uvira in 1998 on a chartered relief flight from Nairobi via Goma, the "headquarters" of the rebels against Laurent Kabila. Though cleared by rebel leaders in Goma as required, the rebel soldiers at the dirt airstrip, about ten miles north of Uvira, would not allow us into the town or let our plane leave "because we have not been informed about your coming". We eventually persuade them to let two colleagues go into the town to talk to their boss. The rest of the team got a message later to go into the town, but the leader of the rebels at the airstrip would not let the plane take off as was planned. The pilot decided to spend the night on the plane at the airstrip, a very dangerous place because it was isolated and aid workers had been killed a few weeks earlier by Burundi Hutu rebels near this airstrip. The pilot would not leave his aircraft alone with the rebels as guards because he could not trust them.

We went to town and tried to assess the needs of the displaced Congolese population. Most of them were in transit, purportedly in the hope of catching a boat to Kalemie (former Albertvillle) but planning to disembark at the Tanzanian port of Kigoma as refugees, a trick Antiok and I had tried 34 years earlier. Good luck to them.

But our problem with the rebel's administration in Uvira was not yet over. We were told in the morning that we would not be allowed to leave Uvira until Bukavu, the capital of Southern Kivu where Uvira was located, gave permission. World Food Programme (WFP) representative used their radio in Uvira to communicate with their office in Bukavu. But WFP in Bukavu was told by the rebels that they did not take instructions from Goma, the administrative capital of North Kivu. So, they got in touch with their office in Nairobi which got in touch with our office (World Vision's) in Nairobi which got in touch with our office in Kigali which got in touch with the Rwandan government in Kigali which got in touch with Bukavu which got in touch with Uvira. By mid-afternoon, the international relief and the UN network was fully mobilised on our behalf: "The Congolese rebels are holding expatriate relief workers prisoner in Uvira," so circulated the message. The whole world would know about us in the next twenty-four hours and the rebels would lose international sympathy for their cause.

We received a message of release late in the afternoon, but the travel documents we received in Goma in lieu of our passports were locked up in the office of a senior rebel leader who was nowhere to be found. They broke in but the relevant documents were not there. The boss, now worried about himself in case we didn't depart as instructed by Bukavu, commandeered one of WFP four-wheel drive vehicles to search for his assistant all over the town. But he had no luck. In the end he was forced to issue a hand-written document explaining that our Goma documents had been misplaced by his office, that we should be allowed to return to Goma and retrieve our passports as planned. We were very doubtful about the authority of such a document. But it allowed us to take off from Uvira airstrip with the runway in half darkness, we entered Kigali (Rwanda) for a night in a hotel and had allowed us to leave Rwanda for Goma in the morning there to retrieve our passports and depart for Nairobi. But I still think that the publicity of our case was a lot more authoritative than the note from a minor rebel leader in Uvira.

As for Uvira itself, it had been almost destroyed by repeated battles over the years, not least by the latest one between Kabila and his former allies.

In and Out of Tanganyika (now Tanzania)

We stayed on board in Bujumbura. Burundi port security and the steamer immigration personnel came on board to check our travel documents. They looked at us suspiciously for a few seconds, checked our tickets and disembarked.

We travelled all night along the eastern side of Lake Tanganyika and docked at Kigoma early in the morning. We disembarked, showing our onward tickets back to Congo, to Tanganyika's immigration officers and they let us into the town, just like other passengers in transit. The boat departed at about noon while Antiok and I hid in the corner of a market.

We revealed ourselves to the authorities late in the afternoon, long after the boat had gone. A police officer escorted us to the office of the District Immigration Officer in Kigoma. We told him we were refugees from Southern Sudan on our way to a school not very far from the town. We handed him the letter of acceptance from the Catholic school in the district, believing that such a letter would make him look kindly at our wilful missing of the boat, but no.

"Do you realise that you have broken Tanganyika's immigration laws! How dare you come into Tanganyika just like that without official documents? This letter is rubbish!" he tore it up. "You stay here until the boat returns tomorrow. We will put you back on it to Uvira." He then locked us in his office and told a policeman to make sure we did not escape. He got into a Land Rover and drove off.

Left alone in the office that was getting darker and darker with the fading daylight, we were confused and frightened. The idea of being forced back to Congo while so close to a school that would take us was particularly devastating to our hopes of ever getting an education in an English-speaking country. It made our long efforts to get to East Africa totally meaningless and disabling. Although we had some tinned corn-beef, hunger seemed to have vanished.

We tried to talk ourselves to sleep on the concrete floor of the office, but sleep was impossible. The evening was very hot, and the mosquitoes were on the attack in the darkness. The policeman was at the door because we could hear him slap himself now and again; we knew he was like us being eaten alive by mosquitoes.

The immigration officer let us out at about 8.30 in the morning but told the police officer to keep us nearby and to make sure we did not escape. He kept coming out of his office, looking at us as if we were rotten eggs, disappearing for an hour or so, then returning and looking at us again. Something about us was giving him a headache.

We opened the can of corn-beef and ate it while we kept our ears open for the boat. No boat came. He called us into his office at

3.30pm and told us that we were to be taken to Dar es Salaam, the capital. "If it were left to me, I would return you to Congo!" he said and called in the police officer who had been guarding us. "You take them to Dar es Salaam on the train this evening. You must hand them over to the central police station there. Here," he took some money out of his pocket, "buy some food for them before boarding the train." He waved us out of his office. I never could understand his hostility.

Our moods changed suddenly from misery to excitement. Not only were we going to a national capital and the biggest city we had ever seen, but we were also going by train, the first time to see one and travel on it. We travelled all night, stopping in small and large towns along the route. People came out even very late at night to sell food and other goods to passengers through opened windows. Our police guard bought some peanuts and fried bread and gave us some to eat. He was neither friendly nor hostile: just watchful.

Three policemen met us at Dar es Salaam Railway Station and, after a short talk with our escort from Kigoma, they put us in a windowless police van, and we drove away. A short while later we alighted in an enclosed police station, unable to see what was going on beyond the walls of the compound. One of the policemen told us to sit on a bench next to an open door; and there we remained for much of the day. Policemen came in with people they had arrested, took them in through the door and took them away again. We expected to be called in for questioning, but nothing happened.

A policeman came with food at about 4pm. I asked him what would happen to us, but he did not know. "I don't know," he said, "you wait."

So, we waited.

At 7pm, a policeman took us around a corner of a building in the same compound and locked us up in a small cell behind the building. "Someone will sort out your case tomorrow."

But other than being fed twice a day in the morning and early evening, nothing much happened for three more days. We were just about getting very desperate when an official-looking man in civilian clothes came in to see us. He found us sitting on our usual bench in front of the door.

After a few questions about our identity and the reasons for being in Tanganyika, he heaved a sigh: "Have you told the police what you are telling me?"

"Yes," I said, "we told them we were from Sudan, but they did not ask any more questions."

"That was the message we got from the police and nothing more," said the man. " Then we got a message this morning about you from the immigration officer in Kigoma. I am from the immigration office here in Dar es Salaam. They should not have locked you up here at the police station. I don't know who gave them orders."

He then turned his attention to a senior police officer standing by the door: "You know you should not have kept these boys in detention for four days without telling us? You will hear from the minister about this. Come with me."

We picked up our bags and followed him out of the police station.

He took us into a small hotel just behind the police station and gave instructions in Kiswahili to the manager/owner. "He will give you a room to share and food tonight and tomorrow morning. I will come for you at ten o'clock tomorrow morning. You are the responsibility of UNHCR."

My attention was caught by a view of the Port of Dar es Salaam: the giant ships moored alongside towering cranes, the wide lagoon and the open sea beyond it. It was more than I could have imagined the ocean to look like. I noticed Antiok's gazing at the same scene. "Is that the Indian Ocean?" I ask absentmindedly.

"What? Oh," said the man from the immigration office, "that's the Indian Ocean. Never seen an ocean before? But Sudan's on the Red Sea! Anyway, I will see you tomorrow."

"Come. I will show you your room then you can go and see the ocean if you like," said the hotel manager.

We were soon out of the hotel and dodging cars on the road between the hotel and the quay on our way to the beach. A long sturdy stone wall separated the sea from the road and the pavement along which many people, mostly Indians, were walking up and down at a leisurely pace. We would soon come to know that these evening walks by the ocean were a regular habit for many Indian families in the city.

For that moment, however, our attention was almost totally claimed by the wonders of the ocean: the gentle slapping and hissing of the seawater over a beach of shingles. The roar of the distant waves in the open sea thundered over the port. We went down cobbled steps to the beach and watched gentle waves coming in and out like a living thing.

Three noisy boys came down the same steps, discarded their clothes and jumped into the ocean, diving and yelling at each other as they surfaced. Antiok and I looked at each other, discarded our shoes and clothes and tested the water first with our toes, then feet. It was lovely and warm, a cooling feeling in the very hot and humid atmosphere of Dar es Salaam. We dived, surfaced and yelled at each other just like the other boys.

"It is all salt!" I shouted my discovery to Antiok.

"It is all salt," he shouted back at me.

We move to a shallower spot. "I knew the sea water was salty," said Antiok, "but I didn't know it was so salty you couldn't drink it."

I told him, "I have read stories in which people died of thirst in the ocean."

Out of the water and dressed, I discovered that my watch was not ticking. I took it off my wrist and examined it. The water had found its way into the watch. I tried to shake it off; then tried to wind it up. The winding knob snapped off, a sad end to my long-cherished property.

The immigration man came in the morning and took us by car out of the city to an expansive refugee camp called Mungulani, a few miles south-east of Dar es Salaam. More than a thousand refugees lived in the camp. They came mostly from South Africa and Mozambique. Among the refugees were a few southern Sudanese who had come to Tanganyika via Uganda or Kenya. The Sudanese were almost entirely Jieng, among them a young man called Mathew Mading Riak, who claimed he had been "flying jets" in the Ethiopian Airforce.

Mathew was short by Jieng standards, but he made it up with his enormous ego. To listen to Mathew was to witness a man in total self-possession.

"I am going to America. I am going to fly JETS!" he said with special emphasis on the word "jets".

When he walked, he swaggered in carefully calculated steps the Jieng associate with the word "*atheng*", a complex term, referred to in an earlier chapter but may be taken here to mean "a Jieng gentleman, weighed down by dignity."

We liked Mathew immediately we met him. He was funny and seemed to know a lot about aeroplanes and Americans. "They eat wheat," Mathew announced, "that's why they are big and clever." The Americans, he told us, were "my tutors in Ethiopia when I was flying JETS!"

There was an "African American Institute" just across the road from the refugee camp. Antiok and I went there on the second day at the camp to see the Principal, an African American. On the third day we were given a test in Maths, English and General Science at the level we told them we were at when back in Sudan. I found the test very easy, and this was borne out by the results two days later: English 100%, Maths 98% and General Science 97%.

I was very pleased with the results; so was the principal. "If it were up to me," he said, "I would admit you at once, but we have to wait for your permit to remain in Tanganyika. This is a government requirement before any refugee is admitted. But you can use the library whenever you like."

I went to school every weekday after breakfast to use the library for the next five weeks. Often, I stayed there all day until the school closed. Sometimes Antiok came to the library with me but left early, often to go to town with Mathew. Some evenings they disappeared together, not telling me where they were going. Soon they began to converse in jargons, speaking about things they had experienced together. I felt left out and wanted to know what was going on, where they went to some evenings. I thought they went out drinking in the local township not very far from the camp; but why the secrecy I sensed?

"We go to visit some friends," Mathew explained unconvincingly. "Antiok says you would not like them."

Still thinking that he was talking about drinking friends I told him that I had nothing against drinking. "It is just that all these bottled beers don't taste like beer. Give me Jieng brewed beer and I will drink it." They looked at each other and then looked at me doubtfully.

In the evening, however, they invited me to come to the township. The first house we came to we stood outside, and Mathew whistled to make our presence known. No one came to see us. In the next house, we could see by moonlight four women sitting in the centre of the compound of two huts. "*Karibu*," (welcome) they said in chorus as soon as we stopped moving on. "*Karibu, Karibu*," they all called. We waited where we were. One woman got up, walked up to us and took Mathew's hand, "*Karibu*," she cooed and led him straight into one of the huts.

Another woman got up and walked up to Antiok and I. "I am out of here," I said to Antiok and walked away. It was now clear to me what it was all about, sleeping with prostitutes. Antiok remembered my reaction to his misadventure in Bukavu. No wonder he had been so secretive. He caught up with me and we returned to the refugee camp.

Anyway, no more was said about the matter in the following days. Mathew and Antiok probably thought me a coward and they were right. I feared catching a sexual disease because I had never got over the ordeal of my half-brother, Atem Langel, with sexual disease that almost made him impotent and almost killed him during his long treatment. The possibility scared me to death and the two of them left me out of their evening adventures in the township; but they continued looking healthy.

One day, Antiok and I were sitting in the shade of a tree in the compound of the refugee camp when three South African refugee girls walked towards us. Antiok got up and hurried away into the house where we lived. One of the South African girls ran after him and Antiok disappeared behind the door. The girl, swearing obscenities after Antiok, returned to me. "You tell your friend, if I catch him I will cut off his testicles. I will kill him! He is a coward! Tell him that." She looked tough and I have no doubt that Antiok would find her a tough nut to crack. "He may kill you instead," I told her. They laughed and walked away.

"Why does she want to kill you?" I asked Antiok later.

"Who? That South African girl? Her name is Willarmie. She is crazy. I have done absolutely nothing. I only asked her if she would like to be my friend and she goes crazy." That was all I ever got out of Antiok regarding Willarmie.

I left Mathew and Antiok to spend their time the way they thought fit and I continued to go to the institute while hoping my residence permit would come soon so that I could attend classes. The principal himself was getting fed up with the waiting. So, he told me one afternoon to "come to classes tomorrow. I am admitting you with or without the permit."

I told Antiok and Mathew the good news of my admission to the institute, but they were not really interested.

I made special efforts to brush myself up in the morning and wandered across the road to the institute with other refugees attending the school. The principal welcomed me into a class he thought appropriate for me. I didn't really care what class it was because I was confident that my true level would soon be self-evident. I was just happy to be in a real classroom once again with English as the language of instruction. My confidence was overflowing.

Two hours later, however, I was called out of the classroom and told to go back to the refugee camp because we were wanted by the government ministry responsible for residence permits in Tanganyika. My anxiety level rose higher and higher as I walked towards Mathew and Antiok as they waited for me at the camp. It could be that our permits to stay in Tanganyika were ready or it could be the unthinkable. Either way the suspense was unbearable.

We got into a police van like the one that met Antiok and I at the railway station. Mathew told us that he did not think there was good news waiting for us. "You know the Sudanese Minister for Foreign Affairs (an Arab he noted) was here for two days last week. Maybe he has made a deal with the government of Tanganyika to have us returned to Khartoum. Other Southern Sudanese in schools in this country have been brought back to Dar es Salaam."

Fifteen of us were arraigned before the person we rightly assumed was the minister responsible for refugee residence permits in Tanganyika. He was dressed in an expensive dark suit with a blue shirt and a red tie. He was in a massive chair with his black-shoes-and-red shocked-feet resting on a glittering desk while conversing gaily with someone on the telephone. We remained standing while he joked and laughed with the person on the other end of the line. At last, he replaced the telephone, took his feet off the top of the desk, leaned forward and, with a severe expression surveyed our faces one by one. "Why are you in Tanganyika? What is wrong with Sudan?"

"Your Excellency," said Mathew, "you know there is a war going on there and the Christians are being persecuted by the Moslems."

"Nonsense," said the minister, "Moslems are peace-loving people. We have them in this country, and they never fight with anyone. How come they are different in Sudan?"

"Because they are Arabs," said Mathew with emotion in his voice.

"So, they are Moslem and Arabs? That's what makes them persecute Christians? Do you know what I think? You are being deceived by imperialists who promise you an independent Southern Sudan. They do not like any talk of African unity. Divide and rule, that's their policy. You Southerners are causing all sorts of problems for the Sudan. Sudan will never be divided. No country in Africa will ever be divided! You are ordered to leave Tanganyika within two weeks! If you are still here at the end of that time, we will deport you back to Sudan!"

He called in his assistant and directed him to have us issued with expulsion orders. "They must leave within two weeks, or they will be deported to Sudan."

We returned to the refugee camp with our expulsion papers wondering what to do next.

A white missionary we had never met before came to the camp in the afternoon. He had news about the expulsion of all foreign missionaries from Sudan. He also heard about our expulsion from Tanganyika. He and his Church would pay our road transportation to any neighbouring country we wished to go to. "That's all we can do," he said and added that he would come back in the evening to find out what we had decided.

Some of us decided to go to Kenya; others to Uganda while two boys who had come to Tanganyika via Uganda and Kenya wanted to go to Congo despite our story. Perhaps we had painted Congo in better colours than we thought?

Mathew told us he was going to Northern Rhodesia (Zambia) to meet up with an American friend in the Copperbelt. "From there I will fly to America to fly JETS!" he said and laughed.

"I think we will go to Northern Rhodesia with you," I said and Antiok agreed.

"You know it is not yet independent," said Mathew, "and the British are not a friendly people. Not like Americans. We may not get in."

Anyway, we told our benefactors our decision and they seemed to have no objection to buying bus tickets for the three of us to go to the border town of Tanduma. Five days after the expulsion orders we were on our way out of Tanganyika to Northern Rhodesia/Zambia.

Government of Tanganyika: Five weeks after our departure, the government of Tanganyika publicly denounced the expulsion of Southern Sudanese from the country.

Ministerial Refugee: While working at the Africa Centre in London some years later, the Secretary General of the centre invited me to lunch at the centre with "a very important refugee from Tanzania. He is coming to lunch with his daughter." So, I met once again with the minister who expelled us from Tanzania, who was now like me a refugee in UK; but with the roles slightly reversed: I was now his host and he my guest for at least an hour. He did not recognise me, of course, and he went on and on about "the intolerable persecution of our brothers and sisters in Southern Sudan by Arab Moslems." - and he was in the company of his pretty teenage daughter! I congratulated myself long after for having resisted embarrassing him with his past.

In and Out of Northern Rhodesia/Zambia

We walked from Tanduma to the Northern Rhodesian border town of Nakonde. Not a single government official, not to mention immigration officers, was at the border. We, including Mathew, were completely surprised by the ease with which we entered a British administered territory.

We walked up to an Evangelical Church and declared our presence in the country, the cause of our departure from Sudan - the full story. The local evangelist, a Zambian, was very polite. He listened to our story with great sympathy. After that he took us to his house and introduced us to his wife and three children. They fed us and gave us accommodation without asking about our plans. They were excellent ambassadors for Zambia because, from then on I have always thought of Zambians as a very polite and generous people.

I took a walk in the town in the morning and ended up at a nearby secondary school. I introduced myself to the headmaster, an African, and handed him the results of my recent test at the African American Institute in Dar es Salaam. "These are excellent results. I will be happy to welcome you to my school any time, but I am sure they will want you to go to Lusaka first to clear yourself with the government there. Come back then and we will take you."

When I returned to the Mission, a local government official was already there, talking to Mathew and Antiok. He greeted me cordially, got on his bike and rode off.

"We have to go to Lusaka to report our presence to the government there," Mathew explained to me. "My brother Evangelist here will help us with transport to Ndola, then you will go to Lusaka while I go visit my American friend in Kitwe. That's where he is, in the Copperbelt. Then I will come to Lusaka."

The Evangelist put us on a bus free of charge to Ndola and gave us some money "for food. Go to the Catholic Mission in Ndola," he said to Antiok and I "because you are Catholic. They should be able to help you with transport to Lusaka."

The bus was overcrowded and moved very slowly; but we were very happy to be on it. We travelled all night and arrived in Ndola early in the morning. Mathew found a lift to Kitwe from "a Zambian brother" within half an hour of our arrival at the Ndola bus station. "Look for the Catholic Church. They will help you with transport to Lusaka. I will catch up with you there," he said and waved us goodbye as his new friend drove off north to Kitwe. We were not to see Mathew again in Zambia.

We found a Catholic Mission soon enough but every priest we tried to interest in our story was simply not interested. In the end we confronted a Bishop on the veranda of the Mission compound. He looked at us briefly and told us to "go away" and walked off. We had the feeling that they did not think we were from Southern Sudan but local beggars who had been a nuisance to them in the past. None of them was willing to listen or interested in us, no matter how long we hanged around.

We had not got anywhere by the end of the day, and we decided to go to the railway station, just to see what it would cost to go to Lusaka by train. The result: All the remaining cash our Evangelist friend gave us for food would buy the cheapest ticket to Lusaka. "We better buy the tickets with the money and hope for the best," Antiok suggested, and I seconded it. "If we don't go this evening, we may not have enough left tomorrow for transport to Lusaka. I don't think these missionaries are going to do anything for us."

We arrived in Lusaka very early in the morning. Very few people were out and about. So, we stayed at the railway station for about two hours then walked into the city. The streets were wide, tarred and very clean with trimmed lawns, flower gardens and many flowering plants and trees. The walls of most buildings were copper-red, and many monuments had copper plaques on them, a testimony to the central position of copper in the national economy.

We spied the spire of a Church just above treetop level at a distance and we walked to it. Just across the road was the Church in a Mission compound that we recognised as Catholic because they almost always looked the same. Once you have seen one Catholic Mission complex in those parts of the world you have seen them all.

The people who lived in them, we learnt on that journey, did not always respond in the same way to those in need like us. Some had been generous; others had been damn rude, almost violent. And we were very hungry that morning. So, we approached the residents of the Mission with extra caution, bordering on shyness. We turned into a gravel path leading into the Mission's compound. The gate was not locked; so, we opened it and entered. There appeared to be no one in the compound, so we sat on the concrete steps of the Church building of the Mission and waited.

Presently a priest, dressed in a dark cassock and a white clerical collar, hurried out of a building on his way to another part of the compound.

We stood up automatically, hoping he would notice us, but he hurried on.

"Father!" I called shyly after him. There was no answer. "Father!" I called slightly louder.

"Go away!" He yelled back at us and went through a door.

We stood there and waited. Soon he returned on his way back to the building he first came out of. "Father!"

"I told you to go away!" He turned to us in a rage, this time determined to throw us out.

"Now get out of here!" he waved us away with his hands like a woman chasing birds from the field.

"We are refugees from Sudan, Father and…"

"Get out of here, I tell you! I don't want to see you here again when I come back." he said and disappeared behind a door.

We picked up our bags and walked out slowly and silently from the Mission. We stood at the edge of the tarred road and wondered what to do next. "We should look for a government's office and let them know we are here. Maybe they will help us," I said unconvincingly.

What Mathew told us about the British weighed heavily on our hopes. We expected to be thrown out of Northern Rhodesia rather than helped by the government.

"You know what Mathew said," said Antiok. "The British are mean people. I am sure that priest is British."

There were big buildings down the road that could be government offices. So, we turned left and walked along the tarred road towards the buildings. A priest dressed like the one who had just chased us out the Mission passed us by in a great hurry. He put envelopes in a red box just ahead of us and turned back towards us. He appeared not to notice us, and we had no intention of engaging another priest, but he stopped suddenly in front of us.

"My God!" he exclaimed. "You are Dinkas! I know you are Dinka boys from Southern Sudan! Come! Come with me. Come." He hurried back into the Mission compound we had just been chased out of. "Come!" We tried with difficulty to keep up with him. "I am Father O'Brien from Ireland. Come, come in."

He yanked open the door of the building the priest who chased us away had entered. "Come here! Come meet these Dinka boys from Southern Sudan. They are being persecuted in their own country. All foreign missionaries have been deported from Sudan by the Arab government. Come in, come in, boys sit down here. Have something to eat."

We sat at a long wooden table. Fr. O'Brien opened a side cupboard, pulled out a large wooden tray full of roast beef and put it the middle of the table. He then put on the table bread and butter and knives and ordered the priest who kicked us out to "bring tea for these boys. Can't you see they are starving." He carved thick pieces of beef and put them on a large plate in front of us. "Eat. You must be hungry."

We ignored the bread and picked up a piece of meat each and begun to eat.

"Look," said Fr. O'Brien, "Let me show you."

He picked up a piece of bread and buttered one side. He then placed a piece of beef over the buttered side, picked up another piece of bread, buttered it and placed the buttered side over the piece of meat so that the meat was between the two pieces of bread.

"That's a sandwich. Have you never had a sandwich before? Look."

He sliced the sandwich from corner to corner into two. He handed me one half and the other to Antiok. "You eat. I will make them for you."

The other priest came in with a big pot of tea, cups, a spoon and sugar. He poured the tea for us and put two spoons of sugar in each cup. We asked for more sugar. "So you are from Southern Sudan," he said, "I thought you were Lozis."

"No, they are not," explained Fr. O'Brian. "That is a mistake made by Europeans. They don't look like Lozis. They are Dinkas and they look different."

They sat across the table and watched us eat while at the same time Fr. O'Brien educated the other priest about the persecution of Africans by Arabs in Southern Sudan. On my part I felt embarrassed. I had always felt embarrassed when being watched while eating by those who were not eating. Fr. O'Brien seemed to notice, and he poured himself and his colleague some tea. They also buttered pieces of bread with butter and jam and began to eat while talking.

"We belong to the Jesuits. Ever heard of them?"

"No," I replied, "our Missionaries were from Verona. They were Italians."

"We are Irish, from Ireland. Do you know where it is?"

"Somewhere in Europe, near England."

"That's right, but it is better than England. It is a Holly Island of Saints! You hear that now?"

"How do you know so much about Sudan and the Dinka, were you a priest there?" I ask Fr. O'Brien.

"Goodness no. Never been to Sudan in all me life. But we all know what is going on there now don't we?"

It was past mid-day by the time we finished telling bits and pieces of our story thus far. With no sleep on the crowded train, the anxieties of the morning, a full stomach and the retelling of the problems we had gone through on the way to Zambia, we felt exhausted, and it showed.

"I will take you to your house," said Fr. O'Brien. "You must be very tired."

"What about the government?" I asked. "They want to see us."

"Now don't worry y'r head about that. I will see to it me self."

"Your house" was a small round thatched hut next to an isolated Church building beside a rail track. There were two cotton mattresses on the cement floor. Fr. O'Brien handed us a blanket each.

"This is where you stay until we can sort something out for you. I will bring you some rice and fish and cooking pots to use. Meanwhile have a rest." And then, as an afterthought, "Mass is served in this Church every morning and the big Mass is on Sundays. See you in the evening."

Though sleepy, a train came by every fifteen minutes or so. Lying on our stomachs on the mattresses we could watch them go by through the open door: "Chuck-chuck cluck, chuck-chuck cluck-cluck," they rolled north or south. Fascinating! The rails were close enough for us to see clearly the large metal wheels rolling over them. They were mostly goods-trains; some were very long and heavy. Soon we began to count the wagons on each train and betted from which direction the next train would come.

A road crossed the rails from west to east and cars cued up and waited behind a barrier when a train was about to come.

There were many small mud-walled houses with corrugated iron roofs a little further to the left of the railway. A lot of people were moving about among those houses. Loud music and laughter emanated from those quarters. We were confident that the room was dark enough for us to observe the interesting things going on outside without us being seen unless someone came close. It was the sort of thing lions loved to do.

Fr. O'Brien returned in the evening with rice, dry fish and other things we were likely to need for our feeding. "Have a good night boy. See you in the morning. By the way, have you any school documents, anything to say what level of education you were at? "

We handed him our test results from the African American Institute in Dar es Salaam. They would not tell him what level of school education we were at, but they were the only educational records we had in our possession. He put them in his pocket without reading them and skipped off whistling to his car.

We attended Mass in the morning. As it was a weekday, only a few people turned up, but Fr. O'Brien did not seem to mind. I offered to serve as the Alter Boy in the next services, which seemed to please him very much. I could understand that. Serving Mass served our cause as bona fide Catholics.

We had a short conversation after the Mass about the level of school education each of us had achieved when we left Sudan. "That explains the difference between your test marks," he said and skipped off, whistling the same tune as the evening before.

Two weeks later Fr. O'Brien arrived very early in the morning: "Wakey, wakey! Boys! Wake up! You are going to school!"

Hurriedly we dressed and emerged from the hut. "You are going to school today!" he said excitedly. "Jacob is going to Canisius College and Antiok, you are going to the last year of our primary school not very far from Canisius College. Get ready. Someone will pick you up at 8 o'clock." He skipped off, whistling his now recognisable tone.

"He enjoys whistling, doesn't he?" Antiok remarked and I agreed.

Canisius College was about two-hours' drive off the main tarred road south of Lusaka. I was to remain behind at the college while

Antiok continued his way further south to his school. Despite our different personalities, we suddenly realised now of parting how close we had been on this epic journey. We had become more than friends, something like brothers who took each other's presence for granted until it was taken away. I felt sad to see him go even when I knew it was only temporary. He felt the same. But we consoled ourselves with the hopeful thought that we would be together again soon at the end of the first term.

"In a year's time, God willing, you will join me here at Canisius College. Work hard," I wished him goodbye.

"I will," he waved back with tears in his eyes. I had tears in my eyes.

The school system we left behind in Sudan was 4 x 4 x 4 (elementary, intermediate and secondary) = 12 years before university. The system in Zambia was roughly 6 x 6 (primary and secondary) = 12 years before university. When I left Sudan in the final term of my third year at intermediate school, I was ready for the fourth year (the final year of intermediate school) - I was in fact more than ready because I was one of the few third-year students selected to sit the secondary school exams a year in advance. Putting me in First Grade (7th year of schooling) at Canisius College was like putting me back into Third-Year intermediate school back home. I explained this to the Principal, an Irish priest, but he told me "Not to worry. All will sort itself out in the long run. Let's see how you do by the end of the first term."

Canisius College was a cut above Kuachjok Intermediate School. It was what I imagined of Rumbek Secondary School would be like. The food was good. The accommodation was good. There were plenty of books to read and the teachers, mostly Irish priests, were friendly, disciplinarian and supportive of a serious approach to learning. This College, I was informed, was one of the two top schools in the country. The other one was Manali in Lusaka. I had no reason to doubt it.

Two sons of David Kenneth Kaunda (KK), soon to be the president of an independent Zambia, were at the college. "They wouldn't be here if it were a cheap school," so I reasoned. Anyway, I would have settled for anything. Canisius College was for me a dream school, an unexpected bonus.

Sports were taken very seriously with the view to developing talent in areas of interest. Because of my height and background in the art of spear-throwing, I soon outdid my college colleagues in javelin. So, I was one of the team throwing javelin for the College at a One-Day Athletics Competition between Canisius College and Manali Secondary in Lusaka. I was second; a boy from Manali was first.

"With a few more instructions and a bit of weight," said my sports instructor, "I am sure you will be the best!"

I loved Canisius College, though much of what I was learning during the first term was what I had learned in the Third Year at Kuachjok Intermediate School. The end of term examinations put me at number two in my class with zero in Tonga, the local language. Ignoring Tonga, I was sure the principal would push me up one grade next term.

My college colleagues went home for the holiday. Meanwhile, Antiok joined me at Canisius College. For him and I, the college was our home, although it would have been nice to go to Lusaka for a break and to see Fr. O'Brien. We therefore planned to work hard in the Mission's garden and save any cash we earned for a day's trip to Lusaka before the second term.

However, a young priest arrived one morning and told us that we were wanted in Lusaka "by Immigration." We tried to find out from him if he knew anything about the intentions of the government, but he said he had no idea what they intended to do with us.

We found out soon enough. A young white immigration officer in Lusaka handed us an open brown envelope each on which the initials: HMS stood prominently in a corner. We gazed at the envelopes, not certain what to do next. "Open them, they are for you," said the young officer and went back to whatever he was busy doing when we came in.

I fished out of my envelope a piece of bluish paper with an address and the initials HMS in the right-hand corner. It read in parts:

To Whom It May Concern

Subject: <u>PROHIBITED IMMIGRANT</u>

I hereby declare that Jacob J. Akol is a prohibited immigrant of Her Majesty's Territory of Northern Rhodesia and must therefore depart from the said territory at the earliest possible convenience.

Our expulsion orders from Tanganyika were not on such a pretty piece of paper or so decorated with big words like "prohibited" and "immigrant." I asked the young officer what they meant exactly; but he picked up a thick English dictionary from his desk and threw it at me; and he resumed whatever he was doing, probably writing more letters of expulsion. I looked up the words, hoping to discover they did not mean what I thought they meant. No luck: they meant exactly what I thought they meant: We were being kicked out of Zambia without mercy. These were the British Mathew had warned us about! What to do now?

I looked at Antiok and his expression of disappointment was unmistakable. He had a very good report from his new school, and he was looking forward to joining me at Canisius College the following year. We looked at the young priest who held out his hand for the papers. We gave them to him. He read them quickly and shook his head sadly.

"At least they have not put in a time limit," he said and added by way of explanation: "They have not stated the date when you should leave the country. Let's go see Father O'Brien."

"Father O'Brien is not in," said a worker, "but he has left a note for you, Father." He handed the note over to the priest.

"Father O'Brien will be at St. Vincent de Paul's Mission Centre this evening. He will meet you there but he would like you to buy some clothes and look well because he wants you to meet some missionaries that may help you go to any African country you wish to. He knows about your expulsion. The Immigration informed him yesterday."

The young priest took us to a big shop in Lusaka to buy clothes, but we were not really interested in clothes because we were still shocked by the news of expulsion. So, he guided us through the shop and made choices for us, which was just as well because we would have been worried about the cost. In the end, each of us ended up with a pair of trousers and a jacket, two of shirts, two of vests, a pair of underpants, a pair of black shoes and a pair of socks. "You may never have the chance to buy these things and you will need them wherever you go," he said and paid a lot of money to the happy shopkeeper.

He took us back to the Jesuits' Mission to take a shower and dressed for the evening. "Well, well," said the attentive young priest when he saw us in our new clothes, "you look smashing!" But we didn't feel "smashing". We felt awkward in the jackets, the first time we had ever worn such expensive-looking pieces of cloth on our backs. "Let's go," he said. "We don't want to keep Father O'Brien waiting now do we?"

We entered a large hall at the St. Vincent de Paul Centre. Although there were many chairs and some sandwiches on a table in a corner, there was no one in the room. The priest told us to sit down while he went to look for Father O'Brien. Shortly after, we heard the familiar whistling tune we had come to associate with Fr. O'Brien coming from a corridor off the main hall. He entered with a lot of other priests, some wearing cassocks we had not seen before.

"Well, well, my boys," said Father O'Brien, "don't you look well now in your new clothes! But enough of that, I will not keep you in suspense any longer than necessary: Well, boys: This is the beginning of the end of the long road from Sudan. No more suffering and travelling from country to country. The Irish Government has agreed for you to go to Ireland! St. Vincent de Paul here has kindly donated air tickets for you. You will leave for Ireland tomorrow noon. Isn't that marvellous!"

We were dumfounded but only for a moment. "Will we be able to go to school there?" asked Antiok.

There was general laughter and we joined in, not quite sure what it was they found so funny in the question. "In Ireland," explained Father O'Brien, "all children must go to school!"

It transpired that Fr O'Brien and his Mission got to work on our behalf as soon as we went to school in Zambia. They found a school for us in their Mission in Wyoming, but the US Government would not agree for us to go there. On the other hand, the Irish Government agreed to take us though there was no school yet for us.

But Zambia was to become independent in a month's time and the future of democracy in the country did not seem promising. Already Kaunda, the president in waiting, had been breathing fire and reportedly had threatened the opposition leader, Harry Nkumbula, with the rope: "I will hang him if he continues to smear ZANU (Zambia African National Union party) with malicious and treasonous accusations!" Although our missionary friends had not said so, they were nevertheless worried that come the nationalist government we might be thrown out of the country with nowhere to go. Then it seemed was the right time for us to leave Zambia.

The following day, we were queuing up to board the flight to

London at Lusaka Airport when a familiar whistling tune pierced through the buzz and bustle of the airport and in came Fr. O'Brien, as cheerful and in a hurry as always.

"Now, now boys, " he pulled us out of the long queue and told the young priest who had helped us check in to keep our place in the queue. "You OK now boys? You got all your documents?" We nodded in the affirmative. "Good. BOA staff will take care of you. They will put you on a plane to Dublin tomorrow and Father Martin will meet you at Dublin Airport. Been on an aeroplane before?" We shook our heads. "This is a jet. It should be a smooth flight all the way. Nothing to worry about. You alright now boys?"

"Father," I said, "what is that tune you always whistle?"

"O that, it is called *IT'S A LONG WAY TO TIPPERARY*. It is an Irish song: 'It's a long, long way to Tipperary! It's a long way…' You will hear more about it when you get there. Goodbye now boys. God Bless you." He skipped out of the door, whistling the tune of the song from which the tittle of this book had been derived.

Athuai, Antiok: Antiok left me in Dublin after two years in school and went to London. While he did odd jobs here and there in England, I was working as a labourer at the Irish Glass Bottle Company in Ireland; but I joined him in London eight months later. While we did various low-level jobs during the day, we also volunteered in the evening to run the then "Southern Sudan Association" and its publication "Grass Curtain" in London, with Antiok as "Distribution Manager" and I as "Secretary/Treasurer" of the organisation. We also studied for Ordinary Level School Certificates some evenings. But, following the Addis Ababa Peace Agreement in 1972, an anonymous donor paid for Antiok and I to study for one-year full time for O & A levels. Antiok, however, was homesick and decided to return to Sudan at mid-term; but his expectations were not met, and he soon returned to England. He married an English girl called Liz, with whom he had a daughter called Awien Majok (women sometimes have ox names just like men). He and Liz later divorced and he married a Jieng girl called Susan with whom he had a son called Yai.

Riak, Mathew: I saw Mathew in the mid-70s in Juba, Southern Sudan. He found his way to America from Zambia alright, but I don't know exactly what he did there. Back in Southern Sudan, he was not "flying JETS." Instead, he was flying a small twin-engine propeller plane for the Southern Sudan's High Executive Council. He was still very much in love with America and things American and he was as funny as ever, now with his broad American droll and the Jieng swagger greatly enhanced by Black America's own. While I wrote scripts for Radio Juba, Mathew sometimes disappeared over Southern Sudan in the little plane during "test flights", only to learn later that he had "crash-landed" in a field near his home in Rumbek area, hundreds of miles from Juba. Suspicious to say the least, but what could President Alier (of the Southern Region) do about Mathew? "I am the only pilot in the whole of Southern Sudan. He has no other pilot to replace me with," Mathew joked and we laughed uproariously at the expense of our employer, the Regional Government.

www.ingramcontent.com/pod-product-compliance
Lightning Source LLC
Chambersburg PA
CBHW031236290426
44109CB00012B/315